PETER'S WAR

PETER'S WAR

*A New England Slave Boy
and the
American Revolution*

JOYCE LEE MALCOLM

Yale University Press
New Haven & London

A Caravan book. For more information, visit www.caravanbooks.com

Published with assistance from the Annie Burr Lewis Fund.

Designed by James J. Johnson and set in Adobe Caslon type by Keystone Typesetting, Inc. Printed in the United States of America.

Library of Congress Cataloging-in-Publication Data
Malcolm, Joyce Lee.
Peter's war : a New England slave boy and the American Revolution / Joyce Lee Malcolm.
p. cm.
Includes bibliographical references and index.
ISBN 978-0-300-11930-5 (cloth : alk. paper)
1. Peter, 1763–1791 or 92. 2. Child slaves—Massachusetts—Lincoln—Biography. 3. African American boys—Massachusetts—Lincoln—Biography. 4. Farm life—Massachusetts—Lincoln—History—18th century. 5. Lincoln (Mass.)—Social life and customs—18th century. 6. Lincoln (Mass.)—Biography. 7. African American soldiers—Massachusetts—Biography. 8. Massachusetts—History—Revolution, 1775–1783—Participation, African American. 9. United States—History—Revolution, 1775–1783—Participation, African American. 10. New England—Race relations—History—18th century. I. Title.
F74.L7M35 2009
973.3′444092—dc22
[B]   2008037295

A catalogue record for this book is available from the British Library.

This paper meets the requirements of ANSI/NISO Z39.48-1992 (Permanence of Paper). It contains 30 percent postconsumer waste (PCW) and is certified by the Forest Stewardship Council (FSC).

10 9 8 7 6 5 4 3 2 1

For my sister, Ellen, with love and thanks

We hold these Truths to be self evident; that all Men are created equal and independent; that from that equal Creation they derive Rights inherent and unalienable; among which are the Preservation of Life, and Liberty, and the Pursuit of Happiness.

THOMAS JEFFERSON,
First Draft, Declaration of Independence, 1776

Contents

Preface

Some years ago I came across the single, frail sheet of paper signed and sealed in Lincoln, Massachusetts, in 1765 recording the sale of a "sartain neagro servant boy named Peter about one year and seven months old." Few eighteenth-century documents for such sales in Massachusetts survive. None that I know of record the sale of so young a child without his mother. Other scholars had seen the document and noted it, as I did, before passing on to other subjects. I made a copy and got on with my work, a complicated project meant to pin down the people and setting of the Concord Road on April 19, 1775, when the running battle between British soldiers and local residents raged along it. Josiah and Elizabeth Nelson, who bought Peter, lived on that road. Once I completed my task I moved on from one research project that pricked my curiosity to another. But I never forgot that bill of sale for that tiny boy. It opened a hidden and totally unexpected window on slavery. As another sabbatical leave approached I thought again of that sale and decided to see whether I could find out more about Peter—Had he lived beyond infancy? Why would anyone purchase a child who could not be even moderately helpful, let alone a servant, for many years? Who were his biological parents? Could his buyers, Josiah and Elizabeth Nelson, who I discovered were childless, raise Peter as anything but their own son? One question led to another, and before I knew it I was off on a fascinating, albeit sometimes frustrating, hunt to retrieve the life story of one long-forgotten eighteenth-century boy.

I have been able to find out a great deal about Peter and the key events of his life. But unlike an author blessed with books, or at least diaries or letters, written by her subject, I was not to discover a single letter written by Peter. Nor did I expect to find any. Little in the way of written records survives for the great majority of people from any era. In the end I have discovered Peter's

footprints but not his voice. I have set those footprints down in the landscape
he inhabited, among the people he knew and the dramatic historic events in
which he participated.

And dramatic these events were. Paul Revere was waylaid by British
scouts just west of Peter's home, and while the first battle of the American
Revolution exploded along the road where he lived, he hid with the Nelson
women and children in the woods nearby. Friends, family, and neighbors
fought in that battle and in the war that followed. At twelve Peter marched off
with the men of Lincoln to join the patriot army gathering in Cambridge. He
was present at Bunker Hill, witnessed the surrender at Saratoga, and fought
at Yorktown. While Washington and members of Congress were originally
ambivalent about the propriety of slaves serving in the American struggle for
freedom, first the British then the American armies were soon enticing slaves
and free blacks into their ranks. Black soldiers fought on both sides for their
freedom. To highlight that fact and the ambivalence it caused for both blacks
and whites, I have included the story of Titus, a New Jersey slave who found
freedom by joining the British army.

There are frustrating gaps in the records of Peter's family life. Mystery
remains, for example, about the fate of his mother, Peggy, and his sister.
There is uncertainty whether Josiah Nelson ever fought in the battles his
descendants later claimed. Since there is no other source for his participation,
I have assumed he did not fight. For ease of reading I have provided an Essay
on Sources at the end of the book rather than inserting notes. Despite the
gaps that deep research could not fill, I believe enough hard evidence survives
to justify this attempt to recover Peter's poignant story and to bring him and
his world to life.

This book could not have been written without the information amassed by
generations of scholars who have written on the era or compiled and cataloged
essential primary materials. The Essay on Sources lists those works that have
been essential for this book. Beyond these debts I am especially grateful for the
generous assistance of colleagues, archivists, reference librarians, and my family. David Hackett Fischer advised me on ways to tackle this subject, and
Graham Russell Hodges shared his exceptional knowledge of slavery in the
mid-Atlantic states. John C. MacLean answered various questions about
Lincoln history, and Donald L. Hafner cleared up the mystery of Elizabeth

Nelson's background. Cindy Williams and Pauline Maier listened and raised key questions. Grateful thanks are due to Robert George and the fellows and staff of the James Madison Program at Princeton, who granted me a fellowship and welcomed me into their midst as my research began, cheerfully exchanging ideas on the subject. Members of the Washington, D.C., Legal History Roundtable invited me to present my findings and offered valuable advice. I especially thank Adele Logan Alexander, who served as commentator. Bentley College generously provided the sabbatical leave that helped me launch the project. My graduate assistant Beth Sweesy was a great help tracking down various items. The enthusiasm of my agent, John Taylor Williams, and of Christopher Rogers, Laura Davulis, Laura Jones Dooley, and their colleagues at Yale University Press, has made the work a real pleasure.

I am grateful for the help of archivists and reference librarians. Among those deserving special mention are Richard Kollen, archivist for the Lexington Historical Society, who opened the society's library on numerous Saturdays to give me access to its treasures. Jeanne Bracken, Lincoln's reference librarian, checked her collection many times for me and shared her enthusiasm for the records housed there. The librarians of the Massachusetts Historical Society combed their archives for tidbits on William Smith, Abigail Adams's disreputable brother, and Terrie Wallace, the curator at Minute Man National Historical Park, took time from her many tasks to help me with their archives. In New Jersey, Marie Heagney of the Morris County Library and Ruth Lufkin of the Bernards Township Library in Basking Ridge provided expertise and ordered numerous books to help my sister, Ellen Ghasemi, with our research.

It is traditional for an author to thank his or her family, and certainly the families of scholars deserve thanks. But in this case it was truly a collaborative effort. Lisa Arienne helped me launch the project. George served as a summer research assistant and immediately made one of the key breakthroughs. My sister-in-law, Jackie, shared material on slavery in New York State. Mark was, as always, supportive in low moments. My husband, Neil, lovingly endured numerous interruptions to give advice and good counsel. Above all this book owes more than I can say to the enthusiasm, diligent research, and comments, of my sister, Ellen. She was intrigued with the subject from the start and keen to help, undertaking research of all sorts and patiently reading every chapter. Sharing the enterprise with her has been a true joy.

CHAPTER ONE

The Hardship Sale

We had lived together as a family of brothers for several years . . . had shared
with each other the hardships, dangers, and sufferings incident to a soldier's
life; had sympathized with each other in trouble and sickness; had assisted in
bearing each other's burdens or strove to make them lighter by council and
advice . . . we were young men and had warm hearts. I question if there was a
corps in the army that parted with more regret than ours did, the New
Englanders in particular. Ah! It was a serious time.

JOSEPH PLUMB MARTIN
Ordinary Courage: The Revolutionary War Adventures of Joseph Plumb Martin
(narrative published 1830)

ON THE LONG WALK HOME to Lincoln, Massachusetts, that
bleak December of 1783, Peter had, for the first time in a long while,
ample leisure to reflect. Not that there wasn't constant danger for a
black soldier trudging the nearly 230 miles to eastern Massachusetts. Once
the regiment descended from its headquarters at West Point, with its commanding view of the majestic Hudson, the soldiers found themselves im-
mersed in the chaotic aftermath of the war, the bitterness, destruction, and
deep divisions it had left. They were never certain what welcome they would
receive as they approached another cluster of houses, another neat farmhouse,
banked with firewood for the winter, its windows glowing invitingly, another
bustling roadside inn, the sounds of local banter carrying out onto the dark-
ening road.

The first part of their journey had been the most dangerous. The loyalties
of New Yorkers were sharply split. The state had been among the last to sign
the Declaration of Independence. Its great city of New York was the only
capital that remained under British control throughout the war, its population swelling from twenty thousand in 1775 to fifty thousand during the war as

Loyalists and fugitive slaves flocked to put themselves under British protection. Twice during those years it had nearly been destroyed by fire. Even after the British surrender at Yorktown, bands of Loyalists and slaves sallied out from New York to loot, kill, and burn villages in the so-called neutral ground of New Jersey. New York was also the state with the greatest number of slaves north of the Chesapeake. Many from the region had fled to the British on the promise of freedom. Now kidnappers were out in force, on the lookout for fugitive slaves or any blacks they could sell as slaves. Thieves were eager to snatch the modest discharge money in Peter's pocket, which, along with his musket and tattered uniform, was his final reward for eight years of service. All in all it was fortunate that Congress insisted the disbanded soldiers be accompanied by their officers. Of course, Congress was not worried about the hazard faced by the soldiers, black or white, but was nervous about the danger battle-hardened veterans posed to civilians. Still, traveling together for the last time was a comfort.

The residents of the rich farmlands of Connecticut were more hospitable, but even there many resented the demands Congress had made on them for men and provisions. Some had carried on an illicit trade with the British in New York, happy to be paid in solid currency. Their sour looks and turned backs when they saw Peter's troop made their views plain. It was a relief to reach the woods and rolling fields of central Massachusetts. The New England landscape was not at its best in December. Its glorious autumn foliage was past, with only the oaks clinging to their leathery brown leaves. The fields were frozen and bare. The grain had been harvested, corn cut, pumpkins cooked, apples picked. It was a landscape painted in shades of brown and gray, punctuated by white birch and the dull green of pine trees, a landscape awaiting the softening touch of snow. But the people were welcoming and had contributed a disproportionate number of men to the cause.

As Peter and his comrades hurried to reach their destinations before the onset of winter snows, their numbers steadily dwindled. At nearly every crossroad some men veered off, eager to walk old, familiar roads toward their homes and families and another life.

There had been no grand military parade when the Continental Army was disbanded. Most of the men had been sent home in June. But their general's moving farewell to his remaining veterans stuck in the memory. Washington addressed Peter and his companions, men branded then and since as the dregs of the country, as those he held most dear. He recalled their "unparalleled perseverance" through "almost every possible suffering and discouragement" and marveled how men from such different parts of the continent had become "one patriotic band of Brothers." "Who," he asked, "will exclude them from the rights of Citizens and the fruits of their labor?" Who indeed, the blacks among them must have wondered. At the last, Washington recommended them all to their grateful country and prayed "to the God of Armies" that they, who had secured innumerable blessings for others, might find justice here and Heaven's favor hereafter.

It was fortunate the journey to Lincoln took so long because in the course of it Peter had to become a civilian again. The mile after slow mile, interspersed with bluff and poignant farewells, provided time to put the hardships, friendships, losses, and exhilaration of army life behind him, to try to blot out wrenching scenes of southern blacks abandoned by the British, and the amazing sight of some three thousand northern blacks setting sail on British ships for Canada and freedom. It was time to consider what awaited him at his journey's end. Thoughts of Lincoln conjured up a lost world, growing up in the comfortable Nelson home that looked out on the bustle of the Great Road to Boston. Back came memories of his families, white and black, of adventures with friends, of daily prayers, farmwork, and school. In many ways his childhood was little different from that of other New England farm boys of the time. Sometimes, it had been easy to forget the difference between slave and free and, beyond that, the racial barrier that made him always the outsider. The early, awkward adjustment his owners, Josiah and Elizabeth, had raising a young child for the first time, let alone a black child, would be lost on him but the later, awkward adjustment would not. He had gone off to war as a boy of twelve, proudly striding at Josiah's side. But the childish, peaceful world he had known before the war had changed irrevocably and so had he. The army had become his family. It was uncertain whether there was any place for him in Lincoln, but it was all the home he now had.

Peter had been sold to the Nelsons on January 29, 1765. He was just over a year and a half. He would have remembered none of it. But constant reminding, by those who did remember, who wanted him to remember, would have seared the event into his soul. He could never forget, nor could they.

Know all men by these presence that I Joshua
Brooks of lincoln in the County of middel sex
and provence of the maschusits bay in new ingland
gentelman for and in consideration of the sum of four
pounds to me in hand before the in sealing hear of
paid by Josiah nellson of lincoln yeaman in full satis
faction whear by sell convay and deliver to him the s
Josiah nellson his eirs and asines for ever a sartan
neagro servant boy named peter about one year
and seven months old and I the said Joshu brooks for my
selfe and for my eairs exetors and administrators do
covenant and in gage to and with him the said Josiah
nellson that before the in sealing hear of I am the
true and proper owner of the afore said peter and I
do warant to secure and defend him the said Josiah nellson
and his eairs against the lawfull claims or demands
of any parson or parsons what so ever in witness whear
of I the said Joshu Brooks with mary my wife haue
hear unto set our hands and seals this twenty ninth day
of Janwary anodomony 1765
in presence of us

John Brook   Joshua Brooks
                                         her
Lucy Brooks   Mary X Brooks
                                        Mark

Bill of sale for Peter.
Courtesy Lincoln Public Library, Lincoln, Massachusetts

Documents of the sale of slaves in New England are rare. Most must have been prudently discarded long ago. Yet for more than two centuries the single, frayed sheet of paper that recorded the sale of Peter, mute testament to the singular story that was his life, lay amid the handful of deeds and other papers carefully saved by the farm family that bought him. Now boxed with these papers, alongside shelf upon shelf of identical boxes of family papers in the vault of the Lincoln town archives, the portal into Peter's existence hangs on this one intriguing, enigmatic, and, for him, humiliating document.

The bill of sale described him simply as a nineteen-month-old "neagro servant boy named Peter." The sale of so young a child, without his mother, was extraordinary. True, New Englanders believed slave children ought to be purchased young, to ensure that they would have the proper upbringing and be thoroughly instructed in Christian virtues. Yet seldom this young. Sometimes the death of the mother occasioned the sale, but there had been no death here. Apart from the wrenching sadness of the separation of mother and child, which the Puritan community and Peter's owners certainly appreciated, the sale clashed with another Puritan virtue—it was improvident. Peter would have to be sold cheaply or even given away. In the South, where large numbers of slaves lived on the same property, owners were happy to have children. These were their future workers and ultimately valuable. An older Negro woman was assigned to look after the young children of slaves while their parents worked. But in Massachusetts there were few, if any, people who owned large numbers of slaves. Someone, black or white, would have to devote years of care to Peter before he deserved the designation "servant." It was cheaper to buy a grown slave who would be useful at once. Why had this premature, painful sale occurred? And who would be willing to buy the toddler and take on the considerable responsibility of raising him?

The answer lies in a further mystery, for it was the owners of Peter's father, Deacon Joshua Brooks of Lincoln, and his wife, Mary, who sold the little boy, not the family that owned his mother. Lexington church records provide a clue to why Peter was sold at so tender an age, and sold by his father's owner. They record Peter's baptism before the church congregation on the morning of October 2, 1763. Since the Nelson family attended the Lexington rather than the Lincoln congregational church, Josiah and Elizabeth were almost surely among the worshippers on that fall day as the Reverend Jonas Clarke, watched anxiously by Peggy and Jupiter, cradled their tiny baby in his arms and blessed him. Josiah and Elizabeth along with the rest of the congregation agreed to help raise the little infant in the knowledge of God, the couple not yet aware how personal that responsibility would become.

But there is more in the records. On November 6, 1763, slightly more than a month after Peter's baptism, Peggy and Jupiter were back in church, this time to baptize a daughter, also named Peggy. They were the parents of twins. That explains why Jupiter's master came to own Peter. Each master claimed one child. Peggy had to part with her son but was able to keep her small daughter for a few years longer. Girls were quieter than boys, and little Peggy would eventually be able to help her mother with her household duties.

Jupiter's owners were a respectable, God-fearing couple, as Joshua Brooks's proud title, "deacon," made plain to all. They were prominent in the community, members of the extensive and prosperous Brooks clan that clustered in such numbers on both sides of the boundary between Lincoln and Concord, its neighbor to the west, that the area was designated Brooksville. Although the deacon and his wife, out of courtesy to their slave, Jupiter, would have journeyed to Lexington to attend Peter's baptism in the Lexington church, Joshua and Mary would have seen little of him since. Peter would not have recognized them. Nor had Peter seen his father very often, for his parents were owned by different families and lived in different towns.

Peter's mother belonged to William Reed, Esquire, long-serving member of the Massachusetts Bay general assembly representing the good people of Lexington, the substantial town bordering Lincoln on the east, toward Boston. Reed was a lawyer and justice of the peace, captain of militia, veteran of the recently concluded French and Indian War, and father of ten. That year he was also the moderator of the Lexington town meeting. He and his wife, Sarah, were even more distinguished than the Brookses. Peter had been born in their home. They were an older couple and did not need or want a small, lively black toddler underfoot, pestering them and his mother, keeping her from her work. None of the extensive Reed family of Lexington was interested in having Peter either. Nor were Joshua and Mary Brooks, Jupiter's owners, willing to keep Peter. With seven grown children with families of their own, Joshua and Mary had both done more than their share of child-rearing. None of the Brooks children were interested in taking Peter, even for the sake of sparing their parents this unpleasant transaction. However, a buyer had been found. And so, on a wintry Tuesday in January, Jupiter had fetched his tiny son from Lexington and brought him to the Brooks's comfortable home, to a house full of strangers, to be sold to Josiah Nelson, a local farmer, and his wife, Elizabeth. Josiah had agreed to pay four pounds cash for the little boy, the going rate for a cow and her calf.

Nine years before this sale, "with the consent of their masters," Peggy and Jupiter had married. It was a fine, traditional wedding in the Lexington meetinghouse, the church Peggy attended every Sunday with the Reeds. As custom dictated, the banns announcing the couple's intention to wed had been posted on three successive Sundays before the ceremony. Everyone in the congregation knew of the impending union. Massachusetts law, unlike that of the southern colonies, recognized slave marriages. Masters were encouraged to consent to the unions. Indeed, the Puritan community was in agreement that it was far better for adult slaves to marry than to be tempted into promiscuity. They were pleased to recognize the unions and to accept the children born of these families into their congregations, there to be baptized and molded into upstanding members of the Christian community. But the black bride and groom were still slaves, and their convenience was unlikely to have been uppermost in anyone's mind but their own. In the case of Peggy and Jupiter, theirs was a long-distance marriage.

Long-distance marriages were common of necessity among the slaves in the rural townships of eighteenth-century New England. The African-American community was small and scattered. Few people owned more than one or two slaves to help in the fields or the kitchen. A town might have only ten or fifteen altogether. Marriages like Peggy and Jupiter's meant a fair amount of travel, usually for the husband, if the couple were to see each other. In their case it was some four miles, but other couples could be separated by much greater distances. Sometimes, of course, the chance to travel was a welcome break for Jupiter. It was an opportunity to leave the farm and work, if only briefly, a chance to be on his own, to travel alone, to see other places and meet other people. But he could not always be spared from work, and the notoriously erratic New England weather would often interfere. In poor weather, along muddy or snow-covered roads, a journey of even a few miles, almost always on foot, could be daunting and treacherous. Eventually, husband and wife might manage to live together through a sale or emancipation. Emancipation, however, was tricky from the owner's point of view. He not only lost a valuable asset, but Massachusetts law insisted he post fifty pounds

sterling, a substantial bond, to ensure that a freed slave would not become a
burden on the local community. So Peggy and Jupiter lived apart and hoped.

Although the children of slave marriages would eventually become valuable, they were not welcome. Indeed, in the New England colonies and New
York, slave women who were barren were preferred. Ironically, it was the close
relationship between New Englanders and their slaves that made the babies a
problem. Slaves and their owners usually lived in the same house. They
worked together, ate together at the family table, gathered together, morning
and evening, to pray. This kinder, family-like arrangement made it more
likely that Negro children would be separated from their parents since their
presence was keenly and continually felt within the confines of household life.
At nineteen months Peter was weaned, walking, and full of energy.

Peggy and Jupiter had been married seven years before Peter's birth.
There is no evidence that they had any children before he and his sister were
born. It is unclear why. Peggy may have been as young as fifteen at the time of
her marriage. In an era when puberty was several years later than it is in the
modern world, this would mean that it could have been some time before she
could bear children. It is more likely that the couple did not want to have
children who would be born "servants for life," were unwanted by their
masters, and would almost certainly be sold to another family. Or it might
simply have been that their opportunities to spend time together had been
limited. If that had been the case, Peggy's pregnancy may have been the result
of war. Peter's birth coincided with the conclusion of the French and Indian
War in which Peggy's owner served. It is tempting to suspect that Reed's
absence allowed the couple a greater opportunity to be together. Jupiter's help
around the Reed home would be welcome while William was away.

For the Brooks family, the sale of the toddler was a hardship sale. For
Elizabeth and Josiah Nelson, the couple who bought Peter, it was a hardship
purchase. Both in their late thirties, they had been married fourteen years but
were childless. Sitting with their family and neighbors in church every Sunday, season after season, year after year, watching the baptisms of other people's babies, Elizabeth and Josiah must have felt that God was punishing
them by denying them children. Their daily work was harder, and their hard
work seemed to be to no purpose. Buying the tiny slave no one wanted could
be seen as an act of charity on their part, God's work. On the other hand,
owning a slave would be a mark of Josiah's growing wealth and status. Because
Peter was so young, he was a bargain, at least in the short run. And he would

someday be a help. But he was also a child for a childless home, and at thirty-seven Elizabeth was a woman in need of a child.

The bill of sale contained four signatures. Joshua and Mary Brooks signed as the sellers, Joshua's brother John and his wife, Lucy, signed as witnesses. Mary, who like many women of the time was illiterate, signed by making her mark, and then she and Joshua set their seals to the contract. The "sartain neagro servant boy" was thereby sold, conveyed, and delivered to Josiah Nelson. The document made plain the social distance between sellers and buyer. Joshua Brooks was designated "gentleman," Josiah, "yeoman," an independent farmer, respectable enough, but no gentleman. Unlike the Brooks and Reed clans, the Nelson family of Lincoln and Lexington were not especially distinguished or prolific. In 1765 there were just three Nelson families there. Thomas Nelson Senior and his two grown sons were living on adjacent farms that straddled the Lincoln-Lexington boundary line and both sides of the Great Road linking the colony's western towns to the port of Boston.

Josiah was a prudent man and would have assured himself that the child was sound and healthy before completing the transaction. This necessitated an awkward examination of a squirming little boy, all the more uncomfortable since he had little experience of small children and was a stranger to Peter. Neither of the two women most central to the sale, Peter's mother, Peggy, and Elizabeth, the woman who would now raise him, appear to have been present. Peggy's absence is not surprising, but Elizabeth's is. Joshua and Mary Brooks both signed as the sellers, but only Josiah was the buyer. Of course Josiah would not have bought Peter if his wife objected. Elizabeth was probably too embarrassed to be present. However she might like to disguise the purchase of Peter as an act of charity or good business, the fact was that she was personally taking on the task of raising this Negro child, was buying a slave child, she who had no child of her own. Worse, how could she ignore the grief Peter's parents were feeling about this forced and permanent separation, this sale. Anyway, there was ample excuse to remain at home. Much had to be done to prepare for the toddler's arrival. Taking Peter into her home would impose a heavy responsibility on her, one no first-time parent is ever fully prepared for. But raising this particular child, this "servant for life" as Massachusetts residents preferred to call slaves, sorting out his place in her childless home and heart, would be more difficult than she could have imagined.

With the document signed and the business over, Peter was bundled up against the cold and Josiah left for home. The situation was uncomfortable and there were good reasons not to linger. Peter, like any exhausted child, would have begun crying for his mother and getting progressively harder to console. And night comes early in midwinter. The route back to the Nelson farm led over a steep hill, and the roads were icy and snow covered. To accommodate extra passengers, Josiah had come by horse-drawn sleigh. Jupiter likely accompanied him on the journey, to hold Peter and comfort him. Once at the Nelson homestead, though, he would be anxious to depart, giving his sleepy little son a final hug before turning to walk back alone, in the growing dark, as the farmhouse door opened and Peter disappeared.

Peggy and Jupiter had no further children.

CHAPTER TWO

Growing Pains

PETER'S MEMORIES of Lincoln revolved around the house, a handsome, two-story structure that had been, but was no longer, his home. It was a roomy house, if anything rather large for the three of them. Its windows faced south to catch the sun's warmth on frigid winter days, while the tall shade trees that surrounded it afforded relief from the stifling heat of summer. Inside, the traditional central chimney bisected and warmed the rooms, suffusing everything with the pleasant scent of wood smoke. The house stood just north of the Great, or Concord, Road, the main route to Boston, by season a snowy, muddy, or dusty thoroughfare winding between stone-walled fields and orchards. It was the perfect vantage point from which a child could eavesdrop on the steady parade of travelers—people, wagons, and animals—passing the farm.

The large barn behind the house was home to the family horse and to Josiah's prized pair of oxen, as well as his small herds of cows and sheep. There was a pen for the pig, although until 1770 the Lincoln town meetings routinely voted to grant swine the run of the town. House and barn were surrounded by Josiah's lands, which extended back over the gentle slope behind the buildings and south, across and along the road in front in each direction. The various small parcels outlined with rough stone walls were typical of the colony's family farms. On the north and west the house and barn were flanked by the family's tilled field. Here the land was flat and the location handy for all the work required to coax a crop out of the sandy, rocky Massachusetts soil and haul it to the protection of the barn. East of the house, between it and the more modest dwelling of Josiah's brother, Thomas, was a grassy meadow. Lincoln was famous for the fine grass its farmers sold to the cities along the coast. Beyond these fields to the north lay their hilly pastures

Josiah Nelson House, burned 1908. Photo by George A. Nelson.
Courtesy Minute Man National Historical Park

and a scattering of wood lots, while the front windows of the house looked south, over the road, to more pastures and the family's apple orchard. Every spring and summer the orchard, with its gnarled trees and long grass strewn with buttercups and dandelions, had been a lovely place to linger and play. In the fall it was littered with fragrant fruit, ripe for eating or crushing into cider. It was so fruitful, so peaceful a spot, at least until that April day in 1775 when they had frantically buried two British soldiers there.

The Nelsons, father and sons, were tightly knit, hardworking, and ambitious, at times overreaching, at times beset with troubles. Peter would have heard family tales about the old Nelson family house with its solid oak frame and a chimney with a brick oven and three fireplaces, one of which was so big it took a team of horses and two or three men to haul a log for it to the Nelson door. He would probably not have been told, but as he grew older heard whispers, that some years before he joined the family Thomas Senior had been unable to pay his debts and had nearly lost the family farm, including the large portion he had been given by his father-in-law. A judgment was taken out against him, and the property was sold to a Boston merchant. The family was permitted to remain. It took seven years of scrimping and saving before Thomas Junior, on behalf of his humiliated father, was able to pay off the debt and reclaim title to the family land. Members of small communities like Lincoln and Lexington are unlikely to forget such embarrassments. After that the Nelsons tended to keep to themselves.

There were other, deeper, problems that a sensitive child would only gradually come to understand. Thomas Senior, one of seven children, and his wife, Tabitha, had just three children of their own, twins Thomas Junior and Tabitha, and five years later Josiah. Both Thomas Junior and Tabitha seem to have had some weakness or disability. Thomas never served in the militia, a responsibility of all able-bodied men, and worked only a modest farm. He supplemented his income running a hop-house with Josiah and selling liquor from a little shop on his land. Josiah married at twenty-five, but Thomas waited until he was in his mid-thirties to wed Lydia, a woman two years his senior. His father built them a modest house, where their children, Lydia and Jonathan, were born. Thomas's twin sister, Tabitha, remained a spinster. At the time Peter was purchased, Tabitha was living with her parents in the family homestead. It was Josiah who was the hope of the family. Through dint of continual effort and scrimping, he and Elizabeth had managed to purchase parcel after parcel of farmland.

Elizabeth's family, the Flaggs, came from nearby Concord. She was one of eight children, their births stretching over twenty years. Elizabeth and her twin sister, Abigail, were the youngest. Their brother Jonathan, closest to them in age, died when only eleven. Their father, Eliazer, owned land in the little town of Grafton, some twenty miles west of Concord, which he sold to his sons when they came of age. Peter never met Eliazer, who died when Elizabeth was just sixteen. Sometime after his death Elizabeth's mother, Deborah, took her two youngest daughters and moved to Grafton to live with their brothers.

Elizabeth and Josiah would have known each other all their lives, but once she moved to Grafton their opportunities to meet would be rare. The memory of that lovely young girl must have haunted Josiah. His father helped him build the handsome home they now lived in, and when Elizabeth was twenty-two they married. The absence of children to inherit the land they were amassing, to fill the house, those "heirs and assigns" all the property deeds referred to, had been a continual worry to Josiah and a reproach to Elizabeth. For an eighteenth-century farm couple children not only gave parents the pleasure of sharing their lives and establishing a family but filled a serious, practical need. They were necessary to help with the strenuous, unrelenting work required to run a farm. And they were counted on to look after their mother and father in old age so their parents would not suffer the disgrace of being thrown upon very public, and often grudging, local charity. Little Peter would eventually be a help, but he was a slave and in everyone's eyes no substitute for children of their own.

Josiah, Elizabeth, and the little boy, alone in that fine house, lived a close family life. They gathered for their meals around the table positioned in front of that central hearth where morning and evening Josiah led them in prayer. "Lord make me thankful. Lord make me worthy of thy gifts. Lord keep me safe. Remember to honor thy Father and thy Mother."

Their farm was the westernmost of the Nelson farms. All three households worked together in the fields and kitchens. Josiah and Thomas also ran the round, stone hop-house they had built along the south side of the road, on the western perimeter of Josiah's land. For Peter the shared labors meant playmates. Lydia Nelson, Thomas Junior's wife, came visiting with her two children, and Elizabeth took Peter next door to Thomas's farm. Sometimes they all worked together at the senior Nelson home. When nineteen-month-old Peter appeared at Elizabeth's door, Lydia's daughter, another Lydia, was six and a half, and her son, Jonathan, barely four and a half. The three children grew up together sharing chores, complaints, and expeditions to the markets and shops in Concord, Lexington, and even Boston. Jonathan, the only boy of the younger generation, was the apple of his grandfather's eye. The future hopes for the Nelson families revolved around him, sole son, heir to three farms. Jonathan was a fine boy but never very strong. Some time after Peter arrived, John and William Thorning, boys closer in age to Lydia than to Peter, moved with their parents into the vacant homestead on the west side of Josiah's farm. They had two sisters as well, Mary, three years older than Peter, and Abigail, a year younger. In 1769 little Sally was born. The Thornings were a hardworking family, but not well off. Several years before they took possession of the North Lincoln farm, their father, John, had been warned out of Lincoln as an indigent. But they were determined to make good. The Thorning boys helped with the work and as they grew older were available to hire out to farmers like the Nelsons who were short-handed. With Sally's arrival, when Peter was six, there were eight children living in the three neighboring farms, making that small stretch of road a lively place.

When their chores were finished, Peter, Lydia, Jonathan, and their friends were free to amuse themselves. With the exception of schooling, lessons in farmwork, and a few appropriate tasks, even stern Puritan households permitted children under seven to occupy much of their time with childish things. The countryside provided all sorts of exciting and even useful possibilities. Wild blueberries grew in nearby marshes; there were lakes and ponds lively with fish where they could while away a summer afternoon batting at dragonflies and sneaking up on bullfrogs. In the woodlots and fields, deer, raccoons, skunks, possums, beavers, and a host of other small creatures went about their lives trying not to be noticed. Every spring and autumn brought immense flocks of ducks and geese to Concord's river meadows, a stop on their great migrations, filling the air with their raucous chatter. When the children were permitted they could wander a short distance down the road toward Lexington and watch the blacksmith at work in his shop or check on travelers coming and going at the Bull Tavern across from the smithy.

On Sundays the three Nelson families journeyed to church in Lexington, where the Reverend Jonas Clarke, the town's respected and feisty minister, preached on topics religious and political. It was Clarke who had married Peter's parents and baptized Peter and Peggy and Clarke who would minister at the crucial moments of their lives.

For Elizabeth Nelson, those first days after Peter's arrival must have been difficult ones, constantly reminding herself to treat him as their "servant for life" rather than as her child, maintaining a suitable emotional distance from the toddler. But what was a suitable distance, anyway, and how was one to achieve it? Under the circumstances this mental effort was bound to fail. She was too busy, as she added to her list of chores the tasks of feeding, training, caring for, and constantly looking after the lively little black boy. Happily, she could call on her sister-in-law, Lydia, mother of two, for assistance. The sisters-in-law shared the busy working lives of colonial farm women—feeding humans and the farm animals in all weathers, gardening, putting up preserves, sewing, spinning, making butter, cheese, candles, ministering to the sick, bartering for necessities. Peter added to the complexity, anxiety, and joys of these daily routines. Tabitha, Thomas's twin sister, living with her parents in the old family homestead, offered another pair of womanly hands. Like her mother, she was named for the Tabitha in the Bible, a very good woman and a disciple of Christ who, the Scriptures say, was raised from the dead by the apostle Peter. Did it give Peter a special place in Tabitha's heart? Her help would be appreciated caring for the three children and joining Elizabeth and Lydia with each season's household projects. The activities and company provided a welcome break from life with her aging parents. The three women found time to laugh, fret, and gossip as they worked. But no one in the family had experience raising a slave child, let alone one so young.

Unlike Elizabeth's relationship with Peter in those first years, Josiah's would have been more distant, not unlike any eighteenth-century father for that matter. His work was outdoors, and boys began to help with fieldwork only when they were around seven or older. The responsibility of raising this Negro boy to be an upright, pious, hard-working man like himself would weigh on Josiah. The welfare and reputation of his family was his personal responsibility. In addition to the labor of farming, he was on the lookout for more land, still buying and selling parcels, and earning extra income managing the hop-house with his brother. Middlesex County was a large hop-growing area, and a number of taverns catered to the tired and thirsty travelers on the Great Road. A short walk to the east of his farm stood the Bull Tavern and, less than two miles to the west, the Hartwell Tavern. The hop-house was a brilliant investment. Having pulled himself up from the ranks of laborer to husbandman, then to yeoman, Josiah was now the proud owner of a slave. When he purchased Peter, Lincoln's population of some 650 residents had only 28 slaves, and they were the property of the most prosperous and prominent men in the town—gentlemen. However fond he might become of Peter, he had to be mindful of the social distance between them. Peter could never be his heir.

A close and caring relationship with Peter within the home was one thing, the public display of it outside the home another. Nothing was more public in that small world than the weekly gathering of the community at church on Sunday. For Peter, those Sundays were a stark reminder that he was not like the other Nelson children, and he and everyone knew it.

Since Josiah's and Thomas Junior's farms were in Lincoln they would ordinarily be expected to attend the Lincoln church with other town residents. But the Nelson sons and their families continued to accompany their parents to the Lexington church. Before 1754, when the town of Lincoln was carved out of Concord and Lexington, the Nelson homesteads were all in Lexington. However, the new town's line went right through the Nelson lands, leaving Thomas Senior's homestead on the east, in the town of Lexington, his sons' farms west of his in the town of Lincoln. The Nelsons had always felt a part of Lexington. Anyway the Lexington church was more convenient, and its minister a far more stirring and popular preacher. The Reverend Clarke cut an impressive figure in his immense white wig and clerical gown. When he was excited by his subject, it was said his voice not only reached the top gallery of the church but could be distinctly heard by those in the neighborhood around the meetinghouse. His congregation was delighted to have so personable and able a minister after it had endured the fifty-year-long ministry of his predecessor, the Reverend John Hancock, a rigid disciplinarian. Hancock was renowned for insisting that church members who had sinned confess before the entire congregation before being admitted to the sacrament. The sinners were usually young engaged couples guilty of fornication. Their public statements of repentance were carefully noted in the church records, forgiven but not to be forgotten.

The decision to attend the Lexington church had an important impact on the family. Although the younger Nelsons lived in Lincoln, their Sundays in Lexington meant that their social and economic contacts were more often with the people of Lexington. And yet they were not citizens of Lexington and had no share in its governance. Being on the border of both communities, they became a marginal people in each.

Sunday was a particularly painful day for Peter. All men might be equal before God, but they were not equal in church. Congregational churches were rigidly hierarchical in their seating arrangements. Wealthy parishioners had prized seats or pews close to the altar or in some other special spot. They even handed these down in their wills. So blatant was this economic and social hierarchy that when the Lincoln church first laid out its seating arrangements, people got to choose their seats according to their assessed wealth, the richest choosing first, the poorest left the least desirable seats toward the back.

In Lexington men sat on benches on one side of the church, women on the other side, children at the rear, "where they might be inspected." A few wealthier families built pews against the walls. Christian charity was shown, though. Old people were given benches at the front, the wealthy people next. But whatever the arrangement for the whites, in every church the black congregants sat in a separate section, either at the back of a church or, if there was a balcony or gallery, up above. Negro heaven, it was sometimes facetiously called. The Lincoln church had a gallery, the Lexington church two tiers of galleries, one for the poorer whites, the second shared by the blacks and the town's stock of gunpowder. Both the Reverend Clarke in Lexington and the Reverend William Lawrence in Lincoln were happy to baptize blacks and welcomed them into their congregations, Clarke even refusing the customary offer of a slave to tend the ministerial farm. So the Negro heaven was full. The entire Lexington congregation, however, shared the discomfort of sitting on hard wood benches during those two-hour sermons, and most of the year everyone shivered with cold since there was no provision for heat.

As a black and a slave, Peter's place at church was with his people. His roots were doubly reinforced on Sundays by his mother, Peggy. She and his sister lived in Lexington and came to church with their owners, the Reeds. Peggy would help him up the stairs to the Negro section. There were other slave children there, and adult blacks, both slave and free. Since the Negro community was so scattered and busy with work during the week, the Sabbath gave them all a rare opportunity to meet and socialize. On Sunday mornings Peter was Peggy's son again. White boys were placed at the back of the church near the blacks. This helped the tithingman ensure a modicum of decorum from the most likely disturbers of the congregation during the Reverend Clarke's lengthy sermons. With his long crook at the ready, the tithingman could poke rambunctious boys and rouse any snoozing ones, or even an occasional sleepy adult. As Peter got older the presence of these other boys must have eased his self-consciousness about the seating arrangements and enlivened the services. But the ambiguity between being the Nelson's child, part of their white world of fiercely independent and free people, while belonging, indelibly, to the black underclass, a servant for life, would be painful for a child to contemplate. If the Nelsons were a marginal family, he was the most marginal member.

Education was something of an equalizer. From the age of four or five, Peter trooped off to the North Lincoln school with Jonathan and other boys and girls. By the age of six, boys, including slaves and servants, were expected to know the alphabet. Reading and writing was essential for a "decent Christian education." Arithmetic was essential for their working lives. True, at Lincoln town meetings there was continual grumbling about the cost of schools and tussles over where they should be located. But the aim was to have a school for the younger children in each district for several weeks every summer.

The tiny building that served for the school in North Lincoln was some two miles to the west of the Nelson farm, a healthy walk on a hot summer morning. On their way the children trudged past the fields and orchards of neighboring farms and hailed their neighbors as they went. The most interesting of the lot were William Smith and his wife, Catherine Louisa, newcomers who arrived in Lincoln in 1772. The young couple with baby Louisa Catherine in tow suddenly taking over one of the largest farms and handsomest houses in town excited a great deal of curiosity and a goodly dose of envy and bemusement. Billy, as he became known, was the son of the Reverend William Smith and his wife, Elizabeth, of Weymouth. Both parents were well off, and their children had every advantage. Billy's talented sister, Abigail, married the bright young lawyer John Adams. But Billy, the only son, had no head for books or money and, although only in his twenties, was already an embarrassment to his family. A letter described this pastor's son as "a person of slight significance . . . he did not even go to Harvard." Slight he was in fact, at just five feet, seven inches. And irresponsible. Though a poor businessman, Smith was a success with animals. Brother-in-law John Adams wrote that the struggling Boston merchant kept "2 Dogs, 4 Rabbits, six tame Ducks, a dozen Chickens, one Pidgeon, and some yellow Birds and other singing Birds, all in his little Yard." Above all Billy was a charmer, endlessly feckless, endlessly forgiven. Doubtless it was that charm that drew Catherine Louisa to him. With no head for business or finance, Smith quickly, and repeatedly, fell into debt. The 120-acre spread in Lincoln was a gift to Catherine Louisa from her mother a year before the couple wed. Smith's finances soon became so desperate that he mortgaged his wife's farm to his long-suffering father, the Reverend Smith, and then sold it to him a year later. When the couple finally moved out to Lincoln in 1772 to work the farm, it was the Reverend Smith's farm they were working. Two years later Billy's father-in-law, William Dodge, for reasons no one could fathom, leased him another 43 acres for five years, and again the Reverend Smith took over the lease to pay his son's debts. The size of Billy's holdings in Lincoln instantly made him one of the town's largest landowners. The failed merchant who knew little to nothing about farming worked the land with the help of his slave, Cato.

Clearly much depended on Cato's abilities. To his credit though, Smith was ready to try his hand at other vocations to add to his income. One year he served as the children's schoolmaster, and the town paid him for building a desk for the schoolhouse, presumably for the schoolmaster's use.

What Billy Smith lacked in business sense or farming know-how he made up for in political zeal. He was a member of the Sons of Liberty, and there were suspicions he had been persuaded to move to Lincoln to help shift cautious, loyal town opinion into the oppositionist camp. All in all, Smith was the subject of much curiosity. Before his brief stay in Lincoln was over, his doings were to cause considerable scandal and provide his neighbors with many more hours of disapproving gossip.

Next on the children's way to school came the Hartwell farms. In contrast to the Smiths, the Hartwells were old-timers with plenty of farming skill. Old Ephraim Hartwell's father had settled the family along the Concord Road when that section was still part of Concord, and it was probably his old house in which his grandson, Samuel, Ephraim's second oldest son, lived with his bright young wife, Mary, and their small daughters. Mary was one of the best-educated local women and, despite the demands of her own housework and little ones, occasionally took a turn serving as schoolteacher. Samuel's house and barn were on the north side of the road, although, like most Great Road farms, his had fields on the south side. Samuel was a kindly and talented man. In addition to running the substantial farm his father had given him, he was a clockmaker and locksmith. His fascinating little blacksmith shop was right next to the road where the children might peek in if they weren't late for school.

Next they came to the homestead of Ephraim Hartwell, patriarch of the family. He had started life as a shoemaker and had risen, with his father's gift of land and his own purchases, to style himself "gentleman." His oldest son, Jonas, was away studying at Harvard College—sometimes sons with little aptitude for farming were sent to college—but Ephraim's other grown sons, John and Isaac, still lived on the family farm and helped their father with the work. Although Ephraim called himself a gentleman, he had turned his parlor into a tavern and used the house as an inn, putting up travelers in one of the upstairs bedrooms, something no real English gentleman would ever think of doing. Their slave, Violet, helped Ephraim's wife, Elizabeth, cope with the work. The Hartwell farm was one of the largest in Lincoln, with its two-acre orchard, the biggest tilled field in town, and no fewer than six oxen. Farmers like Josiah considered themselves fortunate to have two such beasts.

Ephraim was held in high esteem by his neighbors and repeatedly served Lincoln as a town selectman, as a town meeting moderator, and in other key offices. Until extreme old age he was also regularly elected "sealer of leather," monitoring its quality, perhaps a testament to his early shoemaking talents. His sons, Samuel, John, and Isaac, were all well regarded and would all play an important part in the war to come. Ephraim's property was right next to the schoolhouse. When the children reached that part of the hill, they had arrived. They filed into the tiny building and put themselves into the hands of that summer's teacher.

The walk to school gave Peter the chance to see the other slaves who lived along the Great Road or were hired out by their masters to work on its farms and in its shops. The neighborliness and rhythms of a small farming community gave them the chance to get to know one another. All the adults would know Peter. Slaves occasionally helped out at Samuel Hartwell's blacksmith shop, and at Ephraim's home turned inn, Violet bustled about juggling household and tavern duties. Once the Smiths arrived Peter might also spy Cato laboring in the fields. There were no slave children living along the route. Simply spotting these other "servants for life," exchanging a word or two, provided some thread of connectedness while they doubtless kept an eye out for Peter. It is unlikely that there were any other black children at school.

The schoolhouse was built next to Joseph Mason's small home just beyond the Hartwell inn, close to the western boundary of Lincoln. Mason was a man with a small farm and a large family. He was a currier by trade with a talent for music and supplemented his income by teaching. From time to time his wife, Grace, Mary Hartwell, or some other neighbor took over the teaching. Under his tutelage the children toiled over their slates during the hot summer days, with the door to the single room left open to catch any passing breeze. They read the basic primers of the time, works laced with heavy doses of religion and moral sentiments. There was work to be done on the farms during the summer, but education was prized, and Mason's mixed crop of students was a valued summer harvest.

Death was a regular visitor to Peter's world. Religion taught him that each child of God must be prepared to meet his or her maker at any time, sound advice in an age when young and old were struck down with impartiality. Few children reached their teenage years without the loss of a parent or close family member. Peter was fortunate. Although the deaths began when he was four, at first his parents, black and white, and younger family members were spared. The first passing was not unexpected. On May 30, 1767, Josiah's mother, Tabitha, aged eighty-three, died. She and Thomas Senior had been married for more than fifty years. She was laid to rest three days later in the new Lexington churchyard, the first of the Nelson family to be buried there. As three-year-old Peter stood among the mourners that day, surrounded by adults buried in their own thoughts, he was far too young to notice that not a single gravestone in the Lexington cemetery marked the resting place of any of the congregation's African Americans buried there.

Carved on the tombstone that marked Tabitha's grave was the familiar, if somewhat old-fashioned reminder, presumably selected by her husband:

> Time was I stood as thou dost now,
> And view'd the dead as thou dost me:
> Ere long you'll be as low as I
> And others stand & Gaze on thee.

Thomas took the message to heart. Her death heralded the passing of a family generation and jolted him into dividing the bulk of his property between his two sons, leaving the serious farming to those with the strength for it.

Other deaths followed, the next affecting Jupiter. In 1768 Deacon Joshua Brooks, Jupiter's owner and briefly Peter's as well, passed away at the age of eighty, much lamented. He had been one of the Lincoln town founders, driven by his anxiety to separate from the Concord parish and especially its evangelical minister, a proponent of the Great Awakening, the so-called new light that was changing church practice. He remained a leader of the new community, active year after year in its politics, its business life, and its church. When the first Lincoln church needed a bell, Joshua donated the money. By the time of his death, however, he had already given the tannery and much of his property to his son, Joshua Junior. Jupiter's fate is unclear. Few records on the fate of slaves survive, but because he isn't mentioned in the will he seems to have been given to Joshua Junior already as his share of the deacon's property. The death of an owner was always the most perilous time for a slave, when a sale might be needed to pay off debts as part of an estate settlement.

Jupiter had belonged to the Brookses for more than twelve years when Deacon Joshua died, and New England families did not like to sell their slaves. Nor had the Brooks family any need to. They were prosperous and had all sorts of work needing doing at the tannery and slaughterhouse and on the family farm, sufficient reason to keep Jupiter. Still, any change could make matters more difficult, even falling under the control of a different master in the same family. Fortunately, Joshua Brooks Junior was a kindly, vigorous man, perhaps less rigid than his father. During the coming war he and Peter often served together. Of course, a sale to someone living in Lexington would have brought Jupiter closer to Peggy, or the pious deacon might have emancipated him on his death, as some owners did. But beggars can't be choosers, and neither could slaves, and there was much to be thankful for serving a good family and remaining near Peter. Whether he and Peter were able to meet often, or have time together, is uncertain. The Nelsons are not likely to have welcomed close contact between father and son. Peter had to be raised with their values and in their way, and Jupiter may have been reluctant to press the matter or unable to. Brief chance meetings, even sightings, could help assure Jupiter his son was well and reassure Peter that he was not alone.

Peggy's mistress died the following year. Sarah Reed was seventy. She was described on her tomb as the paragon of an eighteenth-century woman—"for Maternal Tenderness, peaceful Disposition, Meekness of Spirit, Prudence in Affairs, Piety to God, Charity to ye Necessitous and other Graces & Virtues which rendered her both amiable & useful in Life . . . an Ornament to her sex." If all this were true, she must have been a caring mistress. Her passing left Peggy with considerably greater duties and responsibilities for her aging master, who lived another ten years. William's numerous children and relatives were close at hand, however, if the need arose. Another passing, another funeral.

As 1770 drew to a close, the final death of Peter's early childhood occurred when Thomas Senior, then eighty-five, died. For many long-married couples the death of one soon leads to the death of the other. But Thomas was of sterner stuff and survived his wife by three years. He was, of course, fortunate to have his daughter, Tabitha, looking after him. His death left her alone in the small family house. Thomas had built this modest, more frugal house for himself, his wife, and his daughter and had abandoned the grand old family home once his sons were married. In addition to the house, he left Tabitha a small meadow, a pasture, a woodlot, and a cow, a modest legacy but enough for a single woman. Her brothers would be expected to see that she was comfortable.

On a gray, rainy November day, Thomas was laid to rest next to his wife. His gravestone bore the same ominous warning, somewhat differently phrased, as hers did:

Behold and see all that pass by,
As you are now so once was I;
As I am Now so you must be,
Prepare for Death and follow me.

The somber messages on the Nelson gravestones proved prophetic. A peaceful chapter was coming to an end. In 1770 the world began to close in on Peter. He was growing up and becoming increasingly aware of the tension between his status as an only child in a white household and as their black "servant for life." That alternative between a future of liberty or one of obedience was to be resolved in a surprising way as the little workaday farming communities he knew were drawn into the battle of nerves between the colonists and their mother country, a parallel and much larger struggle between a future of liberty or obedience.

Change and menace came from every direction—the markets they frequented, the travelers they met, the passionate debates in once-sleepy town meetings, the Sunday sermons of the Reverend Clarke, even the arrival of William Smith with whispered links to the Sons of Liberty. With all these changes came the whiff of death.

CHAPTER THREE

The Four Horsemen

Ye have not harkened unto me in proclaiming liberty every one to his brother,
and every man to his neighbor: Behold I will proclaim a liberty for you, saith
the Lord, to the sword, to the pestilence and to the famine; and I will make
you to be removed to all the kingdoms of the Earth.

JEREMIAH 34:17, cited in "Extract of a Letter from a
Gentleman in the country to His Friend," Boston, 1773

WAR, PESTILENCE, AND DEATH—three of the four terrible
Horsemen of the Apocalypse Peter knew from the Bible—had
been marching toward Lincoln from the time of his birth. The
fourth, Famine, would catch up with him later, in the Continental Army. By
1770, when he was seven, the first three had spurred their horses into a canter
and would soon arrive.

The events that brought War and Death to the Nelsons' door were hard
to unravel afterward, there were so many, and harder still because New England's white population had one set of concerns and its slaves another. Yet
the language and goal were the same—freedom. Unlike most children, Peter
overheard the passionate discussions of both races and like them he understood little of heated debates over taxation and individual rights. He did know
that at bottom were fears by the whites that they would be enslaved and hopes
by the slaves that they might be freed. Year by year the adults in his life, black
and white, grew increasingly anxious and upset. When political events raised
fears among whites about being oppressed and enslaved, Lexington's Reverend Clarke proclaimed those days of prayer and fasting or of thanksgiving
that added excitement to their workaday country life. The slaves in the congregation wondered whether the answer to those prayers would help them.

Pestilence was a stealthier horseman than the others and arrived with less fanfare, although its appearance would cause just as much anguish. Of course pestilence of one sort or another was a constant worry. No one, young or old, rich or humble, was immune. That lesson was driven home for Lincoln residents by the tragedy of the prosperous Hartwell family. Years earlier, in the fall of 1740, all five of Ephraim and Elizabeth Hartwell's young children died of "throat distemper" in just twenty-two days. The family's wealth could not save them or take away the pain. The Hartwells now had four fine, grown sons, yet those first little ones had not been forgotten. In the mid-1770s, though, just before war began, smallpox, a pestilence with a capital "P," appeared. It was many times more terrible than throat distemper. Peter later came to know its cost. Smallpox scarred, maimed, blinded, and killed. And as it disfigured, its victim endured excruciating pain. It was highly contagious and especially dangerous because victims were contagious before they had symptoms. Smallpox had taken a toll in the 1750s. It caused anxiety throughout the 1760s but returned in force in 1774 and remained a threat throughout the war, making life at home nearly as dangerous as life in Washington's army.

But that danger lay in the future. In the meantime it was the political events that the older generation particularly recalled. Looking back, Peter could see that the approach of those Horsemen, the events that propelled the white community from opposition to the mother country into open resistance and then violence, coincided with key moments in his life. The year he was born, 1763, marked the glorious and decisive triumph of British and American troops over the French, ending the French and Indian War. French Canada became British. New Englanders rejoiced. They need never again fear the French with their Indian allies sweeping down along their shores, burning coastal towns, or advancing through the forests attacking isolated western settlements and brutally slaughtering entire families. Massachusetts children heard tales about those poor children spared in these massacres by savage Indians only to be taken by them as human souvenirs. Now the nightmare was over, their towns would be safe, and vast western territories lay open to settlement. Yes, it was a joyful time, a hopeful time, a good time to be born. Or so it seemed.

Yet that joy had vanished almost immediately. Left with the bill for the victory, King George and disgruntled British taxpayers demanded the colonists shoulder the costs for their own defense. The old Navigation Acts designed to control American exports and ensure profits for English merchants, the acts so long and blithely ignored in the colonies, were now to be strictly enforced. These transport laws seemed unfair, and their sudden enforcement was deeply resented. Why should they be restricted in the products they produced? Why did they have to transport goods directly to Britain, where they were redirected to the purchasers? Colonial smugglers were helping their countrymen. Indeed, prominent smugglers came from some of the best colonial families, even the descendants of Lexington's former minister, the stern and godly Reverend Hancock.

Military matters were even more ominous. All able-bodied white men aged sixteen to sixty were, with few exceptions, required to be in the militia. Josiah served with the Lincoln militia. The rules on whether slaves were obliged, or even allowed, to serve, however, kept changing. Some people were opposed to giving slaves military training; others felt it was the duty of free men, not slaves, to protect their community. Many masters simply didn't want to spare their slaves from their daily chores. Some enslaved men, especially those owned by militia officers, drilled with the rest, proud to carry a gun and serve alongside the white men of their town. Jupiter doesn't seem to have had that opportunity, at least at first. Parliament now passed new, worrisome militia acts that allowed the king to shift citizen soldiers from serving officers of their choosing to serving under the command of British army officers. The strict discipline and brutal punishments inflicted on British soldiers was well known. It may have been justified for the British rank and file, who were often the most desperate characters, sometimes taken right from jails. But the colonists were not of that caliber. The new laws also gave those officers the right to disarm the local militia regiments, seize their guns, their personal weapons, and send them home humiliated and defenseless.

Militia service was unpopular as men had other things to be doing. But it was better to shoulder the burden of defense themselves than to rely on hardened, professional soldiers. Professional armies could not be trusted to respect popular rights. Citizen soldiers would never oppress their own people. Everyone knew that. That is why there was such alarm after the French and Indian War when the British army did not return to Britain. Had the army been sent to guard their western frontiers there would have been less concern. But the soldiers were kept in American cities. People policed by a professional army, as so many unfortunate European nations were, were people whose rights were in danger or already defunct. The English Bill of Rights—the colonists' birthright—clearly stated that no standing army should be maintained in time of peace without the consent of Parliament. The problem was that Parliament did consent to this army in the colonies, and the colonists had no representatives in Parliament. The Massachusetts legislature, the General Court, had not consented, and would not consent. "To have an army continually stationed in the midst of a people, in time of peace," the Reverend Simeon Howard fretted, "is a precarious and dangerous method of security." Sober Massachusetts heads nodded in agreement. No good would come of it.

And no good did. To maintain this unwanted army, unwanted taxes were levied. In 1764 and 1765 direct taxes were placed on sugar and other imports, and in 1765, the year Peter was sold to the Nelsons, the infamous Stamp Act, worst of them all, was passed. It was the first internal tax, a bad precedent, and was levied on the paper for legal documents and newspapers. The proceeds of these taxes were earmarked for the support of the British army based among them, insult added to injury. Repressive taxes to support an army to oppress them.

It was nearly impossible, even for busy farm families like the Nelsons, to ignore these dangers. Every Sunday the Reverend Clarke hammered home the peril to the Nelson family, to Peggy's Reeds and their neighbors, to the slaves sitting in Negro heaven, to all the good people of Lexington, drawing lessons from the Bible for the menace of the times. Clarke was a leading spokesman for opponents of British policies, including the network of Committees of Correspondence begun in Boston in 1764 and the so-called Sons of Liberty formed a year later. He was a friend of those ringleaders, Samuel Adams and John Hancock. These Sons of Liberty planting their liberty poles in town after town, inciting tarring and feathering, first formed in 1765 to oppose the Stamp Act but remained to prod the colonies into greater and greater protest and finally war. Boston was home to the first Committee of Correspondence. Its Committee of Correspondence urged other towns to form their own committees to spread news and work jointly. They peppered local town meetings with calls for protest. Those meetings, where the free men of each community gathered to legislate for their town, took place several times a year in the local meetinghouse, their church. Now the men of Lincoln found among the list of articles for consideration—alongside those dealing with whether the swine should run free, who would hold various town offices, which indigent persons had been warned out of town, how much to spend on roads and schools—requests by the Boston activists to put Lincoln on record in support of their protests.

Nodding agreement with the Reverend Clarke in church and complaining to neighbors about the British was no longer enough. Decisions had to be made, votes taken. The Reverend Clarke was an eloquent writer, and he drafted passionate letters of protest to be sent in the name of the Lexington town meeting. Concord's own minister, the Reverend William Emerson, was no less committed to the vigorous defense of political rights and enthusiastically endorsed the Concord town meeting's bold measures. But Josiah and Thomas Nelson, the Hartwells, the Brookses, and their neighbors, wedged between impetuous Concord to their west and tumultuous Lexington to the east, were cautious men, loyal but cool-headed. Until 1775 Lincoln was led by Tories, Loyalists, although alongside more moderate men such as the Brookses and Ephraim Hartwell. Charles Russell, the town's richest man and its usual choice for the legislature, was a Tory, as were Captain Ebenezer Cutler of East Lincoln and Captain Joseph Adams of South Lincoln. The Nelsons, with a foot in each town, were fired into fever pitch at church in Lexington and cooled off in Lincoln. Rights were important, but Lincoln men believed that protests should be lawful.

In 1764 just such a peaceful protest against the tax on imports, a boycott of British goods, was organized and spread quickly. Opposition to the Stamp Act the following year, however, turned violent. A Boston mob, led by the Sons of Liberty, burned the stamp distributor in effigy and wrecked his shop before attacking the homes of the royal customs officials, burning their furniture and tossing their books and papers out into the street. Good people abhorred violence. They made that clear. But when Lincoln town meeting members, law-abiding and sensible, were asked whether they would instruct their representatives to compensate "the persons that suffered in Boston by the mob," they voted No.

Parliament was sensible, too, and when it was impossible to collect the Stamp Tax, it voted to repeal it. There were "Rejoicings at Boston," the Reverend Clarke noted, when news of the repeal reached Massachusetts. But New Englanders took no chances, and three days later the Lexington militia spent the day drilling. In July 1766, when the repeal took effect, Lexington celebrated with a day of thanksgiving. The rejoicing was premature. Parliament followed up its reluctant withdrawal of the Stamp Act with the Declaratory Act, which proclaimed its right to pass laws for the American colonies "in all cases whatsoever." A century earlier the same proclamation had been directed at the Irish, not a happy comparison. Suspicious Americans long feared that British leaders might treat their American colonists in the heavy-handed way they treated the people of Ireland. In their joy over repeal of the Stamp Act, however, few in Massachusetts noticed the Declaratory Act. What they did notice was that while a hated tax was withdrawn, the British army remained.

Parliament would not be trifled with, and the following year it passed the Townshend Act, a general revenue act to tax specific goods at American ports to finance "the administration of justice and support of civil government," including that unwanted army. Once again New England towns agreed to boycott British goods. In January 1768, Josiah, Thomas, and the other men of Lincoln's town meeting were asked to join Boston to encourage "the produce and manufactures of this Province and to lessen the use of superfluities im-ported from abroad." After reflection—a move of such political significance demanded reflection—they pledged not to "purchase any one article of any person that imports goods contrary to the agreement of the merchants of the town of Boston."

Boycotts did not satisfy the inflamed Massachusetts legislature. Members drafted a sharp letter of protest against the tax and sent copies to other colonial assemblies urging them to follow suit. Words have costs, and the British were fed up with the quarrelsome province. Their response was swift and angry. Four army regiments were sent to Boston, one soldier for every four inhabitants.

Peter, not yet three, was too young to remember the Thanksgiving pro-claimed at Lexington on July 25, 1766, for the repeal of the Stamp Act, but he may have remembered the fast the Reverend Clarke announced for Septem-ber 29, 1768, "on Account of the times! Fears on every side!" Their prayers and fasting failed to keep the British troops from landing at Boston two days later, followed by what the reverend branded "A Day of Darkness!!" By 1769, while Peter was toiling over his sums in Joseph Mason's small schoolhouse, the people of Boston began calling on one another to arm.

The following March, the very day the boycott of British goods con-vinced Parliament to repeal all the Townshend duties except the tax on tea, a confrontation between British soldiers and a Boston mob turned violent. A lone British sentry standing guard at the Boston customs house on a bitterly cold day was harassed by local toughs hanging around the docks. Snowballs and rocks were thrown. The sentry sent for help. Eight soldiers headed by a young officer raced to their comrade's aid, bayonets fixed. Confronted with the rapidly growing, heckling crowd spraying them with stones and bottles, afraid for their safety, they fired. Five colonists fell dead; one, Crispus Attucks, was a black man. The Sons of Liberty promptly branded the incident a "massacre," and one of their members, the silversmith Paul Revere, quickly engraved a picture of the event, the better to publicize the atrocity. The Massachusetts House of Representatives could not resist reminding the British: "A military force if posted among the People, without their express Consent, is itself, one of the greatest Grievances, and threatens the total subversion of a free Constitution."

There was that word "free," a free Constitution, men born free. Peter, the young "servant for life," knew how thrilled and disturbed local slaves were by the stirring talk of rights and freedoms, how important every statement that reflected, even indirectly, on their plight, was to his elders. In 1764, when Stephen Hopkins pointed out that "one who is bound to obey the will of another is as really a slave though he may have a good master as if he had a bad one," Massachusetts slaves said, "Amen!" They appreciated Richard Bland's outrage that the colonists "were not sent out to be Slaves, but to be the Equals of those that remain behind." Were they not a living example of the tragedy of the slave condition, constantly worried that they might be sold to a cruel master, purchased by a sea captain, or sent to the large plantations in the South or even to the Caribbean, where slaves were often brutally treated and died by the thousands? The depression that followed the French and Indian War meant less employment for blacks, and when there was not enough work, many were sold. Happily, Jupiter and Peggy were owned by wealthy families with plenty of work to do, but other slaves were less fortunate. Even if the sale was a local one, as Jupiter and Peggy knew too well, they were likely to be separated from their loved ones—husbands from wives, parents from children, brothers and sisters from each other. The black community retold the terrible story of two Boston slaves reported in Boston's *Evening Post* in 1746. A Negro man from the North End of Boston and a Negro woman belonging to a gentleman at the South End had "contracted an intimate and strict Friendship together." When the woman learned she was to be sold "into the Country," the paper reported, "they resolved to put an End to their lives, rather than be parted; and accordingly, at seven o'clock (the Wench being at the House of her countryman), they went up Stairs into the Garret, where the Fellow, as is supposed, cut out the Wench's Throat with a Razor, and then shot himself with a Gun prepared for the Purpose." They were "both found lying upon the Bed, she with her Head cut almost off, and he with his Head shot all to Pieces."

Liberty and slavery, those words, again and again, turned up in conversations carried on over Peter's head as he ate at the Nelson hearth and in the hurried exchanges of the blacks surrounding Peggy every Sunday in the dizzying heights of Negro heaven and in hasty, excited remarks after church. As a servant in the Reed household, Peggy was ideally placed to pass on the latest news and gossip from Boston. Massachusetts slaves followed political events closely, hoping for some benefit for themselves. They prayed, fasted, or gave thanks with the rest and wondered how a people so jealous of their own liberty could justify keeping slaves!

While white colonists feared the British might take away their freedom, their slaves had been waging a campaign against the colonists. God even raised up white champions to help. Many Massachusetts clergy argued for a general emancipation, and Massachusetts's own James Otis was a hero to both races. Otis, who famously resigned his post with the admiralty court to defend Boston merchants against general search warrants, argued before Peter was born that Americans "white or black" were "by the law of nature freeborn." Otis scolded the whites for their effort to overthrow the mild form of so-called slavery Britain was imposing on them "while forcing the real thing on their black fellow-countrymen."

Otis was not alone. There was considerable opposition in Massachusetts to the slave trade, and even to slavery itself. In 1755 the seaport town of Salem instructed its deputy to the legislature to call for an end to the importation of slaves. In 1766 and 1767 Boston's representative called for total abolition. And in 1773 the towns of Medford, Sandwich, and Leicester demanded an end to the slave trade. To encourage individuals to emancipate their slaves several towns agreed to waive the bond that needed to be posted when slaves were freed. Lincoln, Lexington, and Concord made no such calls, no such moves.

The Massachusetts General Court did try several times to end slavery. In 1767, while whites chafed over the imposition of new taxes, the lower house considered a bill "to prevent the *unwarrantable and unusual Practice* . . . of inslaving Mankind in this Province and the importation of slaves." But the General Court hesitated, and in 1771, when it finally agreed to a measure to stop the importation of slaves from Africa, Governor Thomas Hutchinson vetoed it. He claimed it was against his instructions, but added that it was unnecessary anyway because slavery in Massachusetts was so mild in nature.

Massachusetts slaves had not waited for others to save them. They were entitled to be heard in court, and several took the initiative to sue for their freedom. In 1770, when James, slave of Richard Lechmere of Cambridge, sued Lechmere for keeping him in bondage, blacks raised money to carry on the suit. James won his freedom. Time after time when slaves sued their owners, white juries gave the verdict for freedom. But that was freedom for a particular individual in a specific case, not freedom for all. Not freedom for Peggy or Jupiter or Peter and his sister.

Then in June 1772, a year after the disappointment of the Massachusetts initiative to abolish slavery, a wonderful thing happened. William, Lord Mansfield, chief justice of King's Bench, England's highest common law court, found that James Somerset, an escaped slave brought to England by Charles Stewart of Virginia, could not be repossessed and shipped to Jamaica to be sold. In a ruling that boomed across the Atlantic like a thunderbolt, Lord Mansfield declared: "The state of slavery is of such a nature, that it is incapable of being introduced on any reasons, moral or political; but only positive law, which preserves its force long after the reasons, occasion, and time itself from whence it was created, is erased from memory; It's so odious, that nothing can be suffered to support it but positive law. Whatever inconveniences therefore may follow from a decision, cannot say this case is allowed or approved by the law of England, and therefore the black must be discharged." The air of England, it was said, was too free for a slave to breathe! Once there, he was free.

Electrified by the decision, slaves in Massachusetts brought a general suit against their bondage. They argued that they could not be enslaved because, as the English judge had recognized, no positive law permitted anyone to hold a human in slavery, and slavery was contrary to common law, inconsistent with natural rights and natural liberty. Mansfield meant his decision to be narrowly construed, but that is not how slaves or their supporters saw it. In 1773 a group of Boston slaves sent an eloquent petition to Governor Hutchinson, his council, and the House of Representatives pleading to have slavery abolished. They admitted that some slaves "are vicious (who doubtless may be punished and restrained by the same laws which are in force against other of the King's subjects) but many were discreet, sober," able "to bear a Part in the Public Charges." "How many of that Number have there been and are now in this Province," they asked, "who have had every day of their Lives imbittered with this most intolerable Reflection, That let Their Behaviour be what it will, neither they nor their Children to all Generations, shall ever be able to do, or to possess and enjoy any Thing, no, not even *Life itself,* but in a Manner as the *Beasts that perish.*" They concluded, "We have no Property! We have no Wives! We have no Children! No City! No Country! But we have a Father in Heaven, and we are determined . . . to keep all his Commandments."

A second petition, entitled "Thoughts on Slavery," asked the legislature to make a law to prevent importation of any more slaves "into this Government and also adopt some Method to relieve those who are now in Bondage in the Province." Using the reasoning in the Somerset case, petitioners claimed that slavery was against the charter of Massachusetts Bay and incompatible with the laws of Christ. Neither incompatibility moved Governor Hutchinson to act. In this instance both his British superiors, content to continue the slave trade to their colonies, and most of his American constituents would have approved of his approach. Caught between the views of his neighbors and the increasingly unpopular policies of his superiors, however, Hutchinson's popularity would quickly evaporate.

The irony of whites jealous of their freedom owning slaves was not lost on the author of a Boston newspaper article published while the petitions were pending. "It has long been a surprise to me and many others," he wrote, "that a people who profess to be so fond of freedom, and are taking every method to preserve the same themselves, and transmit it to their posterity, can see such numbers of their fellow men, made of the same blood, not only in bondage, but kept so even by them." "Can such a conduct," he asked, "be reconcilable with the love of freedom?"

These concerns for freedom shared by all the colonists began to converge, and War, Pestilence, and Death broke into a gallop. The year Lord Mansfield gave his ruling in the Somerset case, the Lexington town meeting, pointing to "the present distressed and alarming state of our Public affairs," unanimously voiced alarm about the colony's Charter Rights against Parliament's "infringement" and resolved, "That it is the natural right & indisputable duty of every man, consequently of every society or body of men, to consult their own safety & to take measures for the preservation of their own Liberty and Property, without which Life itself, can scarcely be deemed worth preserving." They chose a committee of seven, headed by Peggy's master, William Reed, to report to the town. The problem this time was tea. The new British East India Act gave the East India Company a needed financial boost by bestowing on it a monopoly on the sale of tea to America. Even with the tax the company's tea would be cheaper than the smuggled tea the colonists drank. But the colonists, or at least the Sons of Liberty, resented the tax and the monopoly and were determined it should not stand. In January the Lexington town meeting approved a resolution: "That if any heade of a family of this Towne, or any person shall from this time Forward & until the duty be taken off purchase any Tea, or use, or consume any Tea in their families, such person shall be looked upon as an enemy to this Towne, & to this country, and shall by this Town be treated with neglect & contempt."

Lincoln's response was more measured. Lincoln men also chose a committee to "take into consideration the present circumstances of the town with respect to their constitutional rights and privileges in common with all other towns in the Province." They assured the town of Boston, "We will not be wanting in our assistance according to our ability in prosecuting all lawful and constitutional measures as shall be thought proper for the continuance of all our rights, privileges and liberties both civil and religious being of opinion that a steady united preserving conduct in a constitutional way is the best means under God of obtaining the redress of all our grievances." Lincoln people preferred orderly, legal procedures, "a steady united preserving conduct in a constitutional way," but events overtook them.

Late that year of 1773 three East India Company ships carrying the first cargo of tea, 342 boxes worth ten thousand pounds, entered Boston harbor. The day before the tea was to be unloaded, activists unable to get the governor to prohibit the tea from being brought ashore disguised themselves as Indians and boarded the ships. Demanding the keys to the hold from the captains, they hauled the tea chests on deck, smashed them with their tomahawks "so as thoroughly to expose them to the effects of the water," and tossed them into the sea. British ships of war lay anchored in the harbor but, for some reason, made no attempt to intervene while box after box was dumped overboard. Only a few locals tried to retrieve some handfuls of tea for home use.

This destruction was a wanton act of vandalism, and Boston was threatened with retribution if it did not make good the losses to the company. The Boston Committee of Correspondence appealed to surrounding towns for support. The Lincoln town meeting's hand was forced. Their response referred to "the present gloomy cituation of our publick affairs." They pronounced the duty on tea "alarming" not only because it infringed their rights but because "the same our enemies are dealing by us like the great enemy of mankind. viz. endeavoring to ensnare us by those things to which we are not necessitated but by our own contracted ill habits: although if tea were properly used it might be of some advantage." Noting that "the present plan seems to be to ensnare us above said we need only (had we virtue enough for that) to shun the bate as we would shun the most deadly poison: notwithstanding considering so many are so habituated to the use of tea as perhaps inadvertently to ruin themselves and the country thereby and others so abandoned to vice expecting to share in the profits arising from the ruin of their country as to use all means in their power to encourage the use of tea." They commended "the spirited behaviour of the town of Boston" to get the consignees to resign their offices "or any other lawful means" and agreed, in language similar to Lexington's, "not to purchase or use any tea nor suffer it to be purchased or used in our families so long as there is any Duty laid on such tea by an act of the British parliament—and we will hold and esteem such as do use tea enemies to their country—and we will treat them with the greatest neglect."

But the letter went on to explain that should this boycott of tea fail to produce a repeal of the act,

> We trust we have courage and resolution sufficient to encounter all the horrors of war in the defense of those rights and privileges civil and religious which we esteem more valuable than our lives and we do hereby assure not only the town of Boston but the world that whenever we shall have a clear call from heaven we are ready to join with our brethren to face the most formidable forces rather than tamely to surrender up our rights and privileges into the hands of any of our own species not distinguished from ourselves except it be in disposition to enslave us.

Given a "clear call from heaven," moderate Lincoln men were ready to fight rather than be enslaved. Unwilling to burn all bridges, however, their letter concluded: "At the same time we have the highest esteem of all lawful authority and rejoice in our connection with Great Britain as long as we can enjoy our charter rights and priviledges."

Article 2 of that Lincoln meeting, whether to build an almshouse, was referred to the next town meeting.

In 1774, when Peter was eleven, Lincoln began preparations for war. Years afterward the provocation for that final chain of events seemed almost trivial compared to the dire consequences that were to follow. The dumping of the East India tea was met with the severest penalties for the entire colony, driving even quiet men to ally themselves with extremists. Bostonians and the General Court refused to pay for the lost tea. The British were furious. They decided that the entire colony was to be punished until restitution was made for the tea, for losses sustained by Crown officials, and until King George decided that "peace and obedience to the laws" had been restored. The following spring the nature of the punishment was spelled out in a series of acts. The port of Boston, mainstay of the city's and the region's economy, was closed and the colonial government was moved north to the port of Salem, the customs facilities still farther north to Marblehead. Troops were sent to reinforce the already substantial British garrison in Boston.

There was more. The Massachusetts Bay Charter, with its precious guarantee of rights and privileges, was revoked. The Governor's council was no longer to be elected by the legislature but appointed by the Crown and to serve at its pleasure, and no town meetings other than one annual meeting were to be held without the royal governor's written consent. The meeting's agenda had to be approved by the British. Even juries were to be selected by the governor. By June and July the residents of Lexington and Lincoln were being regularly called on to "Fast on the Times."

All these restrictions would have been hard enough to bear if Governor Hutchinson was in charge, but he now stepped down, and on September 1, Thomas Gage, commander of British troops in North America, a career soldier, was made governor of Massachusetts! The long-feared military rule was at hand. Two days before Gage's appointment, on August 30, delegates from every town in Middlesex County convened at Concord to organize resistance. They pledged to lay down their lives, if necessary, "in support of the laws and liberties of their country."

Other colonies came to their aid. In a grand show of solidarity New York promised a ten-year supply of food for the people of Boston. Herds of sheep were sent from Connecticut, and provisions dispatched from distant South Carolina. Colonists five hundred miles away in Virginia suggested a congress of representatives from every colony to agree on a uniform plan for the defense and preservation of their common rights. That fall the congress met in Philadelphia with representatives from every colony but Georgia. Paul Revere delivered to the delegates a copy of the just completed Suffolk Resolves, resolutions drawn up at a meeting of Boston and other towns of Suffolk County. The resolves pronounced the recent so-called Coercive Acts to punish Massachusetts unconstitutional and void and called on those charged with enforcing them to resign. They urged Massachusetts to establish its own government and collect its own taxes and charged its towns to arm and form their own militia, independent of the British government. The resolves concluded with the assertion that subjects no longer owed loyalty to a king who violated their rights.

And so it began. In the autumn of 1774 the members of Massachusetts' former legislature created a Provincial Congress that was to meet in Cambridge and chose a Committee of Safety headed by John Hancock. And the towns debated the purchase of bayonets and cannon and the establishment of minute companies to protect their community on a moment's notice.

That same year, in the midst of the political crisis, smallpox struck. Those who had managed to avoid the disease in the 1750s were now especially vulnerable, along with young children and people over forty-five. The dread pox was so contagious it could be spread by simply inhaling droplets from air around victims or touching them or their possessions, then touching your mouth or nose. The contagion was carried through the air when the floors in sickrooms were swept and clung to the bedclothes used by the sick. Travelers who had been infected often unknowingly spread the disease, since the incubation period was up to two weeks. During the 1751 outbreak it was believed that refugees from Boston infected Concord and other communities as they fled the city. For the Nelsons, the steady stream of travelers on the Great Road to Concord that passed just in front of their home carried with them the threat of exposure.

An expert on the epidemic of the 1770s described those who were susceptible to smallpox as living a life of incessant dread. The surest way to survive the epidemic was to be inoculated with the virus. Inoculation usually resulted in a more mild form of the illness, and then recovery. Some doctors in the colonies began inoculating patients. Special hospitals were set up to permit patients to be inoculated and then treated when they fell ill. But many local communities were afraid to permit inoculation or smallpox hospitals in their area. They had good reason. Many inoculated patients didn't bother to remain quarantined during the two weeks before they became ill, thus often spreading the deadly disease to their neighbors and friends. There were riots in Salem and Marblehead in 1774 after inoculation hospitals were set up in those towns. Terrified mobs forced both hospitals to close. Four Salem men who stole clothes hanging outside one of the hospitals were tarred and feathered because the clothes might have been contaminated. New York and New Jersey permitted doctors to inoculate and set up special smallpox hospitals, but not New England. Instead strict quarantines were observed during outbreaks, and all smallpox inoculation was banned except during the worst epidemics.

That standard was met when the 1774 outbreak quickly became one of the worst in memory. In the crowded Boston streets patrolled by General Gage's army the disease began to spread. Gage's soldiers were largely immune, having been exposed to smallpox in Britain. The local population was not. Now, along with fears for their liberties, Pestilence brought a more basic fear, that they and their loved ones might fall victim to this painful, disfiguring, and often fatal disease. Smallpox would not stay bottled up in Boston for long. By the fall of 1775 the churchyards of Lexington and other towns west of Boston were filling with its victims, friends and neighbors of the Nelsons. For the moment the Nelsons were spared.

There were so many dangers, but some, at least, came coupled with opportunities. Every child knew that God helps those who help themselves and the bitterness between the colonists and the British offered an opening for slaves seeking emancipation—one way or the other. The question was which way. If it came to violence, should Massachusetts slaves join their masters against the British, hoping that they would realize the inconsistency in fighting for their freedom while denying it to others? Or would the British, whose great judge had decreed slavery inconsistent with common law, be a more logical ally? Was there little to be gained risking one's life for either side, since the quarrel between the colonists and the British was not their quarrel? Many slaves were convinced that helping their masters would not help them. All the talk of freedom did not specifically include their freedom. Their own appeals for a general emancipation had been rejected. Writing to her husband, John, that crucial year of 1774 Abigail Adams reported the rumour that blacks had informed the governor they would fight for him if he promised to give them their liberty. This offer, or at least word of it, was suppressed. But the testing time was coming and the people of Lincoln, free and slave, were soon to hear that "clear call from heaven."

CHAPTER FOUR

In the Crosshairs

O N THE LAST DAY OF Peter's childhood a fine April rain fell, helping nudge the reluctant Massachusetts woodland into leaf. On the little family farms clustered around the neat eighteenth-century villages, the familiar, workaday world he knew so well went on as usual—praying, washing, cooking, tending the animals, turning them out, getting on with the annual effort to work the indifferent soil into a grudging fruitfulness. Toward sunset the sky cleared, and in the moonlight the apple blossoms in the family orchards up and down the Great Road were fragrant in the damp air and reflected a cool whiteness. In many ways it had been an ordinary day. But as Peter settled into his bed that evening, wrapped in the soothing darkness, he knew Josiah and Elizabeth would be sleeping lightly, listening for unusual sounds—rapid hoofbeats, strange voices, messengers—the signal they were waiting for and dreading.

The year was 1775, ten years since Josiah had purchased Peter and brought the little boy home, but it was still just the three of them in the spacious house by the side of the Great Road. There were no other children. None were expected. At nearly twelve Peter was finally the helper that designation "servant" on his bill of sale promised. He was devoted to Elizabeth and Josiah and was the only son they would have. As he grew into a sturdy adolescent, tall for his age, the question of his identity became more urgent and troubling. It was typical in both North and South for slave and white children to play together, but once they reached Peter's age, or even before, certainly before sexual maturity, the friendships cooled as each race prepared for its separate fate.

Peter's friendship with Jonathan and Lydia might already have begun to take that turn. How sad it must have seemed to the Nelsons that this slave boy's strapping good health was such a contrast to the frailty of Jonathan, Thomas's boy and the sole Nelson heir. Peter was Elizabeth and Josiah's only child, but he was also their property. His future was unclear. Did Josiah mean to follow the practice of some slave-owners and free Peter when he came of age? Josiah, who prized property? Owning a slave had put him in the ranks of the town's most prominent citizens. The question of Peter's fate troubled the households of his families white and black. As it turned out, the great events about to envelop all of them would decide the issue.

This April night the crisis so long looming in the larger world suddenly burst upon them, placing the Nelsons and their neighbors in the eye of a storm. It had been expected. The sense of tension and menace had become over-whelming, even for a boy fully occupied with farm chores. The stakes in the struggle between Great Britain and the people of Massachusetts had been ratcheted up significantly the previous October, when an emergency provincial congress meeting in Cambridge summoned every town and district in the colony to prepare for military action. Each town was to reorganize its militia to form separate companies of minutemen and make sure they were well armed. These new companies would be independent of British control and could exclude the local Tories or Loyalists included in the regular militia. The minuteman companies consisted of mostly younger men and the best fighters who were to keep themselves in a constant state of readiness, awaiting a call to action from the Massachusetts Provincial Congress's new Committee of Safety, charged with coordinating the colony's defenses. The regular militia would continue, and groups of boys too young and men too old for the militia were to form watch companies to spread any alarm.

The men of Lexington met in town meeting two weeks after the congress's request. The first item on the agenda was "what methode the Town will take to encourage Military Discipline, and put themselves in a posture of defence against their enemies." They agreed to add another two and a half barrels of gunpowder to the town supply, provide ball and flint and a pair of drums to equip a company of minutemen, and to accept the offer of two cannon from the town of Watertown. A committee of three was chosen to get the "said pieces well mounted and as cheap as they cane." Lincoln organized as well, if more slowly. Their meeting in January debated "whether they will pay minutemen in case any are appointed." The answer was "yes," and money was voted to provide each minuteman a bayonet, cartridge box, steel rammer, gunstock, and knapsack. But the British soldiers would arrive before the promised bayonets.

Serious preparations were expected of the minutemen. They were to drill for four hours a day twice a week and be paid for this. The winter was a mild one so the local minute companies were able to drill twice weekly, although during especially cold days they practiced their maneuvers inside a barn wearing mittens. Josiah and nearly all the men and teenaged boys of Lincoln were enrolled in the militia, the minute company, or the watch company. Friends and neighbors now sported military titles: captains, lieutenants, sergeants, privates. For some reason now lost, perhaps because of some infirmity, Josiah's brother, Thomas, was not involved. His son, Jonathan, was a year too young to serve. The region's few Negro men, free and slave, were exempt from militia service. But being exempt was not the same as being banned. Many were willing and anxious to participate and handy with a rifle. For now, few slaves except those owned by officers got that chance. British spies were to discover that most slaves in New England, who seemed to have little reason to get involved in this dangerous dispute, shared the general anger at British policies and especially the colonists' passionate insistence on individual liberty. Although it was unclear what the white man's fight for freedom would mean for them, there was clearly a desire to join the common cause, perhaps with the hope that men fighting for their freedom couldn't, in good conscience, enslave other men.

Black participation in the white men's struggle, however, would soon provoke tense debates among colonial and British leaders. The thousands of slaves living in New York, New Jersey, and points south seldom followed the example of their New England brethren. Among those who chose the other side was Titus, a New Jersey slave, who fled to the British later that year when his Quaker master refused to free him on his twenty-first birthday. Later his path and that of Peter's father, Jupiter, would cross.

The communities of Middlesex County, especially those near Concord, were on full alert because Concord along with Worcester, a town thirty-odd miles west, were collection points for the arsenal of arms and ammunition meant to equip a rebel army of some fifteen thousand men. It was to be a defensive army, but an army nonetheless. Over the winter large quantities of weapons had been manufactured or purchased and stashed at Concord along with ammunition and food. The feverish preparations could not, and would not, have escaped the notice of local Tories, sympathizers of King George. It was only a matter of time before General Thomas Gage, the British commander, felt compelled to send troops from Boston to destroy the growing arsenal. In the meantime Gage was sending out spies to learn what the colonists intended and where their arsenal was hidden. One of these spies was John Howe.

Howe was careful to dress like a Yankee when he was sent out on April 5. His mission was to gauge the mood and hostile activities of the residents west of Boston as far as Concord and Worcester and consult with the government's friends. He pulled on heavy leather breeches and blue mixed stockings, wound a silk handkerchief around his neck, and covered everything with a gray coat. He pretended his intention was to use his gunsmithing skills to make weapons for the cause. A slave woman working in a tavern eyed him suspiciously, certain she had seen his traveling companion, a disguised British officer, in military dress. The officer returned to Boston, and Howe continued on alone. A free black couple, just as staunch patriots as the waitress but less suspicious, put him up one night and helped him on his way.

Howe's chance meeting with one Lincoln couple made the general mood clear. He had entered their small house pretending to need directions:

> I found it inhabited by an old man and his wife. The old man was cleaning his gun. I asked him what he was going to kill, as he was so old I should not think he could take sight at any game. He said there was a flock of red coats at Boston which he expected would be here soon, he meant to try and hit some of them, as he expected they would be very good marks.
>
> I asked him when they were expected out, he said he should not think strange if they should come before morning, he said some supposed they would go up through Watertown to Worcester for we hear they have sent out spies that road. I asked the old man how he expected of fight. He said open field fighting or any way to kill them redcoats. I asked him how old he was? He said seventy-seven, and never was killed yet. . . . Here the old gentleman told the old lady to put some balls in the bullet pouch. She asked him how many. He said 30 or 40, perhaps I shall have an opportunity to give some to them that have not got any. . . . The old man says, Old woman, put in a handful of buck shot as I understood the English like an assortment of plumbs. Here I took leave of them.

When Howe returned to Boston on April 12 to report to General Gage, he was deeply troubled by the depth of anger and the strength of military preparations he had observed.

James Warren, one of the leaders of the Massachusetts Provincial Congress held at Concord that April, was also deeply disturbed. Warren wrote his wife, Mercy: "Last week things wore a rather favorable aspect, but alas how uncertain are our prospects. . . . We are no longer at a loss what is Intended us by our dear Mother. We have ask'd for Bread and she gives us a Stone, and a serpent for a Fish. . . . All things wear a warlike appearance here. This Town is full of Cannon, ammunition, stores, etc. and the [British] Army long for them and they want nothing but strength to Induce an attempt on them. The people are ready and determine to defend this country Inch by Inch."

For the past month Josiah and Elizabeth Nelson had listened each night for riders bringing word that British troops were advancing on Concord. They were not alone in their vigil. The people of Boston, from aristocrats to stable hands and barmaids, kept a wary eye on the activities of the soldiers based there, watching, listening for signs they were preparing to march. At Concord carts and teams were kept on hand to haul the weapons away at the first alarm, and guards were posted at the bridges, in the town center, and on the road from Boston. Night after night riders for and against resistance patrolled the roads—colonial scouts, British spies, local Tories.

Josiah had agreed to play a key role in spreading the alarm. He was now in his late forties, a pragmatic man, but years of British missteps and weekly sermons at the Reverend Clarke's church had molded Josiah and Elizabeth into stalwart patriots. He was also perfectly situated to help his cause. Any British force marching on Concord would undoubtedly choose the Great Road that ran through Lincoln as the most direct route and tramp right past Josiah's farm, which straddled the road where it crossed from Lexington to Lincoln. He had pledged to bring word of any advance to the minutemen of Bedford, the town bordering Lincoln and Concord on the north. Like the men of Lincoln, Bedford minutemen and militia regiments could get to Concord quickly. And so night after night he listened for noises, but on this night Josiah fell into a sound sleep.

At 10:00 p.m. on April 18, a military expedition of six light infantry companies and the grenadier companies of several other regiments, about nine hundred men in all, set out from Boston. By midnight, the soldiers had been rowed across the Charles River to rendezvous on its western bank in Cambridge. Their mission—kept a close secret—was first to seize rebel leaders John Hancock and Samuel Adams, who were known to be in Lexington, and then to march through Lincoln to Concord to destroy the arsenal rebels were amassing there.

The British commander, General Gage, was under orders from London to use all necessary measures to crush rebellious activities, but his spies, among them John Howe, warned him of potential disaster. When Howe, one of Gage's most trusted informants, was asked how large an army it would take to go the forty-eight miles to Worcester, destroy the weapons stockpiled there, and return safely, he was blunt: "If they [the British] should march 10,000 regulars and a train of artillery to Worcester . . . the roads very crooked, stony and hilly, the inhabitants generally determined to be free or die, that not one of them would get back alive." In fact, the British had just four thousand soldiers in Boston. Gage then asked about destroying the stores at Concord, only eighteen miles from Boston. Howe thought that five hundred mounted men might go to Concord in the night, destroy the stores, and return safe, but cautioned, "to go with 1000 foot to destroy the stores the country would be alarmed; that the greater part of them would get killed or taken."

Gage rejected Howe's advice. Indeed, he did the opposite. He decided to send a thousand foot soldiers to Concord, confident that so large a force of professional soldiers would cow any resistance. His men were prepared to do their duty and, like their general, were more than a little contemptuous of the Yankees' military abilities. An officer leading the expedition had recommended: "one active campaign, a smart action, and burning two or three of their towns will set everything to rights."

As insurance, an advance party of ten officers ready to ambush anyone intending to warn Concord of the military expedition had already slipped west of the Nelson home and was waiting in a pasture a few hundred yards from where Peter lay sleeping,

Around 10:00 that evening, just as the British soldiers were preparing to set out from Boston, patriots Paul Revere and William Dawes began their own journey to Lexington. They had been secretly informed that the British planned to send a force of twelve to fifteen hundred men that night to capture

Hancock and Adams and meant to warn the two men, who were staying at the Reverend Clarke's home in Lexington. Their informant had said nothing about the planned raid on Concord. As a precaution, Revere and Dawes, experienced spies and couriers, took different routes. Dawes disguised himself as a farmer with a large, floppy hat and rode a plodding country horse. Sacrificing speed for anonymity, he avoided suspicion. But a pair of British scouts spotted Revere, mounted on Brown Beauty, a splendid mare. He outran them, thanks to his excellent mount, but had to take a long detour. Both men reached Lexington about midnight, rousing minutemen as they went. They found Hancock and Adams and warned them of their peril. But their conversations with Lexington militia officers convinced everyone that the mission of so large a British force was unlikely to be the mere arrest of two rebel leaders. The aim must be to march on Concord. John Parker, captain of the Lexington militia company, sent scouts east to check how close the British expedition was and other riders west to alert Bedford and Concord. Nothing must be left to chance. Better multiple riders than Concord being taken by surprise. So, after barely an hour's rest, Dawes and Revere mounted their tired animals. With the Lexington town bell clanging in their ears summoning the town's minutemen and militia, they headed west to warn the people of Lincoln and Concord that an attack was imminent.

By happy chance, Dr. Samuel Prescott joined them. The young Concord physician had been out courting that night and was on his way home when he met Revere and Dawes. Finding him, like themselves, an enthusiastic "son of liberty," they asked for his help. Prescott readily agreed—a stroke of luck for the patriot cause, for Prescott would be the only one to reach Concord. The three began knocking at the doors of houses along the road, particularly those with a light showing. Prescott roused the residents at a house east of the three Nelson family farms where he found a visitor, his friend Nathaniel Baker, who left at once for home in southwestern Lincoln. Josiah's farmhouse must have been dark, for none of the three knocked on his door.

Just after 2:00 a.m. the peaceful night was abruptly interrupted as the three riders unintentionally set off an alarm. Revere was the first to spot the two horsemen under a tree near the road. He called to Dawes and Prescott, and the trio tried to force their way through. Four British soldiers came out of hiding, swords and pistols in hand, and ordered Revere, Dawes, and Prescott into a field next to the road, threatening, Revere later reported, "if we did not turn into that pasture they would blow our brains out." They had ridden right into the British advance party's trap.

As they walked their horses into the pasture, Prescott whispered to Revere that they should make a dash for it, each taking a different direction. Immediately, the young doctor galloped off to the left, toward Concord, jumped a stone wall, and vanished into the night. Several officers followed, but they were unfamiliar with the terrain and couldn't catch him. Revere galloped in the opposite direction, toward a line of trees at the far end of the field. As he reached the trees, six more horsemen emerged from the darkness. Seizing his reins, they trained their guns at him and ordered him to dismount. In the confusion, Dawes tried to slip away. Two officers spotted him and gave chase. As Dawes galloped frantically into the safety of a dark farmyard, he tried to convince his pursuers that they were being led into a trap, calling to the darkened farmhouse: "Halloo, my boys! I've got two of them." Although this ruse scared off the officers chasing him, something frightened his horse, and he was thrown hard. The animal trotted off, leaving him sore and disconcerted. The farmhouse turned out to be deserted, and Dawes had to give up the mission and walk, painfully, back to Lexington.

The British soldiers had already taken four other prisoners: two men who had been sent from Lexington to trail the advance party, eighteen-year-old Solomon Brown, on his way to Concord to report on their presence, and a one-armed peddler named Allen who was in the wrong place at the wrong time. They questioned Revere closely. To convince the expedition to turn back, he boasted that the countryside had been warned that Gage's men were on the march. The soldiers would find hundreds of armed provincials waiting for them when they got to Lexington Green. Revere's comments startled the scouting party, and after hurried consultation, they decided to leave immediately, hoping to warn the advancing expedition that they might find armed opposition at Lexington. They ordered Revere and the other prisoners to mount, and at 2:15 a.m., with each prisoner flanked by soldiers, the party returned to the road and headed east, back in the direction of the Nelson farm.

Nelson family tradition is clear about what followed. Elizabeth was the first to hear the voices, although she could not make out what they were saying. She immediately woke Josiah, urging her sleepy husband to hurry out and see whether these passing travelers had any word about when the British might march. Pulling on his breeches as he ran, and without shoes or hat, Josiah dashed out the door just as the horsemen drew up to his home. He rushed into their midst calling out, "Have you heard anything about when the Regulars are coming out?" The British officers had had enough of defiant provincials. One angrily drew his sword and shouting, "God damn you, we will let you know when they are coming," slashed Josiah with the flat of the blade, opening a three-inch gash in his head, very possibly the first blood shed in the Revolutionary War. Stunned, Josiah got to his feet, blood coursing down his face. Elizabeth and Peter waited inside, horrified. The soldiers surrounded him, one officer telling him that he was their prisoner "and must come along with us." The party set out once more, traveling east, with Josiah rushing along on foot, forced to keep pace with the mounted party.

Josiah doesn't seem to have known Paul Revere, but even if he had, in the dark and on foot he could see little of the mounted riders. Not far from Tabitha's modest farmhouse, footsore and headsore, he pleaded with his captors—he couldn't walk as fast as they rode, he was barefoot and bleeding. The soldiers replied that they couldn't ride as slowly as he walked. They decided to leave the bothersome farmer in the care of three of their party and trotted off.

As soon as they were out of sight, Josiah turned to face his remaining captors and discovered they were men he knew, local Tories. They had been showing the British where the weapons and ammunition collected at Concord were hidden. Not knowing what to do with him either, the Tories agreed to let him return home on two conditions: he must not light a light (presumably as a signal) or warn anyone of what he had seen. If he did either, they would return and burn his house over his head.

This was a threat calculated to silence Josiah. There had been rumors that the British would punish resistance by setting colonists' homes ablaze. Wooden houses and barns were especially vulnerable, particularly those that were situated, like the Nelson homestead, along a country road where few neighbors would be available to help save them.

Josiah picked his way home to where Elizabeth and Peter were waiting in the dark, uncertain what to do. Their joy at his return quickly gave way to fear over what was to come. Josiah was not deterred by the rough treatment he had received; if anything, it seemed to make him more determined. Whatever the danger, he meant to carry out his commitment. The Bedford minutemen were depending on him, and the safety of Concord depended on them. Elizabeth lit a candle. By its flickering glow she washed and bound his bloody head. It would have taken only a few minutes to bandage the wound and pull on boots and a hat while Peter was sent to the barn behind the house to saddle the family mare. Josiah did not take a rifle or musket with him, an indication that he did not intend to join the minutemen at Lexington or his own Lincoln company at this point. Instead he loaded his large horse pistols and strapped them on. Pistols would do for personal protection. Revere and Dawes had been careful to travel unarmed, and their caution had been justified. After the British captured Revere they had searched him for weapons. Had any been found, the midnight ride might have ended differently. But Josiah had run sleepily, blindly, into the arms of the enemy and ended up a wounded and pathetic captive. He was not going to permit that to happen again.

Once mounted, Josiah did not immediately ride north to Bedford. Instead he set off on the trail of the British party that had taken him prisoner, cautiously following them to Lexington. Although he may have heard useful snatches of conversation from his captors, he could not be certain a British expedition was on the way. It would not do to raise the alarm in Bedford until he got his facts right. He was a brave man but not a rash one.

Around 2:00 a.m., four hours after leaving Boston, the British troops finally began marching the eleven miles to Lexington. Their rendezvous and wait for supplies cost the expedition precious time. Great care had been taken to avoid attracting notice. Along with the advance party, other scouts had been sent out to waylay any suspicious colonists leaving Boston who might carry news of the march. The soldiers were not told where they were going. Even the company commanders did not know the mission. To avoid detection, they plodded through marshes and streams, at times wading in waist-deep water. Already cold and wet, they had a long night of marching ahead of them. The very slowness of the march would jeopardize the chance of taking the colonists by surprise.

As they moved on to the Great Road there were worrisome signs that the precautions to keep their expedition a secret had failed. An officer leading one of the forward units heard shots to his right and left, signals of some kind. Later, in the moonlight, he caught sight of a "vast number" of armed men running through the woods toward Lexington. Gage's plan seemed to be going awry.

As soon as Samuel Prescott had given his pursuers the slip, he returned to the road to complete the mission Revere and Dawes had started—to arouse residents and alert the minutemen all the way to Concord. Prescott soon had considerable help, for his alarm started a chain of couriers who either rode or walked through the dark to alert their neighbors. Hard by the side of the Great Road where it wound up a hill over a mile west of Josiah's farm sat the small blacksmith shop owned by Samuel Hartwell, now first sergeant of the Lincoln minute company. When Prescott reached the shop it was late, and Crispus, a black slave probably lent to Hartwell to help him forge military supplies, was the only occupant. Crispus led the way to the Hartwell house, where a light shone as Mary Hartwell tended to her baby daughter. Samuel began to prepare at once, feeding his horse and gathering his equipment. He sent someone next door to his father's house, to alert his younger brothers, John and Isaac, who still lived at home. Like Samuel, John was a sergeant of the Lincoln minute company, a solid young man greatly respected. Twenty-two-year-old Isaac was a private.

In his hasty conversation with Prescott, Samuel discovered that Prescott had missed the home of William Smith, the captain of the Lincoln company, whose house was set well back from the road. Someone needed to alert Smith while Samuel and his brothers were preparing to leave. Violet, Ephraim Hartwell's slave, was with Samuel and Mary that night, but she was too frightened to carry the message and flatly refused to leave the house. So Mary placed five-month-old Lucy in Violet's care. Leaving her other two small daughters sleeping peacefully, she wrapped her cloak about her and slipped out into the darkness, staying close to the cover of the stone walls along the road. As she liked to recount long afterward, she brought word to Captain Smith, then returned home and calmly made the men breakfast. When breakfast was over she watched as Samuel and his brothers rode off to join their company. Years later she still vividly recalled the sight of the British troops as they marched by later that morning. "I knew what all that meant," she told her grandchildren, "and I feared that I should never see your grandfather again."

What William Smith lacked in business acumen and farming skill he made up for in courage and patriotic zeal. He had been elected captain of the minute company, and this was his moment. Once Mary brought him word of the British advance, he saddled his horse hurriedly and prepared for action. It was his responsibility to gather and lead the town minutemen. Boasting some sixty-two officers and men, the Lincoln company was larger than most. After bidding farewell to his wife, Catherine Louisa, and perhaps peering quickly into the cradle of his year-old son, William, and trundle bed of little daughter

Louisa, Smith galloped south toward Lincoln Center, taking Cato, his slave, with him. Cato was not an official member of Smith's company but was ready to accompany his master and to risk his life in the crisis. His help was welcome. When they reached Lincoln Center, Smith set the bell in the small town church clanging to summon his men.

Word spread quickly from farm to farm as neighbors knocked on doors in the dark or were awakened by the agreed-upon signal. For most towns this was the ringing of the church bell and the firing of a gun, usually three shots. In larger communities the gun signal was relayed from one shooter to another. And in remote parts of Needham, minutemen were summoned by the blare of a trumpet blown by the slave Abel Benson.

Men and boys, fathers and sons, the town's farmers, both wealthy and poor, its tanners, innkeepers, shoemakers, and laborers all grabbed their weapons and equipment and headed for Lincoln Center. A knock or signal woke the Hartwells' neighbors, the Mason family. Joseph Mason and his wife, Grace, lived in a small house bursting with children. Their sons, Jonas, twenty-six, a sergeant in Smith's company, and his brothers Joseph Junior, twenty-four, and Elijah, seventeen, both company fifers, grabbed their instruments and weapons and hurried out to join their comrades. Back near the Nelson farms, Peter's neighbors John and William Thorning, eighteen and seventeen, respectively, only sons of John Thorning, were alerted and set off in the dark for the Lincoln rendezvous.

Samuel Farrar, the lieutenant of Smith's company, was on his way to the mill when he heard the Lincoln alarm bell. He immediately threw his saddlebags laden with wheat grist over a wall and began to rally his men. Farrar's wife, Mary, was terrified the redcoats would set her house on fire. After Samuel left, she turned the cattle loose, snatched her baby and, looking frantically about her, chose her most valued possessions to carry to safety—the large family Bible, a looking glass, and the family silverware. Then she set out for Oaky Bottom, a piece of forestland half a mile in the back of the Farrar property, where she waited in dread for what the day would bring.

As the men and boys of Lincoln hurried off, leaving behind their elderly parents and women and children, they must have realized with dismay how vulnerable their families were. The British soldiers were hardened professionals and would be marching right by those homes and farms. Would they realize the men were gone? Would they take the opportunity to loot, to rape, to burn? If they had encountered violence on their route to Concord, would they be out to take revenge? And if anything happened to the men, what would become of their families?

No one knows what instructions Josiah gave Elizabeth and Peter that night. If the Tories had merely threatened him, he might have decided to spare his wife and the child further worry. But the specific threat to burn his house was a threat to them all. He could not have left them in ignorance of that danger. Josiah would have urged Peter to be brave and look after Elizabeth and sent them to warn Thomas, Lydia, and his sister, Tabitha.

Wherever the three adults and three children of the Nelson clan gathered that night, whether in Thomas's home or Tabitha's, by dawn the women and children abandoned the house and took to the woods. They would not have had to go far. There was a sizable woodlot on Tabitha's farm that bordered the road just over the Lincoln line in Lexington. According to Nelson family lore, the women hid in the woods on the morning of April 19 and remained there until nightfall.

Keeping well out of sight, Josiah tracked the British soldiers back toward Lexington and stopped on a hilltop short of the town, where he could observe events in safety. Gunfire was coming from Lexington Green. Since the British would not arrive until dawn, perhaps the town minutemen were firing off a volley. But the gunshots convinced Josiah beyond a doubt that the regulars had come. Turning his little horse onto the road, he galloped the two miles to Bedford to alert that town's minutemen. Jonathan Wilson, their captain, promptly gathered his company of twenty-six men at the village tavern kept by Jeremiah Fitch, Jr., where they sat down for refreshments before setting out. As they left for Concord, Wilson tried to cheer them up: "It is a cold breakfast, boys, but we'll give the British a hot dinner; we'll have every dog of them before night."

The pause for refreshments undoubtedly led the Bedford minutemen to arrive at Concord after the town's regular militia. As soon as the messengers sent from Lexington alerted the Bedford militia, that company quickly gathered at the home of their captain, on the Concord Road, then marched directly to Concord, sans refreshments. Tradition holds that Cambridge Moore, a free Negro servant of Captain John Moore, accompanied him as a volunteer, one of several other blacks, both slave and free, who made their way to Concord that morning. Once at Concord the two Bedford companies immediately began to help remove the arsenal to places of greater safety. Thanks to Parker's riders and to Josiah, the men of Bedford were among the first to arrive, although not before Josiah's own Lincoln neighbors.

By eighteenth-century standards Concord was an old town, its founders having come directly from England to build the first Massachusetts Bay settlement above the tidewater in 1635. On the north side of the road a high ridge overlooked the fine town center with its cluster of substantial framed houses, its courthouse, meetinghouse, and inn. The first houses had been built beneath this ridge, and by 1775 a line of handsome homes was sheltered there. On this ridge Concord had buried its dead, high and dry, safe from the floods that made the meadows south of the road a swamp. The ridge was also an excellent vantage point. Beyond the center the town was bisected north to south by the Concord River, which had the unfortunate habit of periodically rising above the two bridges that crossed it, severing the farms and towns on the far side from Concord Center and Boston.

As Prescott rode west past the Hartwell and Mason farms toward Concord Center, the Great Road turned sharply south, and he was forced to slow his horse to negotiate a steep descent down a wooded hill that marked the boundary between Lincoln and Concord. Once the road had leveled and turned due west again, he could spur his horse to full speed over a long stretch of flat meadow that local farmers carefully kept drained to prevent its return to marsh. Just before Concord Center, a causeway lifted the road above the surrounding meadow and swamp, leaving all who crossed over it exposed to hostile attack. Prescott, however, was in too great a hurry to ponder the military problem this created for the approaching troops.

He reached Concord sometime after 2:00 a.m. Gunshots were fired, and the alarm bell was quickly set ringing. As befitted its size and status, Concord had two militia companies and two minute companies, about two hundred men in all. They dutifully appeared in the center, groggy, anxious, and excited, to pick up ammunition at the courthouse. Once armed, they assembled at the meetinghouse nearby. When all was in order, and since the British were not yet in sight, they were dismissed to begin the work of hiding Concord's impressive cache of weapons, with instructions to reassemble at the beat of the drum. Hiding the arms was no small task; the arsenal included at least ten cannon. Some cannon were moved to the town of Stow, some weapons to the town of Sudbury. Other munitions were concealed under hay, straw, or manure, secreted in private buildings or hidden in the woods. Desperate to hide a batch of muskets, the sons of Colonel James Barrett, Concord's militia commander, plowed a field on his farm, put weapons in the furrows, and covered them over.

At Concord, Prescott recruited his brother, Abel, to help him. While Prescott rode further west to alert the town of Acton, Abel rode south to Sudbury, reaching it around 3:00 a.m., then rode on to Framingham, arriving an hour later. Within a half hour of getting the alarm, the entire town of Sudbury had been awakened. The seemingly haphazard alarm system proved to be amazingly efficient and effective. Even before the British had reached Lexington Green, towns for miles around Concord had been alerted and were mustering and marching to its aid.

The Lincoln men, the first to appear apart from Concord's military companies, reached Concord about four in the morning. In the dark they gathered—fathers, sons, brothers, cousins, masters, and servants—calling to one another as they arrived, welcoming friends they knew from neighboring towns who began to join them. Together, as dawn broke, they waited for the approach of the British force. The menfolk of entire families turned out. Samuel Hartwell was there with his brothers, John and Isaac. Nathaniel Baker, jolted by Prescott from a pleasant evening of courting, had brought word to his father, a veteran of the French and Indian War, and his four brothers, Jacob, Amos, James, and Samuel. All the Baker men, together with their brother-in-law, Daniel Hoomer, would be in arms at the North Bridge by dawn. There were six men of the Parks family of Lincoln and thirteen members of the extensive Brooks family, including Joshua Brooks, Jr., who owned Peter's father, Jupiter. All together, some seventy-five Lincoln men would take part in the coming battle. Bedford had seventy-seven men in its military companies in addition to numerous other citizens at Concord that day. Thompson Maxwell, Jonathan Wilson's brother-in-law from New Hampshire, who happened to be in Bedford with his wagon that night, joined Wilson's Bedford company. With the exception of eleven men, every Bedford man between the ages of sixteen and sixty was in arms. One exception was Bedford's minister, who was discovered later in the day sitting peacefully by his fireside. The minister of Dedham reported that the town was left "almost literally without a male inhabitant below the age of seventy, and above that of sixteen." After the

Dedham militia left, a group of the town's veterans of the French wars decided to follow. Men too old for the militia came as "unenlisted volunteers," among them Sudbury's Deacon Josiah Haynes, aged eighty, who insisted on participating and marched off briskly with the militia. Among the "unenlisted volunteers" were free blacks and slaves from nearby towns. At least two came from Bedford, two from Lincoln, and two from Concord. The twenty-one African Americans who have been identified were divided almost equally between slave and free. More may have been present, but as volunteers their names were not noted in the records. Most blacks, though, were presumably ordered to remain home to protect the family and farm. The black men both free and enslaved who took part that day were present not as servants but as volunteers. They would fight side by side with their white neighbors.

After all the furious activity as minutemen, militia, and volunteers from miles around converged on Concord, the entire community seemed to hold its breath. Everyone waited: the families left behind on those little farms and the men assembled at Concord, armed, anxious, outnumbered but prepared to protect the town, their arsenal, and their rights. A grave and fearful prospect faced them as they waited for the British troops to appear. To attack the soldiers would be to cast themselves irrevocably as rebels and traitors.

Josiah did not join the minute company at Concord. Nor was he listed as participating in the battle later that day. Having fulfilled his commitment to the Bedford company, his immediate concern would probably have been to go home. He was wounded and had been up all night. His home had been threatened. The adrenaline that enabled him, despite his injury, to arm and ride after his captors, then carry the alarm to Bedford, may have ebbed, but anxiety for his family would have provided that extra surge he needed to carry him home. Once there, it seems unlikely that he would have taken to the woods for the day. It was the women and children who went to the woods. Having assured himself that his family was safe, Josiah probably returned to his house. It represented everything he possessed, a lifetime of strenuous effort, and it had been threatened with burning. He would have wanted to do everything he could to protect his homestead. He was tired, but he was angry and armed.

Josiah had no idea that the woods where the Nelson family was most likely to have taken refuge, Tabitha Nelson's large woodlot, would turn out to be extraordinarily dangerous. But if that was where twelve-year-old Peter spent the day, it would be the last time he permitted himself to be sent off with the women.

It had been a long night for Josiah, Elizabeth, and Peter, and a long and fearful day still lay ahead. The crisis about to engulf them would, in the pitiless way of war, test their devotion to one another and to the cause of liberty.

CHAPTER FIVE

The Killing

THE THREE WOMEN, Elizabeth, Lydia, and Tabitha, huddled together in Tabitha Nelson's woodlot with twelve-year-old Peter, Jonathan, now fourteen, and his sister, Lydia, now sixteen. The early morning sunlight picked its way through the trees, bringing them a view above of tangled branches, beginning to leaf, and pine forest litter below. Unless Peter or Jonathan cautiously climbed one of the larger pines or oaks, the group could see little beyond. The trees offered little cover unless you went deep into the woods, and then there was little to see. That was the beauty of the hiding place, of course, but also its curse. Experts speak of the fog of war that isolates a man, even in the middle of a battlefield, shrinking his vision to his immediate environs. For Peter the fog of war that enveloped him that terrible day meant long periods of suspense interrupted by short spurts of terror and excitement. How fortunate his teenaged neighbors John and William Thorning seemed by comparison, taking their places at Concord with the men of Lincoln to protect their community. By evening seventeen-year-old William would be a hero. Later Peter, like everyone else, would have to piece together the information and misinformation about the fighting and dying that marked the day.

Even had sleep been possible there was little time for it between Josiah's gallop in the darkness of early morning to Bedford and Peter and Elizabeth's rush to alert the rest of the family, complete their morning chores, and dash into the woods. Like other families up and down the Great Road, they roused their sleepy cows for milking especially early. They turned the animals loose, scattered a few handfuls of grain for the chickens, and collected a simple meal for themselves. There was no telling how long they might need to hide or what they would find when they returned home.

As word of the British advance on Lexington and Concord spread, panic grew. Families from Cambridge, across the Charles River from Boston, to Salem, on the north shore, abandoned their homes, fleeing to forests or churches or simply taking to the roads in their carts, bound they knew not where, just away.

Bedford was not on the route the British army was likely to take, and its women did not flee. The town alarm bell rang all day, its harsh clangs later mixing with the sound of gunshots. Desperate to do something, Bedford women busied themselves preparing meals for the force gathering at Concord and seeing that it was delivered. The women of Acton, the town just beyond Concord, also held their ground and cooked. As Acton's men began to assemble at the home of Francis Faulkner, colonel of the Middlesex militia regiment, they helped the women by driving stakes into the grass for kettles. By the time the men marched away, their wives, mothers, and daughters had begun boiling their dinner of beef, pork, potatoes, and cabbage. At first each woman wanted to cook for her own men, but soon they realized it was simpler to pack each type of food separately and let the men help themselves. Older boys stood by waiting nervously. As soon as the food was cooked and packed into saddlebags, they galloped off to deliver it with strict instructions to make a wide detour if they spotted British soldiers.

Just before dawn the hoofbeats of a lone rider galloping east toward Lexington disturbed the quiet of the Nelson woodlot. Not long afterward the panting horse and its rider could be heard galloping hard back toward Concord. Reuben Brown had been sent by the Concord militia commanders to spy out the British force. He reached Lexington in the gray morning light for a hurried conversation with Captain John Parker, standing with his men on the town common, only minutes before the soldiers arrived. When the regulars opened fire, Brown wheeled his horse sharply around, not even turning to see whether anyone had been hit, and raced back to Concord to deliver the grim news. Shooting had begun.

Peter knew most of the men wounded or killed in the chaos at Lexington, at least by sight. He had seen them at church with their wives and children. One of these, Prince Estabrook, sat in the church's Negro gallery. Only about half the town's militia, some seventy men, were drawn up on the Lexington common as the British came into sight. They stood in a double line on the familiar triangular town green with the church on one side, Buckman's Tavern on another. Rifles in hand, they prepared to face a British force of nearly a thousand professional soldiers. When the alarm bell first rang at two that morning, twice that number of men had appeared. Because the British were not yet in sight and the night air was chilly, Captain Parker had sent them away to return at the beat of the drum. Some went home; others crowded into Buckman's Tavern. When the drum beat again at dawn, many were too far away to return in time, and others were in the church getting ammunition. But it wouldn't have mattered. Even at full strength they were pitifully outnumbered and badly exposed, a small group standing in the open hoping the sight of them would persuade the British to desist. That tactic had worked elsewhere, when the British had ventured from Boston to confiscate gunpowder and weapons and found themselves surrounded by hostile locals.

Captain John Parker was a tall, dignified farmer in his forties, a veteran of the French wars, ill with consumption. He would die of it that fall. But this morning he was prepared to lead his men. Among them were seven members of the Reed family, including William Reed, Jr., the son of Peggy's master.

There should have been no violence. Both the British and the Americans were under orders to fire only in defense. The little group of colonists was not blocking the road, and the British officers could have bypassed them and continued on their march to Concord, where their real business lay. Parker clearly thought they might do that. "Let the troops pass by," he ordered his men. "Don't molest them, without they being first." But the young British officer commanding the advance force stopped and had his men draw up in battle formation. Three other officers rode onto the green. Many remembered one shouting, "Lay down your arms, you damned rebels." The Reverend Clarke heard an officer yell, "Ye villains, ye rebels, disperse, damn you, disperse!" Parker ordered his men to disperse. They began to leave, but in the mist and the panic of early dawn, someone fired. Lexington residents were certain a British officer was the first to fire. A full volley from the soldiers followed immediately. The British officers reported later that someone hiding behind the tavern fired on them first. Whatever the truth, instantly all was chaos. In the smoke, men were running. The Americans fled with the British soldiers in pursuit, firing at them as they ran.

When order was finally restored and the British had given their customary victory cheer and marched off, the dead and injured were brought into the church. Jonas Parker and Robert Munroe had been killed where they stood. Jonathan Harrington was shot as he fled home. He managed to drag himself to his doorstep before he died. All told, eight men were killed, ten wounded. Prince Estabrook, a slave and a volunteer, was one of the wounded. Joshua Simonds dashed into the church as firing began and climbed to Negro heaven, where the ammunition was stored. He later told everyone who would listen that he meant to plunge his rifle into the gunpowder and blow it all up if the soldiers entered, and himself with it. Maybe this story was his excuse for fleeing from the carnage. Who could say?

By six o'clock that morning the sound of trampling feet and male voices resounded through Tabitha's woodlot. The king's soldiers, nine hundred strong, were marching down the Great Road toward the Nelson farms, fresh from the chaos and killing at Lexington. Glimpsed from a treetop, their column filled the road for half a mile as it wound between rough stone walls. Nelson family tradition doesn't say where Josiah and his brother, Thomas, were as the troops approached, but both men were almost certainly crouched near the front windows in their homes, prepared to defend them if need be. Fortunately, with all element of surprise gone, the British officers were in a hurry to get on with their mission. Despite their uncomfortable nightlong march, the regulars were a splendid sight in their scarlet coats and white leggings, the grenadiers sporting their signature high, pointed hats, their bayonets gleaming in the bright morning sun. Officers, elegant and proud, surveyed all from horseback. What a contrast to the Massachusetts men in their homespun, earth-colored hunting shirts and trousers who awaited them at Concord. The terror Peter and the others hiding in the woods felt as the long column approached was followed by a feeling of immense relief when the last soldier had passed. God be thanked they didn't seem interested in venturing into the woods and they hadn't set the houses or barns on fire.

Mary Hartwell remained at home long enough to stand in her doorway and watch the soldiers pass. "The army of the King marched up in fine order and their bayonets glistened in the sunlight like a field of waving grain," she told her grandchildren years later. "If it hadn't been for the purpose they came for, I should say it was the handsomest sight I ever saw in my life." Mindful of their purpose, though, as soon as the soldiers disappeared from sight Mary put her two little daughters and baby Lucy into a wagon and set off for her father's house in Lincoln Center, away from what would become the "battle road."

The morning hours dragged by, but Tabitha's woodlot did not remain quiet for long. As Peter, Jonathan, and the women waited anxiously for the soldiers or the minutemen to return from Concord, armed men began filtering into Tabitha's woods. With joy the group discovered the men were Lexington minutemen. Captain Parker, with 120 or so Lexington men, some with bandages covering fresh wounds, would not disperse a second time. Whatever happened at Concord, the regulars were sure to pass by on their return to Boston, and the minutemen were determined to retaliate for the morning's bloody work. The woods along the road where it entered Lexington had plenty of trees to hide them and a curve in the road for cross firing, the perfect place for an ambush. The fierce fighting that would take place there became known as Parker's Revenge.

As the men positioned themselves, Peter and Jonathan may have overheard snatches of their conversation and perhaps approached politely to quiz them about what had happened. The Nelsons soon knew more about the morning's bloodshed on Lexington Green than the Lincoln men gathered at Concord. The Lexington men's outrage and determination were contagious. How frustrating to be left to guard the women, to be told to stay well back once fighting started. But the advice was sound. After the ambush was sprung, the British would fire into the woods and would likely send soldiers to pursue their tormentors. Anyone in the area could be caught in the cross fire.

First to spot the regulars as they crossed the border into Concord were the Concord and Lincoln minutemen standing watch on the ridge north of the town center. This vantage point gave them a clear view of the road as it emerged from the hills of Lincoln and headed west over the marshy meadows on the long, elevated causeway into town. The road was now filling with the scarlet of hundreds of uniforms. Everyone afterward remembered the glint of the sun on their menacing bayonets, the military weapon most minutemen lacked. The bayonets had a triangular blade designed especially to cause a larger gash than a flat blade, a wound that bled more and was harder to staunch.

The militia leaders had disagreed over what action to take. There seemed little to lose by waiting. The arsenal and military rations had been taken away or hidden. Men from neighboring towns were on their way to join them. William Emerson, Concord's young minister, and many younger men were keen for action, but others believed it wiser to wait and see. Unable to agree on an approach, the leaders decided to do various things. One group of minuteman would march out to meet the British, another would be posted on the ridge holding the high ground, and the older, cooler heads of those in the regular militia companies would wait in the town center.

The advancing British spied the minutemen on the ridge, and troops were dispatched to chase them from the high ground. As for the group of minutemen marching boldly down the road toward the British: "We marched down toward L. [Lexington]," Amos Barrett recalled, "about a mild [sic] or mild [sic] half and we see them acoming, we halted and stayd till they got within about 100 rods then we was orded to about face and marched before them with our drums and fifes agoing and also the B. We had grand musick."

To the oddly cheery sound of fifes and drums, the British marched, unopposed, into Concord Center. The Americans prudently withdrew, regrouping on a long hill on the far side of the North Bridge. From there they could see what was happening in the center, and as men from neighboring communities arrived, they could join them. The British commander quickly set about his business. He sent men to guard the South Bridge, three regiments over the North Bridge to search Colonel James Barrett's farm beyond, and another three regiments to guard the North Bridge until the first three returned. The main force meanwhile began to search the buildings in the town center for weapons and supplies. Tories had informed them where to look, but so much had been removed or hidden that they found little. They did discover wooden gun carriages for the cannon and other material in the courthouse. They hauled these out into the road, heaped them in a pile, and set the whole ablaze. The courthouse started to burn as well. Seeing the rising smoke, the Americans waiting beyond the North Bridge thought the British were burning the town. Lieutenant Joseph Hosmer, adjutant of the Concord militia, reminded Colonel Barrett of the British boast that "they could . . . lay waste our hamlets and villages and we would never oppose them." Hosmer demanded, "Are you going to let them burn the town down?" Barrett ordered the men to march over the North Bridge, now guarded by more than a hundred regulars, to see what was happening. They were not to fire unless fired on, and they assumed the British were under orders to do the same.

Long afterward everyone remembered how Isaac Davis, captain of the Acton minutemen, died. The thirty-year-old gunsmith and father of four agreed that he and his men would lead the American column. Striding two abreast to the strains of the provocative Jacobite tune "The White Cockade," they headed down the hill toward the North Bridge. When the bullet pierced his heart, Isaac Davis leaped into the air as if to meet it. His wife was convinced he'd had a premonition he would die that day. That morning, after he and his men had marched off about twenty rods, he had stopped and dashed back. He stood on the doorstep as if he wanted to say something, she recalled, "but as he stood on that threshold where I have often stood and where, in my mind's eye, I have often seen his manly form, he could only say, 'Take good care of the children.'" Abner Hosmer, a private marching near Davis, died at the same time from a bullet to the head. Four other men were wounded. Joshua Brooks, Jr., Jupiter's master, was grazed in the head.

Captain William Smith had asked that Lincoln's sixty-two-man-strong minuteman company be given the honor of leading the column. Had Major John Buttrick agreed, Smith and other Lincoln men would almost surely have died in that first action. But the Acton men were chosen instead, probably because the Lincoln town meeting's caution and stinginess had left Smith's company without cartridge boxes for quick reloading and with only one old bayonet. The bayonet belonged to Nathaniel Baker, whose father had gotten it during the French and Indian War. Abijah Pierce, colonel of the Lincoln minutemen, according to Baker, went to Concord "armed with nothing but a cane" but, after the initial skirmish, "got the gun of one of the British soldiers who was killed at the bridge." That stinginess saved Lincoln lives, though at the cost of lasting historical glory.

The British troops guarding the North Bridge expected the colonists to flee after they fired a warning shot. Yet on they came in good order, and the British fired again, this time in earnest. That was enough for Concord's Major Buttrick. He shouted to his men to fire back. The regulars retreated over the bridge, removing a few of its planks as they went in hopes of slowing the Americans. Unlike the British, who counted on firing in a mass volley for effect, the minutemen took careful aim at the cluster of bright scarlet targets, trying to pick out the officers. Two privates and a sergeant quickly fell dead, and four privates and four other officers were severely wounded. The remaining soldiers panicked. Dragging their wounded, they abandoned the bridge and raced back toward the town center. The Americans crossed the bridge after them, but stopped. The troops who had gone to Barrett's farm were likely to return at any moment. Not wanting to be trapped between the returning regiments and the British troops in the town, the militia withdrew to a hill to the north of the center from which they could watch the British.

The Reverend Emerson, who was so eager for battle, watched it all from his home near the North Bridge—the shots, the deaths, the flight. He saw the two fallen British soldiers, one dead, the other badly wounded. He may have seen, to his horror, Ammi White, a young man who worked for him, bend over the wounded soldier struggling to his knees and smash his hatchet into the soldier's skull. It was a shameful action everyone whispered about later and tried not to believe. But the British soldiers crossing over the North Bridge on their return from Barrett's farm shuddered as they passed the body of their mutilated comrade, and the rumor began that Americans were scalping regulars who fell, cutting off their ears. It added to their terror as they faced the return to Boston.

Two hours passed while the British waited in Concord Center for reinforcements that never came and while more minutemen joined the colonists. Around noon the British commanders, Lieutenant Colonel Francis Smith and Major John Pitcairn, prepared to leave, taking their wounded with them. They also took William Smith's horse. True to his dashing but thoughtless manner, Smith had left the valuable animal tied outside a tavern in the center of town all morning. Now the British mounted one of their wounded men on it and led it away. The officers had seen minutemen converging on the town and were anxious to begin the long march back to Boston and safety.

The colonists lacked the professionals' discipline, but they had the immense advantage of fighting on land whose contours they knew well. Where the ridge overlooking the center ended at a convergence of lanes near the Meriam family farm, the Great Road ran east over that long causeway across open meadows. When they filed over this section, the British army would be fully exposed. Here the colonists planned their first attack. As the British troops ventured out over the causeway, they were hit with a fierce fire. The distance was too great for accuracy, but two soldiers were killed, others wounded. While the army attempted to react, the Americans dashed off to the next likely spot.

Where the Great Road crossed into Lincoln and went over a brook near the Brooks family tannery, it turned abruptly north and ascended Brooks's or, as some called it, Hardy's Hill, a rise so steep that the road had been dug below the level of the banks on either side. The colonists positioned themselves on each side of the corner at the bottom of the hill, hiding behind trees and stone walls. They caught the British column in a deadly cross fire. Next the road wound up the steep hill. Forest covered the west side of the half-mile ascent, and younger trees bordered the eastern side, giving the colonists ample cover from which to fire. The British officers sent flankers out to chase the attackers away, but many soldiers were wounded and many flankers hurt. At the top of the hill, near Joseph Mason's small farm and the little schoolhouse Peter attended, the road took another turn, this time running due east. Again the Americans caught the British in a cross fire. Eight soldiers were killed and others wounded there, earning the spot the title the Bloody Angle. More British soldiers died around the Bloody Angle than at any similar stretch of road over the long trek back to Boston.

British soldiers were not trained for this "Indian-type" of warfare. Eighteenth-century soldiers of the Crown wore the scarlet uniform that marked them as the king's men. They were bound by a military code that insisted that an honorable man fought in the open, shoulder-to-shoulder with his comrades, held fast by discipline, courage, and loyalty to his mates. An honorable soldier and an honorable man did not shoot from behind walls or trees or houses. He did not duck or swerve, even if he saw a cannonball coming at him. It was shameful as well as dangerous to turn and run. Firing as a group with a coordinated volley made sense. Sending flankers out to keep the colonials beyond effective musket range made sense. To Peter and his neighbors, though, it made no sense to wear a uniform that made you a vivid target. It was foolhardy to march in the open when you could take advantage of the terrain and the trees and walls instead. Each side was to learn from the other as the war ground on, but now both were fighting in the most effective way they knew.

In the running battle that broke out, the discipline the Americans had shown at the North Bridge broke down. The running fight and the steady stream of men arriving from other towns made coordination extremely difficult. As the British headed east, the Concord, Lincoln, Bedford, and Acton minutemen were joined by companies from Woburn, Framingham, Sudbury, Stow, Billerica, and other towns. Each minute and militia company and individuals within them acted as they thought best. There was "little or no military discipline and order" among the Americans the remainder of the day, observed Edmund Foster, a Reading minuteman. "Each one sought his own place and opportunity to attack and annoy the enemy from behind trees, rocks, fences, and buildings, as seemed most convenient." The citizen soldiers were helped by neighbors along the road. Both men and women fired at passing soldiers from their homes and farms.

The British soldiers had begun that day behaving as they had been trained. But they were young, untested troops, and at this point they were exhausted and surrounded by enemies hidden everywhere. They fired into houses that harbored snipers and dashed into others and plundered them. They set houses ablaze whose occupants had fired on them. It was a deadly day.

After the British column escaped the terrible cross fire of the Bloody Angle, they reached the more open fields and orchards of the two large Hartwell farms. Captain Jonathan Wilson of Bedford, whom Josiah had awakened only hours earlier, hid behind one of the Hartwell barns with a few of his men and others from Billerica and Woburn, all ready to fire as the column passed. It proved a lethal spot. One of Wilson's companions, Daniel Thompson of Woburn, began firing from a corner of the barn, shooting diagonally through the British ranks to cause greater injury. An enraged soldier spied him and darted around the barn. He shot Thompson as he was reloading. A man from Woburn then shot the British soldier. Jonathan Wilson and Nathaniel Wyman of Billerica were shot and killed. Job Lane, one of Wilson's men, was badly wounded and would be disabled for the rest of his life. With great sadness, a group of Bedford minutemen carried their dead captain and wounded comrade home, leaving others of their company to continue the pursuit. The British column moved east.

Down the road from the Hartwell farms lay William Smith's large spread. A badly wounded grenadier was left along the road near the Smith house. Catherine Louisa helped him inside. He was in great pain over the next three days, pleading with her to end his life. When his ordeal was over, they buried the grenadier in an unmarked grave in a field across the road near Folly Pond. A century later his remains were found by workmen widening that stretch of road. They reinterred them in a nearby field. The exact location has been lost.

The shouts, sharp crack of musket shots, and awful screams of men and horses in pain were getting very near to the fugitives huddling deep within Tabitha's woods. The long British column was moving rapidly toward them, protected by flankers who repeatedly dashed into the fields and woods on either side of the road to drive off would-be attackers. Just west of Josiah's land, near the Thorning farm, the road was bordered on the north by a rough field dotted with trenches and next to it a field strewn with boulders. This was William Thorning's home ground, and he ran and stationed himself in the first field and began firing at the British. When the flankers spied him, he ducked into a trench. Musket shots whizzed over his head. When the flankers moved on, William followed, dashing into the adjoining field and hiding behind a large boulder. He steadied his gun on the rock and took careful aim. As the column continued marching by, William shot, reloaded, and shot again. Two soldiers fell dead just west of Peter's home.

The Nelson farms were next. The column passed Josiah's without incident, but as the soldiers reached Thomas's house, one of them broke in, possibly looking for goods to plunder. As he hurried out to rejoin his regiment, he was shot on the doorstep and badly wounded. No one ever took responsibility for shooting him, but if Thomas Nelson was guarding his home, he certainly could have shot the soldier in the back. It is hard to see how anyone else would have had a clear shot at his doorstep. Family tradition asserts that the soldier was found later in the afternoon when the family returned home. They carried him inside and treated his wound but could not save him. After his death they searched his pockets and discovered a few of their silver spoons. Plundering was against British military regulations, although the soldiers were increasingly ignoring the rules. This undisciplined, sometimes brutal behavior became nearly unstoppable as the column moved farther east. Had the soldier really entered Thomas's little house, one of the smaller dwellings on the road, for plunder? Had spoons really been found in his pockets? This family secret has been well kept. Certainly, the idea that the intruder was a plunderer made shooting him more acceptable, particularly shooting him as he was leaving.

But that was a problem for later. Now the battle reached the woodlot where Captain Parker was about to take his revenge. As the British drew closer, Peter, Jonathan, Lydia, and the three women must have fled as far from the road as they could to avoid being caught up in the battle about to take place. It was as well they did. Parker's revenge did not go as planned, although the first, massive barrage was effective. The British approached the Lexington border, thankful to be leaving the heavy fighting of Lincoln behind. Instead they were greeted with a withering fire from the 120 men waiting there.

Just as one of the British commanders, Colonel Francis Smith, rode up to the van of the column, Parker had ordered his men to shoot. Smith was badly wounded in the leg and fell from his horse. Another officer, the last unwounded officer of the British Tenth Foot, was also wounded along with some of his men. The barrage was so intense it brought the column to a halt. The other ranking officer, Major John Pitcairn, charged to the front and ordered a large contingent of flankers up the rocky, wooded hill and into the fields. Parker's men scattered. Jedediah Munroe, who had been wounded that morning on Lexington common, was shot dead this time and another Lexington man seriously wounded. The combatants then moved on to the next hill.

Peter and the Nelsons had been spared. Apart from Josiah's head wound, they were physically unscathed, and so were their farms. But the day was filled with further tragedy: their neighbors and friends were less fortunate.

A little farther down the road, soldiers burst into Bull Tavern and plundered it. Then, where the road wound up around Fiske Hill, named for the family farm that spread over it, the fighting again became fierce. This time the assault was led by a Cambridge company. Edmund Foster remembered Major Pitcairn, "mounted on an elegant horse, and with a drawn sword in his hand," riding back and forth urging on the soldiers. Americans crouched behind a pile of rails, raised their guns, and fired. The exploding shells frightened Pitcairn's horse, which threw him and then leaped over a fence and bolted directly toward the Americans. They managed to catch the animal and gleefully discovered Pitcairn's tooled brace of pistols fastened to the saddle. These are now on display in the Lexington home of the Reverend Clarke. Pitcairn was hurt from the fall but continued on.

An Acton volunteer, James Hayward, stopped for a quick drink from Ebenezer Fiske's well just as a British soldier emerged from plundering the house. In one of those terrible moments war seems to have no shortage of, the two men spotted each other. Both fired. The British soldier died instantly. Hayward was badly wounded and died eight hours later. Five other British soldiers were killed or seriously wounded on Fiske Hill.

One final hill, Concord Hill, lay before the British as they approached Lexington Center. The soldiers were exhausted, nearly out of ammunition, and no longer retreating in good order. They seemed to have little option but to surrender. Then as Lexington Green came in sight, the soldiers saw their salvation: the relief column from Boston for which they had been praying. With more men and ammunition, their spirits soared and discipline improved. Lord Hugh Percy, commander of the rescuing brigade, leveled their cannon and fired toward the Americans, sending a cannonball crashing into the Lexington church. The combined British forces rested in Lexington to give the exhausted soldiers respite. The reinforcements, presumably under Percy's orders, spent their time plundering and burning nearby houses. One of these was the house where Dr. Samuel Prescott had been courting his fiancée, Lydia, before meeting Revere and Dawes. Lydia lived in Lexington with her widowed mother. Someone had fired from within the house as the army passed. The troops immediately retaliated by setting it ablaze. After a short rest, the army reassembled and marched on. Despite the growing numbers of Americans attacking them, they would manage to fight their way back to Boston.

Everyone later heard of many of the acts of heroism that took place amid the fierce fighting as the British retreat continued that day. As the troops passed one woman's home, she stood firing from her open doorway. When ordered to desist, she replied with insults and more musket shots. She was shot along with everyone else in the house. One of the most amazing incidents occurred when a group of older men thwarted General Gage's efforts to ensure adequate ammunition for his troops. He had taken the precaution of dispatching a convoy of two ammunition wagons with an escort of fourteen men, in case his forces ran short. A group of watchmen in Menotomy (present-day Arlington), men too old or unfit for the regular militia, led by David Lamson, a mulatto, ambushed the convoy and ordered the soldiers escorting it to surrender. When the soldiers whipped their horses to escape, the Americans methodically shot the lead horses and killed the officer in charge and two sergeants. At this point the surviving soldiers fled, tossing their muskets into a pond as they ran. As the Americans helped themselves to the British ammunition and tried to obliterate all signs of the skirmish, the frantic soldiers spied an elderly lady, Mother Batherick, digging for dandelion greens in a vacant field. They asked for her help and surrendered to her. She led them to the house of the local militia captain, Ephraim Frost, where she left them with the request that if they lived to get back to England they were to "tell King George that an old woman took six of his grenadiers prisoner."

Another elderly Menotomy colonist also became a hero that day. Samuel Whittemore, seventy-eight and crippled, lived with his son and grandchildren near the Arlington River. They were awakened early in the morning to the sounds of British troops on their way to Lexington and Concord. Samuel's wife began preparing to flee to the home of a son living in Medford, assuming her husband would accompany her. Instead she found him oiling his musket and pistols and sharpening his old saber. He could not be dissuaded. Insisting he was going "up town," Samuel limped out and waited behind a stone wall for the British to return. When they appeared, he managed to get off five quick shots, killing one soldier before a flanking party spotted him. As they closed in, Whittemore took out his pistols and shot two more soldiers. He was just reaching for his sword when he was caught. One soldier shot him in the face, hitting his cheekbone, while others stabbed him with their bayonets. When neighbors later found the feisty warrior, he had some fourteen wounds. Although he was covered with blood and appeared to be near death, they took him to Dr. Cotton Tufts of Medford. Thanks to Whittemore's natural resilience or the good doctor's ministrations, Samuel Whittemore survived for another eighteen years.

By the time the British reached Menotomy, American officers had finally devised a strategy to make use of the growing companies of men converging on the British column. They concentrated on attacking the rear of the column and then moving to attack from the flanks. They also began sending out their own skirmishers and ordering newly arriving companies to lay a series of ambushes along the route the British were likely to take. During the ferocious fighting in Menotomy, the reinforced British troops faced over 5,500 militia. The fighting and looting grew more intense. There were house-to-house battles as residents fired from their windows and British soldiers retaliated. "They suffered for their temerity," a British lieutenant wrote, "for all that were found in the houses were put to death." Twenty-five Americans were killed and nine wounded in the fighting in the town. The British lost some forty dead and eighty wounded there.

The men and women of Lincoln escaped serious injury that day. For other towns, the casualties were heavy and deeply felt. Lexington suffered ten killed and another nine wounded. Among the militia officers killed were Captain Nathan Barrett of Concord, Captain Eleazer Kingsbury and Lieutenant John Bacon of Needham, and, of course, Captain Jonathan Wilson of Bedford. Abel Prescott, Jr., who had helped his brother Samuel alert the countryside by carrying the alarm to Sudbury and Framingham, was shot on his return to Concord as he passed the South Bridge. His wound never healed properly, and he died of dysentery that August. Deacon Josiah Haynes, who at seventy-nine had insisted on marching with the men of Sudbury, died somewhere between Fiske Hill and Lexington Green.

Children on both sides were also among the dead. Fourteen-year-old Edward Barber of Charlestown fell victim to the British policy of shooting into houses where residents, who might be potential snipers, were seen. During the brutal fighting in Charlestown, Edward had run to the window of his family's house to watch the troops pass. He was spotted by a soldier and killed with a single musket shot, to the horror of his screaming brothers and sisters. Children died on the British side, too. Lexington's Joshua Simonds captured two soldiers, one a small boy who played the fife. The lad pleaded with Simonds not to kill him. Simonds noticed that the boy's coat was buttoned right up to his chin, the fife sticking out. Looking closer, he found that the coat had been buttoned up in hopes of staunching an angry wound. A farm family took in the small soldier. A few days later he died of his injury.

By sunset the British army had suffered 73 men killed, 174 wounded, and another 26 missing and probably wounded, for a total of 273. Some 50 Americans were killed or died of their wounds, another 39 were wounded, and 5 were missing, 94 in all. The American dead and wounded came from twenty-three Massachusetts towns.

When Peter and his family emerged from the woods that afternoon, the wreckage of battle lay all around them. The drifting smoke of burning houses and the acrid smell of gunpowder blotted out the beautiful spring day. Distraught friends and neighbors dashed about, trying to get information about loved ones missing or still fighting. The men of Lincoln continued to pursue the British back to Boston. The dead and wounded of both sides lay on the road and in the woods and fields. American casualties were being carefully carried home to their families or gathered for burial. There was deep anger and great sadness at these losses. The British wounded were taken in and tended, although almost invariably with little success. Their dead were left, at first, where they fell. Two dead British soldiers lay near Josiah's door; another was dying in Thomas's house. There were dead and wounded men on Fiske Hill, eight more around the Bloody Angle, and five lay all night where they had fallen in the dust of the road near the Hartwell farms.

The soldiers of the Crown, of the mighty British Empire, lay lifeless on their doorsteps. What would happen when they were discovered? Would the government charge them with murder, treason, rebellion? Were they guilty of these crimes? Truth to tell, however sure the people of these little Massachusetts communities were of the rightness of their cause, they were desperately afraid of what might happen next. Whatever that was, Peter was determined to play a part. He was only twelve, but he was tall for his age. And boys could and did fight, or at least accompany the older men into battle and help. When the urgent call for aid came the next day, Peter marched with Josiah and the men of Lincoln to join the army.

CHAPTER SIX

Answering the Call

Our all is at stake. Death and devastation are the certain consequences of delay. Every moment is infinitely precious. An hour lost may deluge your country in blood and entail perpetual slavery upon the few of our posterity that may survive the carnage.

Circular letter to Massachusetts towns from the Committee of Safety, Massachusetts Provincial Congress, April 20, 1775

THE COLD SPRING RAIN that night, with its flashes of lightning and rumbles of thunder, deepened the atmosphere of gloom and foreboding. It drenched the lifeless bodies of the British soldiers lying along the roadside and spattered the fresh mounds of earth already covering the American dead. So great was the fear that the British would return to retaliate, even on the dead, definitely on their families, that townsfolk buried their men as quickly as possible. Lincoln was spared this sad chore, but as soon as the British left Lexington, the Reverend Clarke said a quick prayer over the town's fatalities, lying in the church, and arranged for their immediate burial. The bodies were placed in plain pine boxes, and these were quickly loaded onto two horse carts. No time for the niceties. Clarke's daughter, Elizabeth, eleven at the time, recalled the procession to the cemetery. "We followed the bodies of those *first* slain, *Father, Mother,* I and the Baby." The dead men were not buried with their family members: a common grave had been dug in a remote part of the old graveyard, near the woods. "There I stood," Elizabeth wrote, "and there I saw them let down into the ground. It was a little rainy, but we waited to see them covered up with the clods." Her father was not satisfied that the gravesite was safely hidden until the burial mound had been covered with branches of pine and oak and looked like nothing more than a pile of brush.

The Danvers men who died in the fierce fighting in Menotomy were sent home piled on an ox sled. Menotomy's own dead, all twelve of them, were put in a sledge and hauled to its little cemetery, where, as in Lexington, they were laid to rest in a common grave still wearing the bloody clothes they had died in. Cambridge gathered three of its dead and buried them without coffins or shrouds in a trench in the churchyard near the town common. The son of one of the three men leaped into the grave and gently placed his father's coat over his face before the earth was tossed into the pit. Oddly, there was less concern about disposing quickly of the British dead. And so a grim day ended.

Daylight brought no relief. The Nelsons and their neighbors were still trying to take in the enormity of the battle and were busy tending to the wounded and the British dead when a desperate appeal came from the Committee of Safety in Cambridge. The British troops had fought their way back to Boston as dark descended on April 19. It had taken the Royal Navy boats nearly three hours to ferry the wounded soldiers across the river to safety. They were almost certain to march out again and with greater force. When they did, their fury would be terrible. That must not be allowed to happen; they must be blockaded in Boston. Guards had already been posted at Charlestown neck, cutting off the city's link to the mainland, and patrols had been sent there. The Committee of Safety did not mince words. It was "absolutely necessary," they wrote,

> that we immediately raise an army to defend our wives and children from the butchering hands of the inhuman soldiers, who, incensed at the obstacles they met in their bloody progress, and enraged at being re-pulsed from the field of slaughter, will, without the least doubt, take the first opportunity in their power to ravage this devoted country with fire and sword. We conjure you, therefore, by all that is dear, by all that is sacred, that you give all assistance possible in forming an army. Our all is at stake. Death and devastation are the instant consequences of delay. Every moment is infinitely precious. An hour lost may deluge your country in blood.

Failure to respond would doom survivors to "perpetual slavery." There was no going back. They had all gone too far.

Captain Billy Smith quickly summoned the members of his Lincoln minute company who had not remained in Cambridge. They were to leave with the Lincoln militia as soon as possible. Josiah began gathering his clothes, weapons, and food to march with the militia company. This was Peter's opportunity. He insisted on accompanying Josiah. No more hiding in the woods. The initiative was surely his. Neither Josiah nor Elizabeth would have suggested the youngster join the army. Peter would be sorely needed at home. But the situation was plainly desperate, and they agreed he could go, doubtless proud of the boy's eagerness and courage.

The question was whether Smith would agree to take him into his minute company. The members of the minute and militia companies were meant to be at least sixteen. Sometimes boys as young as fourteen were included, usually as fifers or drummers. The Lincoln minute company already had the Mason brothers to play the fife and Daniel Brown to play the drum. With so much to do and more important things to attend to, Smith probably had little time to consider Peter's plea. Somehow Peter was able to convince the captain that he would be useful. Others could vouch for him. Joshua Brooks, Jr., Jupiter's owner, just twenty at the time, was a member of Smith's company. So, too, were John, Samuel, and Isaac Hartwell and Peter's neighbor, John Thorning, and many other men who knew Peter well. It was a testament to the confidence they had in the boy that they were happy to have him along. He was duly enrolled as Private Peter Brooks, his last name, as was customary for a slave, that of his original owners.

Smith's own slave, Cato, joined the company, leaving Catherine Louisa to handle the farmwork somehow. Jupiter was to remain in Lincoln, though. He and Peggy could be proud, if anxious, that their son was marching with the white men. And though Josiah and Peter were leaving, Thomas Nelson was staying, as was Jonathan, although he was older than Peter. Whatever Jonathan's wishes, he was needed and wanted at home. The only son would not be put in harm's way.

No one knew how long they might be gone. Elizabeth would be left to manage the farm alone and see to the spring planting. Thomas and Jonathan would help her, of course, but they had their own land as well as Tabitha's to work, and the weather would not wait. The Nelsons could ordinarily hire one of the Thorning boys next door. John Thorning was marching with his minute company, although William, the hero of yesterday, was staying home to help his family. Elizabeth appreciated the urgency. There was no time to waste. Anyway, it might not take long. Negotiations might end the standoff, and then Josiah and Peter could come home. Cambridge was only twenty miles away. God willing, everyone would return safely.

As Peter and the Lincoln men prepared to march off, the dead British soldiers scattered along the road from Concord to Boston were unceremoniously buried but, unlike the American casualties, seldom in consecrated ground. At dawn the two soldiers Will Thorning shot still lay where they had fallen near Peter's home. Like most eighteenth-century children, Peter had seen dead people. But these battle dead were different. They were terrible to look at. Musket wounds had shattered their bones, and many were bloody and cruelly maimed by their injuries. Josiah agreed that Will's two soldiers could be buried in the little knoll in his apple orchard, across the road from the house. And so they were. That peaceful orchard, fragrant with blossom, took on a more ominous aspect. For decades to come, the knoll where the two soldiers lay was known as "The Soldiers Graves." Then there was the soldier shot on Thomas's doorstep. After he died of his wound, they buried him a short distance "westerly" of Thomas's house. Their homes seemed surrounded by crude resting places hiding the bodies of the Crown's men. The three graves on their own land were unmarked. To the east of the Nelson farms, two more soldiers were buried on the side of the road just beyond Bull Tavern, and the man who died in the deadly confrontation at the Fiske family well was buried near a stone wall on Fiske Hill. "A heap of small stones once marked the spot," historian Frank Coburn wrote in 1912, "but they have disappeared."

Eight British soldiers lay all night in the road near the Bloody Angle. Neighbors buried three that day near the roadside. Ephraim Hartwell and another older man, probably Joseph Mason, hitched oxen to a cart and gathered the five soldiers lying near their farms, meaning to give them a Christian burial. Mary Hartwell was moved at the sight of the dead soldiers when the two men returned with the team. She would never forget the image of the cart and its burden as it headed slowly for the Lincoln cemetery in the town center: "My thoughts went out for the wives, parents, and children away across the Atlantic, who would never again see their loved ones. And I left the house, and taking my little children by the hand, I followed the rude hearse to the grave hastily made in the burial-ground. I remember how cruel it seemed to put them into one large trench without any coffins. There was one in a brilliant uniform, whom I supposed to have been an officer."

The march to Cambridge was tense with excitement but sobering as Peter and the Lincoln men trudged past the smoldering ruins of burned-out houses and heard tales of the violence suffered in the towns nearer to Boston. Everywhere they met men converging on Cambridge from throughout New England—so many that the Committee of Safety ordered some to stay home. Young Joseph Martin, living in Milford, Connecticut, wrote that Milford men who engaged "to go to war" got only as far as the next town when they received orders to return because "there was a sufficiency of men already engaged." Cambridge was soon crammed with citizen soldiers. Within two weeks ten thousand were gathered there.

On April 22, two days after the Committee of Safety's call had gone out, the Provincial Congress met at Concord, well beyond the reach of General Gage's artillery and the guns of the warship *Somerset,* and agreed to raise an army of 30,000 men to defend the country. Some 13,600 were to be from Massachusetts. Two days later, on April 24, Peter and the Lincoln minute company were officially enrolled in the newly organized army, one of ten companies in the regiment of Colonel Abijah Pierce. When the army was reorganized in May, they were moved to the regiment of John Nixon of Sudbury. In all there would be fifteen Massachusetts regiments of foot and a battalion of artillery. On April 26 the Committee of Safety called on other New England colonies to provide as many men as they could to assist Massachusetts.

The new soldiers were housed wherever there was room. They were stuffed into Harvard College buildings and private homes, many others sleeping rough, needing tents. Harvard opened its kitchen to feed men based nearby while taking care to move its library and other treasures north to Andover, well away from Cambridge. Men housed at the college drilled on the Cambridge common just across the road. Supplies were variable. It was a difficult time of year for foodstuffs, and each town sent what it could. Tucked into the wagons of supplies were parcels from families for their men. Some Cambridge residents had left town, and a few militiamen helped themselves to private property. It was necessary to issue a general order to punish any soldier making free with someone else's things.

It was an unusual army. There was considerable coming and going, especially since many men were not far from home, and at first there was little military deportment. The men didn't think an army of citizen soldiers needed the rigid discipline of professional troops. They gloried in the difference between them and the British regulars, and there was much bravado. They were convinced they had the advantage because of their own fervor and the logistical difficulties foreign armies faced in America. In December 1774 the anonymous author "Americanus" had bragged in the *Connecticut Gazette*, "there is not a power in Europe, formidable and numerous as their armies are in that country able to send and support an army of thirty thousand men in America." On May 2, 1775, another Connecticut gentleman claimed to feel "no apprehensions from General *Gage's* ever being able to penetrate into the country thus far, if he was even reinforced with fifty thousand men." Of course, Connecticut was not Massachusetts, with a British army based in its chief city.

The American regiments that actually had to deal with the British were spread from Roxbury and Dorchester in the south to Charlestown in the north in an attempt to ring Boston on the landward side. Watches were kept to ensure a tight siege. Peter and the other boys were kept busy moving supplies, carrying messages, serving officers, and being generally helpful. There was a great deal of digging. Breastworks were thrown up at the base of Prospect Hill. Men were sent to Lechmere's Point, where they could look across the Charles River to Boston.

At first they were all under the command of Major General Artemas Ward, described uncharitably by the American general Charles Lee as "a fat old gentleman who had been a popular church-warden." To be fair, Ward was a highly respected farmer, religious and thoughtful, who suffered from kidney stones. But he was a veteran of the French and Indian War and took care to issue orders only after a council of senior officers had met to discuss them. As for his men, the Massachusetts Provincial Congress sent George Washington a frank description of the army he would find at Cambridge: "The greatest part of them have not before seen Service. And altho' naturally brave and of good understanding, yet, for want of Experience in military Life, have but little knowledge of divers things most essential to the preservation of Health and even of Life. The Youth in the Army are not possess'd of the absolute Necessity of Cleanliness in their Dress, and Lodging, continual Exercise and strict Temperance to preserve them from Diseases frequently prevailing in Camps; especially among those who, from their Childhood, have been us'd to a laborious Life."

The lack of attention to cleanliness had quick and sad results. Camp fever, or typhus, struck the army encampment. Hospitals were established, but the dread disease caused by the unclean conditions was highly contagious and often fatal. Soon it had spread from the army to nearby civilians. Lexington was hit hard. The list of deaths in the Reverend Jonas Clarke's diary that summer makes grim reading:

> July 22 a Negro child out of Mr. John Simond's House
> July 24 Mr. Isaac Winship's Child buried
> July 25 Mr. Marret Munro's Child died
> July 26 David Fisk's Wife died
> August 2 Mr. Jonathan Smith's Child died
> August 21 Widow Anna Munro buried
> August 23 Ebenezer Parker's Child buried
> August 28 Mr. John Munro's Child died
> August 30 Mr. N. Reed's Child died.

Throughout the fall Clarke was busy with funerals. Children were especially vulnerable. That summer Lexington had more fatalities at home than among those serving in the army.

The British military, with a tradition honed over centuries, sneered at their colonists' amateurish military abilities. General Clark famously boasted in the presence of Benjamin Franklin that he could march from Maine to Georgia with just a thousand grenadiers and "geld all the males, some by force and the rest by a little coaxing." Lord Sandwich dubbed the colonial troops "raw, undisciplined, and cowardly." Raw and undisciplined they surely were, but, as the British would soon find out, not cowardly. And the problem of being raw and undisciplined could be cured. Whatever the spontaneous army's weaknesses and hardships, Peter along with the other slaves and free blacks in the ranks found a brotherly camaraderie they were never to know elsewhere.

Despite British confidence, the American blockade created severe problems. The Boston garrison soon ran short of fresh food. In June, General Gage wrote that his supplies from the surrounding country were cut off and he was trying to get some from "Other parts of the Continent." He urged the government to recruit foreigners, Indians, "even to raise the Negros, in our cause." The British, bottled up as they were with the population of Boston, also had problems with disease. An epidemic of smallpox broke out in the city. The British soldiers tended to be immune because of previous exposure to the disease, but many Bostonians suffered terribly.

On a happier note, spirits soared in the American camp when word reached Cambridge that on May 10 their forces had captured Fort Ticonderoga on Lake Champlain. The lightly guarded fortress fell in a surprise raid. Some men had left the Cambridge camp, but their mission had been kept secret until its victorious outcome. Ticonderoga was one of the most important fortifications in the New World. Americans, led by Connecticut's Benedict Arnold and by Ethan Allen commanding Vermont's Green Mountain Boys, overwhelmed the British garrison, Arnold rushing ahead and shouting to the garrison commander, "Come out of here, you damned old rat." The fort's nearly ninety cannon were a great prize, desperately needed for the siege of Boston. In the coming winter, when they could be moved on sleds, about fifty cannon would be hauled through the snow to Massachusetts. Concord's Reverend William Emerson, who had gone along as chaplain to the Middlesex regiment, contracted camp fever and died that fall in Rutland, Vermont.

Ten days after the capture of Ticonderoga, a shadow passed over the black soldiers serving in the army. The Committee of Safety passed a resolution that "no Slave be admitted into this Army upon any consideration whatever." It seemed inconsistent to the committee, and indeed was inconsistent, that slaves should be part of an army of free men fighting for freedom. But blacks, both slave and free, had fought at Lexington and in the running battle from Concord to Boston. It was painful to be singled out in this way. Fortunately, the Massachusetts Provincial Congress set the recommendation aside, but it was a warning of things to come.

While the American army dug ditches and tried to keep fed, equipped, and healthy, General Gage was biding his time, waiting for reinforcements to help him break out of the blockade. Their arrival was solemnly recorded by the Reverend Clarke: May 15, "60 Regulars come in," June 12, "More regulars arrive." On May 25, the Americans were still celebrating the capture of Ticonderoga when three British major generals sailed into Boston harbor to bolster Gage's force. Peter would come to know their names well. General William Howe, a massive man, tall and dark, was the most senior. He had been sympathetic to the Americans, but soldiers obey orders, and he was there to put down the rebellion. A boisterous man who drank, gambled, and womanized, he was nevertheless a fine military leader. His reputation had been made when in 1759 he led General James Wolfe's men up the cliffs at Quebec in the brilliant strategy that enabled the British to capture the French city. The second of the trio, General Henry Clinton, had been born in New York during his father's tenure as its governor. In contrast to Howe, Clinton was a quiet man but also a fine military commander known to have described himself as a "shy bitch." He immediately found fault with the British troops in America. There were too many Irish officers, men whose education left them "inimical to all subordination"; in addition, the officers paid little attention to their men and were expected to carry muskets and defend themselves in action. In Clinton's estimation, an officer could not command "while he is firing, loading, and playing bo peep behind trees." Further, the uniforms were unsuitable for the climate, and the soldiers had little skill with bayonets. It was Clinton's task to work with this imperfect material. The most colorful of the three men was General John Burgoyne, handsome, dashing, popular with his men, and cocksure. With these generals at his elbow Gage became more aggressive. On June 12 he declared martial law, although he promised that rebels would be pardoned if they laid down their arms.

Two days later, on June 14, the Continental Congress responded by taking the citizen army assembled around Boston into the pay of the "United Colonies." The Congress moved to unify the various colonial armies at Boston and called on Pennsylvania, Virginia, and Maryland to contribute a rifle regiment each to the force. Then on June 17, a clear, hot day, Gage made his move.

A direct assault was the surest way to unnerve untested amateurs. So around three o'clock that afternoon 2,200 British troops in close ranks began charging straight up Breed's Hill. Peter's regiment and the rest of the exhausted Americans crouching behind the walls of their freshly dug redoubt waited in silence on the hilltop. When at last Colonel William Prescott gave the order to fire, Peter had his first experience of battle. He was not in the front line, but he was a member of the regiment whose task it was to help the men on the line. And he was there, on the hill, a participant in the sort of formal battle the regulars were so well trained to execute but the colonists were not. It was to be the bloodiest battle of the Revolution.

The Americans had quickly gotten wind of Gage's intention to storm Dorchester Heights to the south and then take Roxbury and Charlestown Heights, which would clear the way for them to attack the American encampment at Cambridge. The Committee of Safety decided to fortify Dorchester and Charlestown Heights at once, but there were too few men to hold Roxbury and Dorchester Heights. By fortifying Bunker Hill on the Charlestown peninsula the committee hoped to disrupt British plans, protect the army at Cambridge, and keep the British blockaded in Boston. Colonel Prescott was ordered to take a few regiments and fortify Bunker Hill, the highest point on the Charlestown peninsula, just across the Charles River from Boston. This meant constructing a redoubt on the hilltop within earshot of the British garrison and within range of the great guns on their warships. It had to be completed before dawn broke, exposing them to British fire, rather a tall order that depended on speed and surprise.

The men were ordered to muster on the Cambridge common at six o'clock that evening. Some twelve hundred men assembled under Prescott's command. The colonel was a tall, lanky, and experienced officer, brave and able. For three hours the citizen soldiers stood waiting for dark to descend and for everything to be ready. At nine o'clock the president of Harvard College blessed them and their mission, and they marched off to the Charlestown peninsula.

A small force of Connecticut men under General Israel Putnam joined them. Putnam, or "Old Put," as he was affectionately known, was, like Prescott, popular and experienced. Tales of Putnam's bravery and exploits abounded. Owner of a small farm and cider business, he was said to have pursued a wolf that was killing his sheep, crawling on his hands and knees into its den. When he spied the wolf's eyes glittering in the gloom, he shot it, then pulled it out by the ears. The recollections of Jacob Francis, a black soldier, help explain the men's regard for Putnam. They had been digging fortifications on Lechmere's Point and had dug up a large stone, which they put on the side of the trench, when Putnam rode up. "The general spoke to the corporal who was standing looking at the men at work and said to him, 'My lad, throw that stone up on the middle of the breastwork.' The corporal, touching his hat with his hand, said to the general, 'Sir, I am a corporal.' 'Oh,' said the general, 'I ask your pardon, sir.' And immediately got off his horse and took up the stone and threw it up on the breastwork himself and then mounted his horse and rode on." But it was Putnam's impressive military experience that mattered now. During the British assault on Fort Ticonderoga in the French and Indian War, General Howe's older brother, George, had died in Putnam's arms. Now Putnam and another Howe were in arms against each other.

After climbing Bunker Hill the men waited as the night slipped away while the officers argued over whether to fortify Bunker Hill, which was higher but just out of range of the British, or the smaller Breed's Hill, then known as Breed's Pasture. Breed's Hill was a more dangerous location, but the British could not ignore it. The hill commanded the harbor and would put the British within range of American cannon. Finally the decision was made, Breed's Hill it would be, and at midnight the men began digging. They dug until dawn. When the sun came up, they were surrounded by the redoubt, its earthen walls six to seven feet high with several rail fences in front of it. The redoubt was not quite complete, but it was protection.

The British had heard their voices during the night, but General Gage felt that whatever was happening could wait until morning for his attention. The redoubt had been erected none too soon. The captain of the sloop *Lively* spotted the redoubt at 4:00 a.m. and opened fire. A second sloop, *Glasgow,* began firing from the Back Bay, and by 9:00 a.m. the British guns on Copp's Hill in the northern part of Boston joined in. British cannon kept firing on the Americans all day, only stopping just before the land attack began. Prescott sent messages pleading for reinforcements, but they had to cross the neck of the Charlestown peninsula under the guns of four British vessels—two sloops and two armed scows. General Ward was reluctant to send the men. When he eventually acted, few men from the nine Massachusetts regiments he dispatched ever reached the fight. Most watched the battle from nearby Bunker Hill.

Peter's regiment under John Nixon was not one of these. When the alarm was raised on June 17, Nixon took three hundred men and dashed for the site. Among the first to arrive, they reached the hill just before the attack. Their position was near a rail fence and breastwork concocted of hay below the gap. Each man was armed with just thirteen rounds of ammunition.

The assault began in midafternoon. The British had waited for high tide. On they came, ferried across the river, regiment after regiment. The redcoats landed on a nearby beach while the navy provided covering fire. At three o'clock the first assault began. The sky was already dark with smoke. The British troops closest to Charlestown had been fired on from nearby houses in the town. In response, Howe ordered that the town be burned to the ground. His battery at Copp's Hill opened fire, striking the town's large wooden church. Neighboring buildings caught fire, and Charlestown was soon aflame. The dreadful sight of the burning houses angered the men watching on Breed's Hill and stiffened their determination.

The British soldiers, bayonets drawn, were led by General Howe and his personal regiment. They didn't stop to fire but charged in close ranks straight for the American lines. A New Hampshire regiment, well drilled in marksmanship, had planted markers on the beach indicating the range from a stone wall. When the British came within fifty yards of that wall, the New Hampshire men opened fire, aiming low as ordered and trying to hit the officers first. Despite the deadly American fire, the British kept advancing, but they could not reach the Americans. Another wave of soldiers assaulted from a different angle, and again the Americans held their fire until the British began climbing the fence of the fortifications. The British fired back. Nixon was shot and severely wounded. His men carried him off the field. He survived the day, thanks to a dollar coin in his pocket. American bullets also found many British targets. Howe was soon left alone on the field as his men pulled back. Behind the redoubt, the American line had held.

Clinton, watching from Boston, was so upset that he had himself ferried across the Charles River with five hundred more men and joined with Howe in a third assault. Peter's regiment and the others were now short of ammunition. They were hungry, thirsty, and exhausted. They could see reinforcements with fresh supplies on Bunker Hill, but these men refused to cross to Breed's Hill. The ammunition of men who fell was shared. Colonel Prescott opened artillery shells and handed out the powder as the British rallied for one last effort. The Americans held their fire until the British were only twenty yards away. As they climbed the hill, the advancing British had to step over the bodies of fallen comrades, and many bullets found their mark. But the British could not be stopped this time, and they forced their way into the redoubt. In this final effort before Prescott ordered their retreat, Peter Salem, a slave from Framingham, aimed at one of the officers rallying the British troops, Major John Pitcairn, who had played such a prominent role in the fatal raid on Concord. Just as Pitcairn was crying, "The day is ours," Salem shot him through the head. Joseph Warren was one of the last Americans to leave the redoubt. As he reluctantly backed away, he was hit by a bullet to the forehead and fell dead.

It was a ferocious battle. The British had won the day, but they had suffered more than a thousand casualties, nearly half the men engaged. Nineteen officers were killed and another seventy wounded. The Americans had suffered, too. Between four hundred and six hundred were killed or wounded. A few men were captured and died later in British hands. The colonists had lost the ground but had exacted a high price. The British were shocked at the Americans' display of courage and seriously hurt by the loss of men. "The loss we have sustained is greater than we can bear," Gage wrote to a friend, the victory "too dearly bought."

Peter knew only that he and his colleagues and neighbors had survived. They had fought until their ammunition ran out and, amid the terrible carnage, had witnessed great bravery from fighters both white and black. Apart from Peter Salem's killing of Pitcairn, revenge for April 19, the outstanding valor of Salem Poor, a free Negro from the north shore town of Andover, prompted a letter of commendation to the Massachusetts legislature. Salem had managed to buy his freedom six years earlier, and he came to Cambridge as a volunteer. During the battle he had shot Lieutenant Colonel James Abercrombie, the highest-ranking British officer killed in the battle. The letter read: "The Reward due to so great and Distinguished a Character. The Subscribers beg leave to Report to your Honorable House (Which we do in justice to the Character of so Brave a man) that under Our Own observation, we declare that A Negro Man Called Salem Poor of Col. Fryes Regiment, Capt. Ames. Company in the late Battle of Charleston, behaved like an Experienced Officer, as Well as an Excellent soldier." The writers, busy men, excused themselves from setting forth "Particulars of his Conduct" but concluded, "We Would Only beg leave to say in the Person of this Negro Centers a Brave & gallant Soldier." The commendation was signed by Colonels William Prescott and Jonathan Brewer and four junior officers. Salem Poor was alone in receiving such recognition.

That letter of commendation to the legislature was written in December. Long before then, on July 3, General George Washington of Virginia arrived in Cambridge to take command of the American army. Southern regiments and southern officers arrived, too. A week after Washington reached Cambridge, army headquarters issued an order that no "Stroller, Negro or Vagabond, or Person suspected of being an Enemy to the Liberty of America, nor any under Eighteen years of Age" could be enlisted. "As the Cause is the best that can engage Men of Courage and Principle to take up Arms," the announcement explained, "so it is expected that none but such will be accepted by the Recruiting Officer." Despite their loyalty and bravery at Bunker Hill, blacks, free or slave, seemed not to be considered "Men of Courage and Principle." When the Committee of Safety had passed a resolution on May 20 to permit only free men to enlist, the Massachusetts Provincial Congress had ignored it. This time the decision was not theirs.

CHAPTER SEVEN

Another Call, Another Answer

Our Dunmore [governor of Virginia] has at length Publishd his much dreaded proclamation—declareg Freedom to All Indented Servts & Slaves (the Property of Rebels) that will repair to his majestys Standard—being able to bear Arms—what effect it will have upon those sorts of people I cannot tell. . . . Sears who is at worck here says there is not a man of them, but woud leave us, if they believe'd they coud make there Escape—Thom Spears Excepted—& yet they have no fault to find[.] Liberty is sweet.

LUND WASHINGTON to GEORGE WASHINGTON, Mount Vernon,
December 3, 1775

WHILE PETER and other slaves and free blacks in Washington's army were smarting at the indignity of being branded unworthy of joining the fight for liberty, British officers were mulling over a very different strategy, one that would ultimately affect everyone, white and black, free and slave, North and South. A young slave named Titus was one of those whose life it changed.

On November 8, 1775, Titus, the second oldest of John Corlies's slaves, ran away from Corlies's property in Monmouth County, New Jersey. The advertisement promptly placed in the *Pennsylvania Packet* appealing for his capture described the fugitive as "about 21 years of age, not very black near 6 foot high." Titus was a mulatto. He had last been seen wearing a gray homespun coat, brown breeches, and blue and white stockings. He had taken with him "a wallet drawn up at one end with a string in which was a quantity of clothes." Three pounds' "proclamation money" was offered for his return. Ironically, the day before Titus disappeared, John Murray, earl of Dunmore,

British governor of Virginia, had issued a proclamation declaring "all indented Servants, Negroes, or others (appertaining to Rebels,) free that are
able and willing to bear Arms, they joining His MAJESTY's Troops as soon as
may be." News of the proclamation took nearly a week to reach Philadelphia,
so Titus could not have known of the offer the day he vanished. But when he
returned to New Jersey many months later, he was fighting for the British.

Titus ought to have been one of New Jersey's more fortunate slaves,
owned as he was by a Quaker. But members of the Society of Friends differed
on the subject of slavery. In Pennsylvania they were ardent abolitionists, yet
despite an edict ending slaveholding among Quakers in 1758, the shift in
Monmouth County was gradual. Members of the local Shrewsbury Meeting
were directed to educate their slaves and to free enslaved males when they
reached twenty-one. If they refused to free their slaves, the congregation
could expel them. A few recalcitrant Friends were willing to part with their
slaves only for cash payments or after their own deaths. Free or slave, however, the blacks were not welcome to worship with the Society of Friends.
Titus's contemporaries, young men owned by John Hartshorne and Richard
Lawrence, had been freed when they reached that magic age shortly before
Titus's disappearance. Although Corlies's description was purposely vague
about the escapee's age, Titus had just turned twenty-one.

Every faith has its wayward members, and John Corlies was of a different
stripe from other Quakers. He was a cruel master with a reputation for
drinking and fighting. He beat his four male slaves, aged twenty-five, twenty-
one, sixteen, and fourteen, for the slightest fault. He and his mother, Zilpha,
owner of two slaves, stubbornly refused to emancipate them. Repeated visits
by the Friends as Titus's birthday neared failed to convince Corlies to free his
property. His visitors reported that "he has not seen it his duty to give them
their freedom." They were probably not surprised, given his refusal even to
follow the Quaker practice of educating slaves. "They have no learning," they
noted of Corlies's slaves, "and he is not inclined to give them any." Although
Corlies was no pacifist and no saint, it was his refusal to free his slaves that
eventually persuaded the Society of Friends to act in 1778: "After a considerable Deal of Labour bestowed on him Respecting his keeping Negroes in
Slavery, [Corlies] still continues to decline complying with the yearly meeting . . . therefore . . . there is the necessity to disown him."

But that was in the future, and Titus was less patient than the Friends.
His options were a lifetime of brutal treatment or flight. It was a hard choice.
Escaped slaves who were caught could expect to be severely punished and

were usually sold to the large plantations of the Deep South or Caribbean. Titus had made himself an expert on the region's waterways, swamps, and back roads and may have been assisted by frustrated Shrewsbury Quakers ashamed of their wayward brother. At any rate, he vanished. He would never be anyone's slave again.

Lord Dunmore was an ambitious Scots laird. He was the same age as George Washington. The two met socially when Dunmore moved to Virginia in 1771 and got on rather well. They enjoying hunting, dining, and attending the theater together, and both were interested in land speculation. Dunmore had joined the British army at nineteen, resigning in midcareer to represent Scotland in the House of Lords. His undistinguished political career in Britain ended in 1770, when he was appointed governor of New York. With high hopes, he and his family set sail, as keen as other emigrants to seek their fortune in the New World. Despite his title and his wife's noble background, the couple's eight children—five sons and three daughters—imposed a considerable financial burden. Within a year of his arrival in New York, Dunmore had managed to obtain some fifty thousand acres of land near Lake Champlain. And so he was not pleased when in 1771 he was reassigned as governor of Virginia, even though the colony was the wealthiest of the kingdom's North American settlements. On his arrival in Williamsburg, Dunmore promptly turned his attention to finding land for his sons in this new location. Disobeying orders, he financed surveys of Virginia's vaguely defined western territories, disturbing the Indians living on that land. His impetuous landgrab worked: the Shawnee resisted. In 1774 he retaliated with a quick military campaign and returned victorious, bearing a treaty ceding to Virginia title to the land west and north of the Ohio River. It ought to have made him a hero with the colony's elite, and briefly it did. On January 19, 1775, Dunmore hosted a splendid ball in Williamsburg in honor of the queen's birthday and the christening of his newborn daughter, and he seemed at the height of popularity. But his arrogant, pig-headed ways constantly gave offense. He quarreled with the Virginia House of Burgesses and upset those he ought to have befriended. He also kept London in ignorance of his activities and of the colony's sentiments about British taxes and the punishment of Boston. William Woodford, a prominent Virginian, took to referring to the governor as "Wronghead." Dunmore was an acquisitive and impetuous man with military ability but few political skills. The proclamation to free and arm slaves was his idea, announced without approval from London.

The logical, though most dangerous, direction for Titus to take, was south to join Dunmore in Virginia. The farther south he traveled, into colonies with larger numbers of slaves and greater fears of uprisings, the more perilous his journey became. The roads were being watched for runaway slaves. Blacks spotted by patrols were stopped and questioned. Titus traveled along the coast, keeping where possible to marshes and away from well-traveled roads. He survived by taking odd jobs and always claimed to be free. Although he escaped before Dunmore issued his proclamation, he hadn't needed anything official to persuade him that the British, not the colonists, held out the possibility of refuge and freedom. There were rumors, well-founded, circulating months before Dunmore's announcement, that the British might offer slaves their liberty. Dunmore made no secret that since 1772 he had been toying with the idea of freeing slaves who came to him. He saw it as the perfect lever to keep Virginia's whites in check. That was the year the Somerset Case ending slavery in England had electrified America's slaves and brought their owners sleepless nights. The slaves of New Jersey began holding mass meetings at night. When masters complained of thefts of food or of their slaves riding their masters' horses to the nighttime meetings, some were boldly informed that "it was not necessary to please their masters, for they should not have their masters long." Although the slaves soon found that the British did not intend to apply the ruling to North America, the political potential of such a move was not lost on anyone, certainly not Dunmore. Dunmore wrote the secretary of state for the colonies, William Legge, that if an enemy could persuade some of Virginia's 165,000 slaves to join them, "a conquest of the Country would inevitably be effected in a very Short time."

Throughout the winter of 1774–1775, as friction grew between the British and their colonists, rumors of slave uprisings proliferated from South Carolina north to Massachusetts. The members of the Virginia Convention hoped threats of dire punishments would keep the slaves quiet. They heralded the new year of 1775 with the announcement "that if any slave, or slaves, shall be hereafter taken in arms . . . the committee of safety shall . . . transport such . . . to any of the foreign West India islands, there to be disposed of by sale . . . or otherwise dealt with according to an act of assembly for punishing slaves committing capital offenses." Insurrection was a capital offense. Virginia slaves found guilty of insurrection were sentenced to "suffer death, and be utterly excluded all benefit of clergy." In April, when war broke out in Massachusetts, it seemed to both blacks and whites that the British might now feel sufficiently desperate to deploy the scheme to turn the slaves against their masters.

Two days after General Gage's expedition to destroy the Concord arsenal provoked war, Dunmore tried his own preemptive strike. It happened this way. In March a group of leading Virginians worried about British policies convened in Richmond and agreed to Patrick Henry's resolution "raising a body of armed Men in all the counties." They then elected Henry and six other colleagues to represent Virginia at the Second Continental Congress in Philadelphia in May. George Washington and Peyton Randolph, speaker of the House of Burgesses and president of the Continental Congress, were among those delegates selected. But Dunmore, with his recent military victory, was still popular, and the convention, doubtless hoping to mollify him while taking these hostile actions, unanimously praised "our worthy Governor Lord Dunmore, for his truly noble, wise and spirited Conduct in the late Expedition against our Indian Enemy . . . [and] important Services to the People who have the happiness to live under his Administration."

It was a waste of breath. Dunmore was not mollified. Word had not yet reached him of Gage's disaster, but where Gage failed, Dunmore succeeded. In the early hours of Friday, April 21, Dunmore's marines quietly left their ship and raided the Virginia magazine at Williamsburg. The munitions depot was surrounded by a high brick wall in the center of town. The marines approached undetected and began to remove the public supply of gunpowder stored there. They were just loading the fifteenth half-barrel of powder onto a wagon when they were discovered. The townspeople awakened to shouts of alarm, and the militia dashed to the depot, but too late. There was widespread anger and dismay, and Virginians promptly requested the return of the powder. It was needed, they insisted, because "we have too much reason to believe that some wicked and designing persons have instilled the most diabolical notions into the minds of our slaves and that therefore the utmost attention to our internal security is become the more necessary." Who those "wicked and designing persons" might be was not specified. Dunmore coolly assured them the powder was in a secure place and that "whenever it was wanted on any insurrection it should be delivered in half an hour."

The next day, April 22, Dunmore played his trump card. Should force be used to recover the ammunition, the governor promised, he would "free and arm the slaves." Indeed, Dunmore said he would receive all slaves "that will come to me, whom I shall declare free." For good measure, he added that he "would not hesitate at burning rebels' houses to ashes and spreading devastation wherever he could reach."

The threat to free the slaves backfired, at least among the white population. It caused such fury among both friends and foes of the British administration that Dunmore feared for his family's safety and sent them to New York. Then on June 6 he himself fled to the ship *Fowey,* anchored off the Virginia coast. Runaway slaves now had to row out to join him. But row out they did. Writing that June, James Madison saw in Dunmore's plan "the only part which this colony is vulnerable; and if we should be subdued, we shall fall like Achilles by the hand of one that knows the secret."

While Dunmore was accustoming himself to life offshore, General Gage, commander in chief of British forces in North America, blockaded in Boston that summer, was also gloomily speculating about making use of "every resource, even to raise the negroes in our cause." In New Jersey a worried resident of Somerset County, northwest of Titus's Monmouth County, was convinced that "the story of the Negroes may be depended upon, so far at least to them arming or attempting to form themselves." He pointed out that the virtual state of war had made the situation worse because the militia were "gone off in such numbers that we have hardly Men in Arms left in those Parts which are least affected to the cause." These threats and rumors of slave uprisings put white North Carolinians into a frenzy of fear all summer. They ransacked the homes of the colony's blacks nightly in search of weapons. In July there was such outrage at the mere rumor that Governor Josiah Martin "planned to free and arm the slaves" that the governor fled the colony.

By autumn 1775, when Titus was contemplating his flight, the idea of using the blacks against the whites began to gain traction in England. In October, Parliament debated a proposal to send a few regiments to the American South, where "negroes would rise and imbue their hands in the blood of their masters." In November the earl of Guilford was defending the use of blacks and Indians, claiming that "there never was any idea of raising or employing" them until the Americans had done so first. Of course, blacks were fighting in New England regiments. Guilford did not yet know that Dunmore had already acted. Typically, the Virginia governor hadn't bothered to seek approval, but then his orders from London were few and far between. He received no instructions that year from May until December. And he was not a patient man. Events had moved quickly, and he had no mind to wait.

Dunmore formally took matters into his own hands on November 7, 1775, when he issued "A Proclamation." It began by denouncing those taking arms against the British as traitors and declared martial law throughout Virginia. Dunmore then commanded "every Person capable of bearing Arms, to resort to his MAJESTY'S STANDARD, or be looked upon as Traitors to His MAJESTY'S Crown and Government." This was far more drastic than anything done elsewhere at that time or at any time during the war. Every man able to shoot who didn't rush to Dunmore's standard was to be considered a traitor, his life and property forfeit. Then came the famous and, for the white population, infamous call to those slaves and indentured servants working for these rebels and able to bear arms to join him and be freed.

The Virginia Convention tried its best to dissuade slaves from rushing to Dunmore's fleet by making the already dire punishment for flight even worse. Any slave aiding the enemy, if armed, would be sold in exchange for gunpowder in the West Indies, where, a writer to the *Virginia Gazette* argued, "their condition will be ten times worse than it is now," or put to work in Virginia's lead mines. Letters published in the newspaper urged that blacks be reminded that the British were the true perpetrators of the slave trade and that the colonists had several times tried to stop it. Once their masters were defeated, they would not be given their freedom but would probably be resold. It was also pointed out that the offer of freedom was extended only to "such as are able to do Lord Dunmore service," not women, not children, not elderly slaves.

Colonel William Woodford, commanding several companies of minutemen near Norfolk, was already under orders "to suffer no persons to pass and repass" whom he suspected "to be inimical." He was "particularly" to "stop and detain all slaves, who may so attempt to pass; if in arms, to proceed against them according to the rules of war, otherwise to send them to their masters being our friends, or dispose of them as prudence may direct." But all Woodford's men and other land and river patrols and the most terrible threats their masters could devise couldn't prevent hundreds of slaves, alone or in small groups, from slipping away from home to join the British governor.

Dunmore's scheme was a diplomatic disaster with the whites but offered the hope of freedom to the blacks. And as Lunt Washington, writing from Mount Vernon, warned his cousin George, "Liberty is sweet."

Titus surely knew the risks of relying on the British, knew of their crass role in the slave trade. On the other hand, the patriots talked of liberty but made no offer of freedom to slaves and were turning them away from their army. He was already on the run and had few options. Patriots would return him to Corlies or sell him in the West Indies. Somehow he managed to elude the patrols. He reached Dunmore safely and offered his service to the British governor. Dunmore duly enlisted him in his new Royal Ethiopian Regiment.

CHAPTER EIGHT

Home Fires and Campfires

KEEPING HOME FIRES burning is not easy. For Elizabeth Nelson, living alone most of that year, it was undoubtedly an exhausting and anxious time. Josiah and Peter were only twenty miles away in Cambridge, but their army life seemed, and was, another world, one threatened by combat and disease. It was uncertain how long they would be gone. But for whatever comfort it gave Elizabeth, hers was a common experience that year and would be an experience shared with many families for years to come. All over Lincoln and surrounding towns, hundreds of families were suddenly shorn of their men and teenaged boys. Women, men too old for the militia, and boys too young for it were left just at planting time to work their family's farm and care for the crops their lives depended on.

The hardship was felt throughout Lincoln's small social world. The prosperous Hartwells were hard-pressed. Ephraim's sons, Samuel, John, and Isaac, were all soldiering, leaving their sixty-eight-year-old father scrambling to hire men to assist him with his and Samuel's sizable farms. For once, large acreage seemed a disadvantage. Worse off was Catherine Louisa, Captain Billy Smith's wife, left alone with her four young children. Billy had taken Cato with him to Cambridge, leaving her to care for home and farm with, one suspects, barely a second thought. A brief visit from her husband in June left her pregnant with their fifth child. Small farmers such as the Masons with their modest homestead and large family were scarcely better off. Joseph and his sons, Joseph Junior, and Elijah, were all with the army in Cambridge. Elijah had served as a fifer at the Battle of Bunker Hill. Jupiter's owner, Joshua Brooks, Jr., was serving in the same company as Peter. At least he had left Jupiter home to help with farm chores and the work at the family tannery. Whether Jupiter would have preferred to serve with his master and son in the army is unclear. Peter may have been enthusiastic about the cause, but that patriot cause, full of talk about freedom for whites and fears of their own "enslavement" by the British, had made no promises to free him. So Jupiter, older and less impulsive than Peter, may have preferred staying home to help with the work. The white men, older boys, and slaves left at home must have had all the work they could handle. Anyone free to charge for his labor, such as Peter's neighbor Will Thorning and Jupiter, in his spare time, would have done well.

Elizabeth was better off than many women. She had Thomas and Jonathan just next door to help with the outdoor work, and Tabitha and Lydia, as always, ready to lend a hand with household tasks. And neighbors helped neighbors. Billy Smith's sister, Abigail Adams, comfortably settled on a farm in Braintree, complained good-humoredly to her husband, John, serving in the Continental Congress in Philadelphia: "I miss my partner, and find myself unequal to the calls which fall upon me; I find it necessary to be the directress of our Husbandery and farming. I hope in time to have the Reputation of being as good a Farmeress as my partner has of being a good Statesman."

Amid the struggle to carry out their daily work, Lincoln residents were also expected to support the men and horses in the army with firewood, foodstuffs, blankets, and hay. The town was sending so much firewood to Cambridge that by the end of the year it was excused from the order to provide thirteen more soldiers. Even so, in December townsfolk were asked to supply three tons of hay and, in January 1776, fourteen blankets. The neighboring town of Bedford that month was sending six cords of wood and two tons of hay daily to the encampment.

The worry of disease added to people's troubles. It was a terrible summer for sickness and for dying, what with camp fever spreading from the army to the towns and that dread disease, smallpox, cropping up in the army and among the population blockaded in Boston with the British troops. Smallpox was one of the many problems that bedeviled George Washington from the start.

On June 18, the day after the Battle of Bunker Hill, George Washington wrote his wife, Martha, from Philadelphia that he had been selected to command the army of the united colonies. With his letter he enclosed a copy of his will. Four days later he set off for New England with the good wishes of the Massachusetts delegation at the Continental Congress for "an agreeable Journey and a glorious Campaign." On July 3, a lovely summer day, the Reverend Clarke noted in his diary, "Gen. Washington came."

The first sight Peter and the other curious soldiers had of their new commander in chief was reassuring. Their general was a tall, dignified Virginia planter, forty-three years old, with military experience and an impressive military bearing. He was described by one Connecticut delegate to Congress as "no harum-scarum, ranting, swearing fellow, but sober, steady, and calm." Washington had ridden north with a group of southern officers and was accompanied by William Lee, a tall, dignified mulatto slave, sporting a turban. Lee was the general's personal servant and constant companion. However different Washington's ways, it was a relief to have such a respected southerner committing himself to the cause, making clear in his person that distant colonies meant to share in their fight. It all boded well.

Washington's first sight of Peter and the crowd of men and boys, white and black, who constituted the patriot army, however, was less happy. He applauded the Massachusetts Provincial Congress for the "virtue & publick Spirit of the whole Province of Massachusetts Bay" and their "firmness, & Patriotism without Example in modern History." But privately he thought little of the men or their officers. "The officers generally speaking are the most indifferent kind of people I ever saw," he wrote Lund Washington, and summed up the whole as "an exceeding dirty and nasty people." "I found a mixed multitude of People here," he wrote his brother John, "under very little discipline, order, or Government." He had served with the British army during the French and Indian War and the scene that greeted him in Cambridge, with its disorderly but enthusiastic New Englanders, was painful to a professional's eyes. Starting with Washington's orders the very next day, Peter began his transformation from a young, rough-and-ready farm boy into a professional soldier.

Washington made it clear that he expected discipline and cleanliness. The general "required and expected that exact discipline be observed, and due Subordination prevail thro' the whole Army, as a Failure in these most essential points must necessarily produce extreme Hazard, Disorder and Confusion; and end in shameful disappointment and disgrace." The men were reminded that the articles of war forbid "profane cursing, swearing & drunkenness." They were told that headquarters "requires & expects, of all Officers and Soldiers, not engaged on actual duty, a punctual attendance on divine service, to implore the blessings of heaven upon the means used for our safety and defence." Officers were to see that their men were neat and clean and to "inculcate upon them the necessity of cleanliness. They are to have Straw to lay on, if to be had."

Peter just needed to learn the new routines. At twelve that is not very hard. Everyone had already come to realize that cleanliness was not only next to godliness but essential for their health. The new rules brought a new sense of care, orderliness, and decency to the camp. In addition to camp fever, which cleaner conditions could eliminate, Washington was immediately concerned about smallpox. He had caught it himself as a young man and having survived was immune, but most of his men were vulnerable. No one was permitted to go fishing at nearby Fresh Pond or visit the pond for any other reason for fear "of introducing small pox into the army." A smallpox hospital set up near Fresh Pond was guarded around the clock by six men. It was forbidden to enter or leave except with the doctor's permission. Every company in the army was to be inspected daily for smallpox symptoms, and any man suspected of having the disease was to be sent to the hospital at once. So many continued to fall ill that a second hospital was established.

For Peter and the other novices, a more serious change was the insistence on strict rules of military behavior. This meant discipline, obedience, and respect for rank, none of it really so difficult for a well-brought-up boy from Lincoln. Many of Peter's comrades, however, were used to coming and going as they wished, citizen soldiers more citizen than soldier. Some refused to obey orders; others brawled, mutinied, and deserted. It took all Washington's determination if not to stop, than to limit their disorderly behavior. All summer while he worried about shortages of gunpowder, repeated warnings failed to stop men from shooting their guns whenever the spirit took them. By August he was out of patience. "It is with Indignation and Shame," began the General Orders,

> the General observes, that notwithstanding the repeated Orders which have been given to prevent the firing of Guns, in and about Camp; that it is daily and hourly practiced; that contrary to all Orders, straggling soldiers do still pass the Guards, and fire at a Distance, where there is not the least probability of hurting the enemy, and where no other end is answer'd but to waste Ammunition, expose themselves to the ridicule of the enemy, and keep their own Camps harassed by frequent and continual alarms, to the hurt of every good Soldier, who is thereby disturbed of his natural rest, and will at length never be able to distinguish between a real and a false alarm.

Some complaints were of high spirits of a less worrisome sort. On hot August days men bathing in the Charles River were informed that Washington "does not mean to discourage the practice of bathing, whilst the weather is warm enough to continue it," but men were not to bathe at or near the Cambridge Bridge, "where it has been observed and complained of, that many Men, lost to all sense of decency and common modesty, are running about naked upon the Bridge, whilst Passengers, and even Ladies of the first fashion in the neighborhood, are passing over it, as if they meant to glory in their shame." Guards and sentries at the bridge were assigned to halt the practice.

After Washington's arrival the men and boys discovered that they would be punished for insubordination, sleeping on watch, and other infractions of military discipline. When they complained, William Tudor, Washington's judge advocate, reminded them that "when a man assumes the soldier he lays aside the citizen, and must be content to a temporary relinquishment of some of his civil rights." The punishments for infractions, however, were sobering. Washington admired the British military system with its brutal punishments for the least infraction. The British courts-martial were authorized to impose sentences of 500, 1,000, or even 2,000 lashes. Somehow, men survived these beatings. Daniel Morgan, captain of the Virginia rifle company that would join the Massachusetts army in August, bore scars on his back from the 499 lashes he had received in the British army for striking an officer. Much to the men's relief, and Washington's regret, the articles of war already in effect in Massachusetts, while patterned on the British model, were far more lenient, having a maximum of 39 stripes. Many crimes were punished with fines or confinement for several days on a diet of bread and water.

Peter could not avoid playing the part of witness to punishments, since public shaming was a key element of them. There were different punishments for officers and the rank and file. Shame in itself was believed a serious punishment for an officer and a gentleman, but being humiliated in front of one's friends and comrades was almost as miserable for all but the most hardened privates. Among the first punishments Peter would have witnessed were those for a group of officers, a colonel and two captains, charged with cowardice during the Battle of Bunker Hill. One captain had his name and place of residence placed in his colony's newspapers, and everyone was notified that thereafter "it shall be deemed scandalous for any officer to associate with him." Another officer had his sword broken over his head during parade, while a third was "drummed out of Camp . . . by all the drummers and Fifers in the Army and never to return." Flogging was the punishment for enlisted men guilty of drunkenness, theft, sleeping on guard duty, disobedience, and desertion. Punishments were usually administered after prayers in front of the offender's entire regiment. Peter's regiment was also rocked by charges that John White, their quartermaster, had been drawing out provisions for more men than the regiment had. A court-martial considered his case and absolved White, but the furor it caused made for plenty of gossip. Not long afterward a lieutenant of their regiment, William Ryan, happily not a Lincoln man, was also tried. In his case the crime was insubordination. He was found guilty and immediately cashiered, presumably with the usual fanfare.

The most painful change for Peter and other blacks in the army was the effort to remove them from the ranks. Washington and his southern officers and even many prominent New Englanders felt slaves and free blacks did not belong in an army fighting for freedom. In recruiting the new army, General Gates had ordered recruiters not to enlist any Negro, free or slave, lumping them with "strollers" and "vagabonds" as unsuitable. This terrible slight came despite the courage shown by blacks, both slave and free, during the fighting on April 19 and since. Peter and other blacks already enrolled in the army could serve out their enlistments, but that was all.

There was no major engagement for the forces in the American camp that summer after the Battle of Bunker Hill. Washington didn't feel able to evict the British from Boston, but the army was on constant guard against any possible British move. Life in camp was by turns exciting and tedious, made worse by the endless false alarms. Peter's regiment was camped at Winter Hill and formed the northernmost wing of the army's semicircle around Boston. Winter Hill together with nearby Prospect Hill just south of it, where a Rhode Island regiment was based, guarded the road from Charlestown. Apart from Boston neck, this was the closest land passage the British could take from Boston. Since the Battle of Bunker Hill, General Howe was in charge of the British soldiers stationed at Bunker Hill and had set up his headquarters in what remained of Charlestown. Washington thought the position Peter's regiment occupied was in an insecure state when he arrived and set them all to work putting up additional lines of defense to secure themselves from the enemy and cut the enemy off from the countryside. Washington found his own lines spanned some ten miles, any part of which might be attacked "without our having one hours previous notice of it." He had insufficient powder to give every man thirty musket cartridges and barely enough for his artillery to last for a single day's "brisk action." The situation was perilous.

As for Peter, when he wasn't busy improving the fortifications, he and his comrades were watching the harbor, monitoring the goings and comings of British ships and the regulars at Bunker Hill and Charlestown. The British in Boston were short of rations, and there were fears that, quite aside from an expedition into the countryside, they would attack coastal towns to steal cattle and other supplies. Peter's regiment and the British troops were so near to one another, and the land was so open, Washington noted, that "we see every thing that each other is doing." Not surprisingly, the men occasionally got into skirmishes with the British. The new defense lines were complete by late August, but keeping watch went on and on. Washington captured the mood perfectly. Once the defensive lines were complete, he reckoned there was nothing to fear from the enemy, "provided we can keep our men to their duty and ma(ke) them watchful & vigilant." But he found this "among the most difficult tasks I ever undertook in my life to induce these people to believe there is, or can be, any danger till the Bayonet is pushed at their Breasts."

The one major campaign undertaken late that summer was far to the north and had little immediate impact on Peter and his Lincoln comrades. General Philip Schuyler was authorized by Congress to invade Canada in hopes that the Canadians might join with the American colonists or, failing that, that the American troops might rob the British of their Canadian sanctuary by capturing their strongholds there. Schuyler sent Brigadier General Richard Montgomery north from Fort Ticonderoga with about seventeen hundred men. In addition Washington agreed that Benedict Arnold, spoiling for action and a command, could assist in the plan with an assault on Quebec. Arnold visited each regiment at Cambridge and asked for volunteers. He managed to recruit some thousand troops bored with standing guard and, like himself, eager for a fight. They set off for the wilderness of Maine.

Apart from training, guard duty, and the new routines, the men often had time on their hands, in some ways too much time. During those summer months, regiments marched into Cambridge from the backcountry of Virginia and Pennsylvania, rough, proud, opinionated men. They were crack shots and arrived armed with knives, tomahawks, and hunting guns of various sorts. Some wore on their brown hunting shirts the image of a coiled rattlesnake and the warning "Don't Tread on Me." They were insubordinate and bigoted, and they exhausted Washington's patience. New Englanders, of course, could be every bit as proud and stubborn as the Virginians, particularly the rugged Massachusetts regiment from the north shore towns of Marblehead, Salem, Beverly, and Lynn. Its men were sailors and fishermen, a mix of whites, blacks, and Indians who plied their trade in the North Atlantic.

Differences between the new southern troops and New England regiments caused flare-ups, especially over race. The Massachusetts north shore regiment, unlike the Virginians, was well disciplined by its captain, John Glover, a prosperous shipowner. But when Glover's sailors in their "round jackets and fisher's trousers" rubbed shoulders at Cambridge with a regiment of Virginia riflemen, many of them slaveholders, there was trouble. Taunts were traded, and racial insults levied at the Marblehead blacks quickly led to blows. Within minutes hundreds of men joined the fight, even biting and gouging. An observer, Israel Trask, vividly recalled that when Washington learned of the riot he and his slave, William Lee, leaped onto their horses and rode right into the fray. "With the spring of a deer," he wrote, Washington dismounted and "with an iron grip seized two tall, brawny, athletic, savage-looking riflemen by the throat, keeping them at arm's length, alternatively shaking and talking to them." The other fighters stopped, then fled at top speed. Trask marveled that hostile feelings between two of the army's "best regiments" were "extinguished by one man." Shared dangers would teach these men from very different cultures to respect one another, but for now ugly racial tensions simmered just below the surface. The situation wasn't helped by the ambivalent attitude of headquarters toward blacks in the army.

By August, Peter and Josiah must have found it difficult to focus on their army duties when Elizabeth badly needed their help to bring in the harvest. Other local men were needed just as urgently by their wives and elderly parents. For a brief time they were able to slip home to help. Although their absence left Washington's forces stretched, he could do little. And luck was with them: the British did not attack. When the harvest was in, the local men returned to Cambridge until their enlistments were up in December.

The issue of enlisting blacks had only temporarily been laid to rest in July. The enlistments of most of Washington's men expired in December and the general was planning to raise a new army of more than twenty thousand men. Should blacks be included? On October 8, a war council again took the matter up, doubtless because there were serious objections to the current policy. The question was put "Whether it will be advisable to re-inlist any Negroes in the new Army—or whether there be a Distinction between such as are Slaves & those who are free?" The council agreed unanimously to reject all slaves and "by a great Majority to reject Negroes altogether." The policy came up again later that month when Washington met with delegates from the Continental Congress and deputy governors of Connecticut, Rhode Island, and Massachusetts Bay. The delegates agreed with the war council that in the new enlistment blacks "be rejected altogether." This decision dismayed not only blacks but many whites who had fought side by side with them. The day after the conference ended, General John Thomas, commander of the Massachusetts troops based at Roxbury, wrote John Adams deploring the bias shown by some from the southern colonies. "We have some negroes," he explained, "but I look on them, in general, as equally serviceable with other men for fatigue; and in action many of them have proved themselves brave."

Then on November 7 Lord Dunmore issued his proclamation inviting slaves to join the British and be free. The news took some time to reach the Congress at Philadelphia and even longer to reach General Washington. He didn't know of it on November 12, when, in accordance with the decision of the conference, General Orders were published announcing "Neither Negroes, Boys unable to bare Arms, nor old men unfit to endure the fatigues of the campaign, are to be inlisted." When the report of Dunmore's actions reached Philadelphia on December 2, John Hancock immediately wrote Washington: "This Day we Receiv'd Advice from Northampton in Virginia, that Lord Dunmore has Erected his Standard at Norfolk, Proclaim'd Martial Law, invited the Negroes to Join him, and offer'd them Freedom, for which purpose he has issued a proclamation from on board the Ship where he Resides."

Washington was alarmed. On December 15 he wrote, "If the Virginians are wise, that Arch Traitor to the Rights of Humanity, Lord Dunmore, should be instantly crushed, if it takes the force of the whole Colony to do it. Otherwise like a snow Ball in rolling, his army will get size—some through

Fear—some through promises—and some from Inclination joining his Standard—But that which renders the measure indispensably necessary, is, the Negros; for if he gets formidable, numbers of th(e)m will be tempted to join who will be afraid to do it without."

The day before, December 14, Virginians themselves decided to take a more conciliatory approach. They published a declaration stating that although slaves "who have been, or shall be seduced, by his lordship's proclamation . . . to desert their masters' service, and take up arms against the inhabitants of this colony," ought to be executed, they would consider a pardon "to the end that all such, who have taken this unlawful and wicked step, may return in safety to their duty."

Washington now became more conciliatory, too. He saw little option but to employ African Americans in his army. As a southern slaveholder he fully understood the danger of arming blacks and the impact it would have if his army moved south. Some blacks in the Cambridge army had implored him to let them continue to serve. It was more diplomatic to claim that their pleas, not Dunmore's invitation to slaves, convinced him to relent. His decision may also have been influenced by Phyllis Wheatley, the extraordinary Boston slave and poet whose poetic tribute to the general reached him that month. He was much struck by the classical learning it exhibited and arranged to meet her. His views of the capacities of the black race were changing. By December 20, he had made up his mind, writing Colonel Henry Lee: "We must use the Negroes or run the risk of loosing the war . . . success will depend on which side can arm the Negroes faster." Lee replied that intercepted letters of Dunmore's "will let you pretty fully into his diabolical Schemes." "If my Dear Sir," Lee continued, "that Man is not crushed before Spring, he will become the most formidable Enemy America has—his Strength will increase as a Snow ball by Rolling; and faster, if some expedient cannot be hit upon to convince the Slaves and Servants of the Impotency of His Designs."

Washington had an expedient in mind. On December 30, he announced a new recruitment policy: "As the General is informed, that Numbers of Free Negroes are desirous of inlisting, he gives leave to the recruiting Officers, to entertain them, and promises to lay the matter before the congress, who he doubts not will approve of it." Free blacks could enlist, but not slaves. He wrote to John Hancock the next day explaining the change of strategy: "It has been represented to me that the free negroes who have Served in this Army, are very much dissatisfied at being discarded—as it is to be apprehended, that they may Seek employ in the ministerial [British] Army—I have presumed to depart from the Resolution respecting them, & have given Licence for their being enlisted, if this is disapproved of by Congress, I will put a Stop to it." Congress considered the matter and two weeks later grudgingly resolved "that the free negroes who have served faithfully in the army at Cambridge, may be re-inlisted therein, but no others."

By then Peter, Josiah, and their companies had returned to Lincoln. Their enlistments were up. They were delighted to be home, and Elizabeth was grateful and relieved to welcome them back. Peter had tales to tell his elders and the neighboring children, Jonathan and Lydia and the three Thorning girls, Abigail, Mary, and Sarah. But his pride at having served with the men of Lincoln, the joy of making Elizabeth and Josiah, Jupiter and Peggy, proud and being looked up to by local children, was shot through with humiliation. There was nothing disgraceful at being considered too young to serve, but being singled out as a slave was altogether different. He knew nothing of General Washington's private correspondence and little of Lord Dunmore's proclamation. What he did know was that he and other slaves, who had risked their lives for the cause, were not welcome to return to the army. They had been effectively drummed out, with the dishonor that eviction entailed.

Winter at home in Lincoln differed little from before Peter had enlisted in the army, but after the army encampment, ordinary work and familiar ways seemed less commonplace. Short, cold days were spent tending animals and hauling firewood, helping Josiah and Elizabeth, working fast to keep warm. There were hurried conversations with neighbors, shared complaints and laughter, everyone rushing to get their chores done, then long, dark evenings indoors with just the three of them, enlivened by occasional visitors. Sometimes they stayed indoors all day as winds whipped snow against the walls and windows, with only a hurried trip outside, plunging through knee-deep snow to the barn to feed the animals. It was a harsh, though beautiful time of year; snow covered everything, softening and smoothing out the hard edges of houses and fences. When weather permitted, there were Sunday trips to church in Lexington with families piled into sleds, then huddling together on wooden benches, Peter high in the gallery with Peggy, and Elizabeth, Josiah, and the rest of the Nelsons on the main floor below, mixing with their neighbors and friends. The Reverend Clarke reminded them all of the eternal truths at length, and they prayed fervently for God's help.

Home seemed more comfortable than before. Families, thankful to be reunited, gathered around their firesides in the evening, safe for the moment. But the danger had not disappeared. The British still controlled Boston and might venture out at any time to burn the towns and ravage the countryside. In October, when the people of Bristol, Rhode Island, refused provisions for a British ship, the town was bombarded and burned. At that point the towns-people agreed to turn over forty sheep for the ship. The same month British ships bombarded and burned the town of Falmouth (now Portland), Maine. Happily, the cold weather made it feasible to bring the artillery captured at Ticonderoga south to Massachusetts. The cumbersome cannon were heaved onto sledges and hauled to Boston, where they could be used to pressure the British garrison and their ships to leave.

There was much talk about the poor residents of Boston living a hand-to-mouth existence, cooped up with the British garrison and with fugitive Loyalists, careful not to catch the eyes of the British soldiers. Apart from enduring the miseries of life with a hostile army and short rations, after Howe took over from Gage in October, residents risked the death penalty if they tried to leave. Worse, smallpox was raging throughout the city. Many Bostonians were sick, and scores of others had been exposed. By 1782 nearly 300 of the city's residents would die of the pestilence. Washington worried about the 150 poor inhabitants let out of Boston that December. Four British deserters had appeared at his headquarters to report that Howe had infected several of the exiles hoping to spread smallpox among the American troops. The pestilence did break out in two of the families that had been allowed to leave Boston. Washington was among those convinced the illness was "a weapon of Defence, they Are using against us." His soldiers taking part in the ill-fated attempt on Canada had reason to agree. They were devastated by the disease. Many died. In some regiments more men were ill than fit for duty. Against orders, desperate men began inoculating themselves to better their chance of surviving the disease than catching it naturally. By January the expedition, leaving sick and dying men behind, began a grim retreat south to Fort Ticonderoga, where the main invasion party had started. The pestilence was closing in on Lincoln from all directions.

With the new year the brief quiet was over, and the outside world intruded again. By February Washington's new army was taking shape. He had some nine thousand Continentals and an additional seven thousand militia he could call on. The Reverend Clarke traveled to Cambridge to enlist. He was not needed immediately and was away for only a few days. That was as well, since he was badly needed at home. Smallpox had arrived in the Lexington area in earnest and was beginning to take a frightening toll of neighbors.

In late February Washington learned that the British had taken possession of every ship in the Boston harbor and seemed to be planning to evacuate the city. The general had been pressed hard by the Continental Congress to move on Boston, but prudence won out. Fortifying unoccupied Dorchester Heights and placing the newly arrived cannon there was far safer than an assault on Boston. The cannon would force the British either to attack, with the memory of their losses at Bunker Hill, or to surrender the city. Washington summoned local militia to help fortify Dorchester Heights and mount the new cannon. On March 4 John Hartwell's Lincoln militia company were called up. Sixty men set off for what turned out to be a brief, five-day stint in Cambridge. This time Peter and Josiah were not among them.

The ground on Dorchester Heights was frozen, so the redoubt's frame was built in camp. The cannon were placed on the heights. Then, under cover of cannon fire, two thousand men moved the redoubt into place to complete the fortification. By the morning of March 5, everything was ready. American artillery now threatened the British ships in Boston harbor. Two days later, as the army in Cambridge observed a day of prayer, fasting, and humiliation, the British began to evacuate Boston. Washington had readily agreed to Howe's bargain that in return for the Americans allowing the evacuation to proceed peacefully, the British would not burn the town. One of the British officers present, Lieutenant William Fielding, apparently unaware of the agreement, was furious that they hadn't "burned it to the ground." He reported that as the British evacuated, "the Rebels were very numerous upon all the Heights from prospect hill near Charles Town, round to Dorcester hills, & never Fire'd a Shot . . . but believe the[y] dreaded some Scheme was laid to draw them in, and very peaceably stood at the distance and never Attempted the Hills nor Boston lines till they saw the Harbour quite Clear of ships and Boats." Fielding added that if they had fired a shot, "the Town Certainly wou'd have been Burnt, as every thing was laid for that purpose." He had no sympathy for the colonists, fuming: "I would be content to lose a leg and an arm to see them totally defeated and their whole country laid waist." On March 17 some eleven thousand British soldiers and sailors with more than a thousand refugees were aboard a flotilla of ships anchored off Nantasket, on Boston's south shore, ready to set sail for Halifax, Nova Scotia. The following day Washington entered Boston for the first time. He was impressed by the strong fortifications the British had built and found that the town was "not in so bad a state as I expected to find it." But the British were not done with Boston. On March 20, doubtless much to Lieutenant Fielding's delight, they blew up Castle William, the island fort guarding Boston harbor. They had made no promises about the fort.

That day, one of those bright, cold days that signal the coming of spring, while jubilant New Englanders were still celebrating the departure of the British, Elizabeth Nelson died.

CHAPTER NINE

The Ethiopian Regiment

FROM THE TIME he arrived in Dunmore's camp, Titus's life changed utterly. The brutalized slave turned fugitive was pressed into military training at once and thrust into battle soon after that. Dunmore's proclamation had stipulated that slaves fleeing to the British must belong to enemies of the government, but no one here knew or seemed concerned about the political views of John Corlies. Titus could tell them whatever he wished. The summer before he reached Virginia, even before he had run away, Dunmore had become a fugitive, cruising up and down the Potomac and around the Chesapeake Bay. He anchored between the towns of Norfolk and Portsmouth or camped around the bay accompanied by a flotilla of the ships of supporters and their families. Much of the erstwhile governor's time was devoted to gathering more volunteers, snatching or welcoming slaves who managed to row out to his ships, and raiding enemy supplies. Oddly, Dunmore's own slaves, abandoned in the governor's mansion, were seized by the patriots and auctioned and sold the following year.

By the time Titus arrived, Dunmore and his men had captured more than seventy cannon and other militia equipment and had defeated the Virginia militia at Kemps Landing in Princess Anne County. In October Dunmore had taken over Norfolk, the largest town in Virginia and a vital port. Its Loyalist population was delighted to see him.

In contrast to the patriot forces in which blacks and whites served together, runaway slaves were formed into a specially created Ethiopian Regiment. The regiment's men, all three hundred of them, were housed in special barracks erected at Dunmore's new headquarters in the Gosport Shipyards on the Norfolk docks. Most of Titus's new comrades had fled from owners in the tidewater area of Virginia or the neighborhood of Norfolk. Few slaves from further north even tried to reach Dunmore. The men of the new regiment were undergoing an exhausting course in soldiering when he arrived. And they needed it. Unlike northern blacks, few of the runaways, Titus included, had any experience of militia service, and only a few were familiar with hunting weapons, let alone the cumbersome military musket and bayonet. They needed to learn basic skills. Dunmore was prepared to see that they got it. The regiment was placed under the command of Thomas Byrd. He and other senior British officers and enlisted men schooled Titus and the rest of the men in traditional, eighteenth-century drills with close order marching, elbow to elbow, to the strains of the fife and drum. They were also taught marksmanship, at least the way it was practiced in the British army, more volley than aim, a maneuver that required a lot of coordination. Dunmore ordered them all special uniforms with the slogan "Liberty to Slaves" emblazoned on their jackets.

As Titus quickly discovered, black men were not the only ones to seek and find shelter with Dunmore's army. Some slaves had managed to bring their wives and children with them. The women were able to find work. Armies needed women to wash, cook, tend the injured or sick, and wait on the officers. Judith Jackson was already an escaped slave when Dunmore's proclamation was broadcast. Unlike Titus, who had escaped only the day after the proclamation was published, Judith had fled her Norfolk, Virginia, master two long years earlier. And unlike Titus, who had only his own safety to worry about, Judith was pregnant when she made her escape and had taken her one-year-old daughter with her. How she managed to avoid detection for all that time and support herself and her children remains her secret. The fact that her master, John Maclean, sailed for Great Britain shortly after she ran away, leaving his business to be managed by a company, surely helped. And Norfolk was a busy and crowded port. Still, those years in hiding and disguise must have been terrifying. Dunmore's proclamation seemed a godsend. Judith slipped into British quarters and offered her services under the terms of the proclamation. It was a rare opportunity to find safety, although a perilous safety as a woman working for an army. She was put to work as a laundress.

Eight years later, when her future seemed assured, she would be discovered. As the war drew to a close, Judith and her little family joined the exodus of black fugitives from the South, more than two thousand strong, fleeing to the British stronghold of New York City. She managed to get the precious certificate for evacuation to Nova Scotia when one Mr. Eilbeck, of Eilbeck, Ross and Company, charged with running her former master's affairs and a Loyalist to boot, learned of her whereabouts. He demanded that she and her children be returned. Yet unlike Titus's story, hers would end happily. A hearing was held, and Guy Carleton, the newly appointed British commander in chief, decided that Judith's years of faithful service to the royal cause entitled her to her freedom.

Titus's new life was exhilarating. He was free. True, the military training was hard work, made more so by his having to catch up to those who joined the regiment before him, but he was used to hard work. And this was not hard labor to no purpose, or only to John Corlies's purpose. The British put a gun in his hands and were teaching him how to use it. With it and his new skills, he could free other slaves and take revenge on cruel owners. He was uneducated and untrained, but he found that military training came easily; indeed, he excelled at it. That was fortunate, since he would put it to use within the month.

Dunmore, always the optimist, was feeling confident as November waned. With one additional regiment and a few more battalions he felt sure "we should reduce this colony to a proper sense of their duty." He had high hopes of raising more men and expected the British high command to send him reinforcements. His opponents, the Virginia Committee of Safety, which commanded the forces of the colony, had been frantically amassing men at Williamsburg and soon had a far larger force than Dunmore. Where he was confident, they were anxious, especially about his base at Norfolk. It seemed time to try to dislodge him. They dispatched Colonel William Woodford with the Second Virginia Regiment to do it. Reconnoitering, Woodford decided that rather than attack Dunmore's base, he would block an assault on Suffolk that Dunmore was rumored to be planning. Before Titus joined them, Dunmore's men had already smashed patriot forces at Kemp's Landing. A day later Dunmore raised the king's standard and declared Virginia in a state of rebellion.

Woodbridge marched his men south of Kemp's Landing to Great Bridge on the Elizabeth River, the shipping point for Norfolk. The bridge there afforded the only good spot to cross the Elizabeth, marshy along most of its banks. Dunmore would have to get past the Virginia men to reach Suffolk. He also needed to control Great Bridge in order to maintain his hold on Norfolk and assure his supply line.

Woodbridge bided his time and dug entrenchments while colonial regulars, minutemen, militia, and volunteers from five Virginia counties along with 250 men from Carolina converged on Great Bridge waiting for Dunmore's men to appear. "On hearing of Lord Dunmore's insolences and outrages," presumably including his promise to free slaves, Woodford reported that some 150 gentlemen volunteers had marched from North Carolina to join them.

Dunmore and his troops, Titus and the Ethiopian Regiment among them, about three hundred men, eventually arrived. They were unaware of the numbers of men waiting for them across the river, but the governor was, as ever, supremely confident. The hard work of building defenses began immediately. Titus and the others labored to erect a stockade fort across the bridge from Woodford's growing army. They demolished five or six houses near the causeway, which Dunmore then fortified with two cannon. Woodbridge had far more men but no cannon and, though the British didn't know it, little ammunition for his troops. The two sides settled down in their fortifications.

The confrontation proceeded in stages. For several days there was a tense standoff. From December 1 to December 8 the two forces skirmished, but each remained on its own side of the river. Then on December 9, Dunmore moved. His soldiers broke from their fortress, crossed the bridge, and attacked. They were startled to find that their commander had wildly underestimated the numbers facing them, or maybe he didn't care. In earlier encounters with the Virginia militia, its members had disgraced themselves and fled. This time they did not flee. They waited, crouched behind their entrenchments, then fired as Dunmore's men dashed across the exposed bridge.

The result, Titus's first taste of battle, was a disaster. According to Edmund Pendleton, a member of the Virginia House of Burgesses, Dunmore's men "met a defeat so complete, and sustained so large a carnage, that they have not yet appeared in action. They retreated on board the ships, and our Army marched into Norfolk without opposition." Fully half of the troops who fought for Dunmore that day were the runaway slaves of the Ethiopian Regiment, Titus's new friends and comrades. Some of the survivors retreated with the British troops, but not all. Pendleton reported that while "the notorious Tories, and some blacks, are gone on board the Vessels in the harbour," others gave themselves up. "All the slaves," he explained, "except what are on board the vessels, have surrendered, on promise of pardon, or been taken in arms, out of whom some examples will be made; and the apprehensions of danger, from that quarter, seem to have subsided." But having accepted their surrenders, the Virginia Convention decided against pardon for those blacks who had been in arms. They were to be jailed, their value appraised, and sent to the West Indies or Honduras to be sold.

The Battle at Great Bridge was the first major battle since Bunker Hill. This time the colonists won. With the loss at Great Bridge, Dunmore could no longer hold Norfolk. He retreated to the fleet with his troops, those men of the Ethiopian Regiment who remained, and some prominent Tories. Titus was among the few survivors of the once proud Ethiopian Regiment.

They did not have far to retreat. Their fleet anchored just off Norfolk. Once the patriots took over the previously friendly town, the British army considered it an enemy stronghold. On January 1 Dunmore had no compunction welcoming in the new year by ordering his fleet to bombard the docks where they had formerly been so hospitably based. For good measure, he sent a landing party to set fire to some 50 selected buildings. "I have the pleasure to assure you that this rebel town . . . is in ashes," one of Dunmore's officers wrote from aboard the sloop *Otter*. "It is glorious to see the blaze of the town and shipping. I exult in the carnage of these rebels." The poor people of Norfolk. Just as the British had no concern about them once Norfolk was in rebel hands, the Americans had little sympathy for the town because of its Tory sympathies. As the Norfolk buildings burned, Virginia's own soldiers cheerfully looted what remained. A month later Colonel Robert Howe, a Virginia officer, punished the remaining Norfolk citizens for their support of the British by setting fire to houses of those reckoned to be Tories. Three days of burning and looting followed, destroying another 860 structures. Titus and the rest of Dunmore's soldiers and sailors watched the city burn from their ships, a sobering lesson about the fickle and fatal fortunes of war.

The Americans were soon ashamed of having so thoroughly destroyed their own city and blamed the devastation on Dunmore and his men. Later that month, the committee of Sussex County pledged to help the inhabitants of Norfolk find shelter and land to cultivate. The loss of Dunmore's base at Norfolk was a blow to fleeing slaves. It was now far more difficult and more dangerous to reach him. Many were captured in the attempt.

It was winter. The British forces could not remain aboard their ships indefinitely. For their new quarters Dunmore chose a place called Tucker's Point just across the Elizabeth River from Norfolk. Titus's months there were terrible ones. The conditions could hardly be more different from his first, exhilarating experience with the British troops when he was warmly welcomed into their midst in the prosperous city of Norfolk. The winter of 1776 was a long, sickly, uncomfortable, and disappointing time. Smallpox broke out and began taking a heavy toll of Dunmore's men. The soldiers of the Ethiopian Regiment were especially hard-hit. Their agony was horrible, and for Titus the suffering of his new comrades was distressing. What a helpless feeling to have to watch from a distance, kept even from comforting his desperate friends for fear he would catch the illness. Dunmore began having his recruits inoculated, but new recruits reaching him brought the illness or quickly took sick and died.

The course of the disease became familiar all too soon. Titus's friends' first symptoms would be a headache, a backache, fever, and vomiting, along with a feeling of exhaustion. After a day or two the fever would drop but would start up again as the first smallpox sores began to appear. These began at the mouth and throat, then quickly covered the body, being especially thick on the face, the palms of the hands, and the soles of the feet, the neck, and back. The victim would suffer excruciating pain. If the pustules ran together, the infected person would likely die. If they didn't, the chance of recovery was good. After about two weeks, scabs would begin to form. These would crack whenever the victim moved, causing more pain and leaving the skin raw. If the victim didn't die within ten to sixteen days, he or she was likely to live. Gradually, scars would replace the scabs. The disease took about a month to run its course, and the patient was contagious until the last scab dropped off. Some who survived were blinded. The one blessing in all this, and not a small one, is that if you survived the disease, you were immune ever after. Somehow amid the terrible suffering and deaths of many of his friends in the regiment, Titus survived.

Lord Dunmore remained fit, but he had troubles of his own. In February he learned to his "inexpressible Mortification" that General Clinton and his forces had been ordered to the "insignificant province of North Carolina" rather than reinforcing the British ranks in Virginia. Ever the optimist keen to be in action, Dunmore offered to go to England to negotiate a peaceful settlement between the motherland and the colonies. The Virginia Convention greeted this suggestion coldly. The Committee of Safety informed Dunmore that it was "neither empowered nor inclined to intermeddle with the mode of negotiation; that we looked to the Congress for management of this important matter"; it suggested that he demonstrate his good intentions by suspending hostilities. Of course, that was unthinkable.

Month after month the Virginians kept a wary eye on Dunmore and his men. Month after month men like Titus who had not yet gotten smallpox or had survived it faced grim living conditions. There was the constant fear of contracting other diseases that ravaged military camps or of injury and death in combat. By the time spring arrived, Dunmore had had enough. He ordered his men back onto their ships. Their little fleet headed north. According to deserters who rushed to report their problems, Dunmore's men were on half rations. They had with them the "shattered remains" of the Ethiopian Regiment. They also had "the Small Pox on board." The suffering and dying continued. Dunmore reported that every ship in his fleet threw one, two, or three dead overboard every night. Scores of bodies drifted ashore.

On May 27 the sickly little army surprised the Virginia rebels by landing on Gwynne's Island in Chesapeake Bay. The entire island consisted of two thousand acres of dry land a few hundred yards from shore. It did afford good anchorage for the fleet, and Dunmore's surgeons hoped it would enable them to isolate the sick. Because the island could be forded on the landward side, Dunmore hoped it would become a rallying point for Loyalists, black and white. Some two hundred recruits did join the Queen's Own Loyal Regiment, but the hoped-for reinforcements from the British army were never sent, while, on the island, it was reported that "dozens died daily from small pox and rotten fevers."

Nevertheless, Washington and the Continental Congress were alarmed at Dunmore's presence on the island. With enemy troops so close to land, they were a serious threat. Washington insisted the Virginians take action to remove Dunmore's force. The Virginians began by massing troops on the mainland across from Gwynne's Island. In many ways the face-off would resemble that at Great Bridge, but this time Dunmore was weaker, his cockiness gone. On June 1 Pendleton wrote Jefferson that Dunmore "with 400 half starved motly soldiers on Gwyn's Island, and 2000 of Our men on the Main-[land] are looking at each other."

While the confrontation continued, a British fleet whose help Dunmore badly needed in Virginia suffered an embarrassing defeat in the attempt to take Charleston, South Carolina. The commander, Commodore Sir Peter Parker, had opened fire on Fort Sullivan and found to his amazement that the fort's palmetto log walls absorbed the British shot like a sponge. They would not splinter. Worse, the Americans, led by Colonel William Moultrie, fired back at the British fleet with unexpected accuracy, inflicting serious damage on their two largest warships and killing many of the crew. The *Actaeon* ran aground and some smaller frigates were damaged, HMS *Sphinx* lost its bowsprit, and Commodore Parker was painfully wounded and lost his breeches. Altogether, the British fleet suffered 261 injured and dead.

If the confrontation at Gwynn's Island resembled the standoff at Great Bridge, the battle on July 9 was in some ways like Bunker Hill in reverse. At Gwynn's Island the Americans attacked the British. It was a formidable task. Titus and the rest of Dunmore's troops were entrenched on an island, and the Americans needed both artillery and boats to vanquish them. Andrew Lewis, who commanded the American troops, eventually managed to assemble ten companies of veterans to reinforce troops already facing Dunmore. He also had every piece of artillery in the area that could be spared hauled to the site— seven large cannon, some more powerful than Dunmore's, and two field pieces. Dunmore was ready for them. Titus and the remnants of the Ethiopian Regiment along with other troops, several hundred strong, were waiting on the western side of Gwynn's Island. Their artillery guarded the closest landward side, and the *Otter* and other ships were poised to fire on any attackers.

Despite the preparations, the battle started accidentally. Dunmore's personal ship, named for himself, drifted within range of hidden American artillery. Lewis ordered his men to fire. After an hour of pounding British targets, the more powerful American artillery overwhelmed and silenced the British cannon. The good ship *Dunmore* was hit nearly a dozen times before the *Otter* helped it slip out of range. Four British tenders ran aground; three were then burned, the fourth captured. Dunmore himself was slightly wounded in the leg by a splinter. Titus and his fellow soldiers escaped a complete and bloody rout because the Americans lacked enough boats to follow up on their triumph and assault the island at once. But the surprise barrage had caused a great deal of damage, and Dunmore's small force was terrified. That night, under cover of darkness, Dunmore and his troops quietly boarded the remaining ships and abandoned the island. Early the next morning the Americans attacked. Some two hundred troops rowed across the channel prepared for a fight only to find silence and a scene of horror. Dunmore and his army were gone, but they had left behind thirty sick and dying black soldiers. Their barracks had been burned in the previous day's battle, and the small island was covered in mass graves. Some of the dead had not yet been buried, and lying among them were dying members of Titus's regiment. The scene was described as one of "misery, distress and cruelty." During Dunmore's stay there, five hundred people had died on the little island.

Dunmore's fleet sailed north, stopping briefly at George's Island in the mouth of the Potomac so the men could take on fresh water. Whenever they came near shore slaves dashed to greet them and give themselves up to British protection, among them three of George Washington's own slaves. The presence of the British ships caused a brief panic among the members of Maryland's Council of Safety, especially after two of the vessels, rumored to be carrying men sick with smallpox, drifted onto the mainland. But Dunmore had no designs on Maryland. He was in no position to invade any place. On August 7 he ordered his ships to separate. Some smaller vessels were abandoned and set afire, others with Loyalists aboard were sent to the safety of Bermuda and the West Indies or set their sails south for Florida. Dunmore, with Titus and the ailing troops, including the survivors of the Ethiopian Regiment and their families, sailed north to join the thousands of British soldiers converging on New York. If Titus had a purpose beyond his personal freedom in joining the British, he would have to bide his time. But the fleet was heading north, toward his old home of New Jersey. And there was every reason to hope he might live to help his people there gain, as his uniform promised, "Liberty to Slaves."

CHAPTER TEN

A Motherless Child

The Lord giveth, the Lord taketh away. Blessed be the name of the Lord.
JOB 1:21

THE FORLORN LITTLE GROUP stood in the Lexington churchyard—Peter with Josiah, Thomas and Lydia with their children, Jonathan and young Lydia, and Tabitha—each lost in thought. The Reverend Clarke led them in prayer. Elizabeth Nelson was laid to rest in the plot Josiah had selected for them, just behind the graves of his parents, Thomas and Tabitha. He later chose the simplest inscription for her stone:

> Here lies the
> Body of Mrs
> Elizabeth Nelson
> (wife of Mr. Josiah
> Nelson,) who de
> parted this Life
> March 20th 1776
> In the 48th year
> Of her age.

Maybe the many months caring for home and farm alone, anxious for the safety of Josiah and Peter, had worn Elizabeth out and made her more vulnerable. Not that any of the mourners needed the Reverend Clarke to remind them that death could come at any time. Death was seldom absent from Lincoln and Lexington that spring. Every few days another family brought a loved one to the town cemetery. In addition to the usual ailments, many were victims of the dreaded smallpox epidemic. Brief entries in Clarke's diary record Lexington's grim tally. On February 13 Samuel Winship died. Four days later Benjamin Bowman died. On March 7 John Bridge died. On March 11 Widow Prudence Winship died. Thaddeus Parker's wife died a day after

Elizabeth. On April 3 Mrs. Simonds died, and a day later Daniel Simonds died along with William Reed III's child, one of Peggy's master's many great-grandchildren. On it went. Few families escaped. But the uncertainty of life and shared sorrow didn't really help.

Death, even if expected, even coming after a long illness, is always a shock. This was Peter's first loss of a loved one, and the one he lost was probably closer to him than anyone else. Peggy and Jupiter were his parents, but he didn't live with them. He and Josiah shared home and work. But it was Elizabeth who had cared for him as long as he could remember and who figured in his earliest memories. Peter had provided her only chance to raise a child and had been the beneficiary of her motherly attentions and concern. He was not quite thirteen, still a boy, although the past year in the army had forced him to grow up quickly. He would miss her terribly.

Later on, after the burial and the good-byes, Peter and Josiah went home to the empty house. No welcome at the door, no happy chatter, no one bustling about cleaning and cooking full of gossip, questions, and advice. Just the empty house. Family and friends offered food and sympathy. It was a blessing there was little time to sit and brood with all the chores to do—at least during the daylight. On a farm there are always chores. Unlike last year, the two men would be home to prepare the fields and do the planting. Unlike last year, she would not be there.

When a decent interval had passed, Josiah would need another wife. A man, especially one with a large farm, needed someone to take care of all the womanly tasks of life. It wouldn't be fair to take advantage of the kindness of his sister-in-law and sister indefinitely. Lydia was busy with her family, and Tabitha, though a spinster, had her home and small farm to tend. But for now there was work to be done—with one eye on the weather and the other on events in the larger world. Unless it could be settled peacefully, the continuing fight against Great Britain was certain to upset their lives again in ways they could not foresee.

Two days before Elizabeth's death, a day after the British evacuated Boston, the Lincoln men assembled at their annual March town meeting. The momentous issue of independence was on their agenda. Immediately after the usual article to select their representative to the Massachusetts legislature, they were asked whether "to advise the person who shall be chosen as aforesaid [to represent them in the legislature] whether (in case the Continental Congress shall declare the United American Colonies independent of Great Britain) they will engage to support such independence with their lives and fortunes." "The vote being put to the town," the town meeting minutes record, "it past in the negative." Lincoln men, patriotic but prudent, voted no. They were willing to serve in the army, however, and they appreciated the sacrifices being made by neighbors, so they agreed to exempt men serving in the army from the town's highway tax. In the legislature the Lincoln representative was outvoted. On May 23 the Massachusetts General Assembly agreed to instruct its delegation to the Continental Congress that the colony would support a declaration of independence "with their lives and the remnant of their fortunes."

John Adams was a member of the congressional committee charged with drawing up the proclamation of independence. "Yesterday," he wrote Abigail on July 3, "the greatest Question was decided, which ever was debated in America, and a greater perhaps, never was or will be decided among Men." It was a daring, even foolhardy move. As Congress was nearing a vote on the matter, members learned that a British fleet with thousands of troops had arrived at New York. Being independent was grand but also terribly disappointing. It meant that the rift between the mother country and the colonies would not be healed. "We might have been a free and a great people together," Thomas Jefferson, author of the Declaration of Independence, lamented in an early draft. The colonies, now states, stood alone against Great Britain, one of the greatest powers in the world. They would be free to trade as they liked, but the British navy blocked their ships, and British merchants were prohibited from trading with them. Basic items crucial to daily life such as salt were soon in short supply. But most disappointing, independence meant there was little hope of a negotiated resolution of their differences. The war would continue.

Copies of the Declaration were sent to every colony to be read to the people. On July 9 New York crowds thronged the huge bronze equestrian statue of George III, erected in Bowling Green six years earlier. Some climbed and toppled it, smashing it into pieces. The pieces were hauled away to be melted down into bullets to fire at the king's soldiers. Two weeks after it was published in Philadelphia, the Declaration was read in Boston. Jubilant crowds tore down the king's coat of arms and broke them. Cannon were fired, and the crowd, in true British fashion, gave three cheers. Church bells rang throughout the city.

As Josiah and Peter tried to adjust to life in their silent house, General Washington and the Continental Congress were struggling with the extraordinary task of protecting the colonies from the shiploads of British troops converging on them. With such a long, vulnerable coast and wild frontiers to defend, a decision had to be made where to concentrate the energies of the American forces. Once the British evacuated Boston, Washington decided to march most of his army to New York City, but he insisted the assault on Canada was a priority. The troops there must hold fast and be given every support. General Philip Schuyler, the commanding officer of the Northern Army, was told to "contest every foot of the ground" and to prevent the enemy, at all costs, from moving up the St. Lawrence River. It was the wrong choice and the wrong advice. The American retreat from Canada had already begun.

Schuyler was a controversial commander, yet the expedition launched with such high hopes in the fall of 1775 was successful at first against the lightly guarded British strongholds. Schuyler's health was poor, and he returned to Ticonderoga, leaving General Richard Montgomery to coordinate strategy with the impulsive General Benedict Arnold. Arnold led a separate force that reached Canada after a grueling overland march through Maine to Quebec. In November Montgomery captured the fort at St. John's and then Montreal. At the end of December, he joined Arnold in an assault on Quebec City.

Everything went wrong. They attacked the lower town in a blinding snowstorm. Their forces numbered some nine hundred men, many of whom expected to go home the next day. Montgomery at the head of one column was killed almost immediately, while Arnold leading the other was wounded in the leg. Daniel Morgan then took command of the attack. The Americans were repulsed, and in the process Morgan and half of Arnold's column were captured. Arnold was not easily discouraged, however, and he settled down with the remaining men to besiege the city. During that bitter winter the American army surrounding Quebec had no adequate shelter and suffered grievously. Bad as the weather was, the danger from disease was worse. Like Dunmore's Ethiopians, smallpox began decimating officers and men alike. Even the coming of spring brought no relief. The smallpox epidemic raged on, and as the number of fit American troops shrank, the British received reinforcements. On June 2 Major General John Thomas, like Montgomery one of Washington's finest officers, died of smallpox at Quebec. Washington ordered a New Hampshire lawyer turned soldier, John Sullivan, to take command. Despite orders to contest every foot of ground, by mid-June Sullivan decided that it was wiser to abandon Canada while he had some of his army left. If he stayed and lost them all, the way south would be open to the British. Benedict Arnold was the last man of the army to leave Canadian soil.

The Northern Army retreated to Crown Point, south of Lake Champlain. General Gates, sent to shore up the defenses there, arrived to find "the wretched remains of what was once a very respectable Body of Troops." He added that smallpox "had taken so deep a root, that the Camp had more the appearance of a General Hospital than an Army form'd to Oppose the Invasion of a Successful & enterprising Enemy." Sullivan struggled to explain the horror of the situation to his superiors: "to give you a particular account of the miserable State of our Troops there and the numbers which Daily kept Dropping in there Beds and Graves would rather Seem like the effect of imagination than a history of facts." A Crown Point doctor noted in his journal: "Since I have been writing, one more of our men has made his exit. Death visits us almost every hour."

Sullivan decided to abandon Crown Point and move farther south to Fort Ticonderoga, where the ill-fated Canadian expedition had started. Ticonderoga was more defensible than Crown Point and could be fortified to withstand a British attack. If the Americans were to have any chance of repulsing an assault, far more men would be needed at once. Congress ordered Continental regiments and militia from the New England area to reinforce the fort. When they were slow to arrive, Sullivan conceded, "They are extremely apprehensive of being infected with the smallpox, and not without Reason as it proves fatal to many of them." It is to this wretched place that the men from Lincoln would be sent.

The sultry weather set in, and long, hazy summer days brought the illusion of normality and the serenity of a world already lost. Illusion it was. Threats were all around. Smallpox continued to take a toll of neighbors, and the war was not going well. The expedition to Canada, for which nineteen Lincoln men volunteered, had failed. The sickly survivors would soon be back at

Ticonderoga preparing the fort for a British assault. It was a relief to turn from the larger concerns to local gossip, and local gossip turned to the doings of John Adams's brother-in-law, Billy Smith. While other men thought themselves lucky to be at home, Smith, father of five since baby Mary was born in February, was pestering John to help him get a commission in the Continental Army. That summer he was made a captain, but he yearned for something grander. He accepted the commission and agreed to serve, awaiting his chance for a more exciting opportunity.

Washington's Continental Army had never reached the numbers he had planned, and now as dangers increased, he urgently needed more men. Massachusetts, with its sizable and loyal population, had the dubious distinction of being assigned the highest quota of troops to recruit. Five Massachusetts regiments of the Continental Army were still at Boston, and Washington ordered their commander, Artemas Ward, to dispatch three to Ticonderoga and two to New York. Ward advised him that smallpox "prevails to such a degree in Boston, and so many of the soldiers got the disorder, that I apprehended the remainder of them must soon be inoculated." A week later he informed Washington that the Massachusetts legislature had given permission "for the Inhabitants to inoculate, and as so many of the Troops in Town had taken the disorder I thought it might be most for the general good to permit the (re)mainder of the two Regiments in Town to be inoculated." Among those rushing to be inoculated, John Adams learned, were Abigail and their children. "It is not possible for me to describe, nor for you to conceive my Feelings upon this Occasion," John wrote. "Nothing, but the critical state of our Affairs should prevent me from flying to Boston, to your Assistance. I shall feel like a Savage to be here while my whole Family is sick at Boston." The Adams family, like Ward's men, were likely to be ill for a month.

By early August the Boston regiments were "generally recovered of the small pox." Ward promised "to have them thoroughly cleansed, and, agreeable to our orders of the nineteenth of July, shall order them to march this week for Ticonderoga." Washington considered "their having had the small pox as a fortunate circumstance." They were urged to take the most direct road to Ticonderoga.

These new regiments would still not be enough to prepare and garrison Ticonderoga. Washington called on the militia of the New England states for help. In truth, he had little respect for militiamen, complaining in a letter to Lund that they were not "worth the bread they ate." But beggars cannot be choosers, and he needed men. Eighteen Lincoln men were recruited to join the expedition. General Schuyler assured them all, "Every Precaution will be taken to prevent their being infected by the small Pox." Years later Josiah's descendants claimed he was one of that number, although no contemporary record testifies to his service. If he did serve, the duty and danger of the expedition was certain to drive thoughts of his lonely home from his mind. He would be gone for five months, from harvest time until well into December. Their quiet house would be emptier still. Peter couldn't manage the farm alone, and others would have had to take charge. Peter could look to Thomas and Lydia, Jonathan and young Lydia, for food, companionship, and direction. Peggy could comfort him briefly on Sundays. But with or without Josiah, the motherless child was surely beginning to feel like an orphan.

It was a long march to Ticonderoga over unfamiliar countryside. The Lincoln men and their regiment headed west across Massachusetts, past Worcester and the rolling fields of the Blackstone Valley, where farmers were busy taking in their harvest, through the rugged Berkshire Mountains into New York State. Approaching Albany the land broadened out, and after Albany they turned north toward Lake Champlain. They marched as quickly as they could, but even where the roads were decent, men on foot accompanied by lumbering baggage wagons don't move very fast. At the fort they were welcomed with pleasure and put to work immediately. Their task was to build a new post, Mount Independence, on the eastern shore of Lake Champlain, opposite Fort Ticonderoga. Trees had to be cleared and defenses constructed. The goal was to make the post "invulnerable." They were all used to hard outdoor labor, but this was different. Clearing the area, hauling logs, digging trenches, and constructing fortifications from sunrise to sundown was exhausting work. Constant pressure to hurry made it more so. There was no telling when the British might launch a major assault from Canada. In addition to the new fort, new fortifications were being completed around Fort Ticonderoga. Fortunately or unfortunately, depending on how you looked at it, the work had to stop from time to time because the weather that August was uncommonly wet and stormy.

The Massachusetts men at Ticonderoga were joined by militia from New Hampshire and Connecticut. The Bay State's troops had arrived, well supplied with "excellent Tents, and a Sufficiency of good Camp Utensils," which, General Gates wrote Washington, "is a great Help to us; and does that Province much Honour." By contrast, the New Hampshire and Connecticut men appeared without tents, and much time had to be spent gathering boards and erecting huts to shelter them.

Although the work was hard, at least the army at the fort was healthy. True to their word, by the time the Lincoln men appeared, the officers had cleansed Ticonderoga of smallpox. By August 28 Gates was able to report that the disease "is now perfectly removed from the army." He and other officers were determined to keep it that way. At Albany, Schuyler ordered a Connecticut general "to remove all Officers and soldiers infected with the Small Pox to a distance from the roads (being used by the militia on their way)." He was clear: "no excuse is to be taken, no plea of danger to the infected is to be attended to, the Life of individuals is not to be put into Competition with that of the States."

The anxious months slipped by, with the men serving out their enlistment and Peter at home working the farm, the servant his bill of sale had promised. October was an unfortunate month. While Ticonderoga was being fortified, Washington's army in New York City narrowly escaped annihilation and began a long retreat. That same month General Arnold led a small fleet into Lake Champlain hoping to keep the British navy from dominating that gateway into New York State. He failed. On October 13 a powerful British fleet under General Sir Guy Carleton, the British commander in Canada, caught up with Arnold's much overmatched ships. After an amazing seven-hour battle, Arnold managed to slip away under cover of fog. He arrived at Ticonderoga with the remaining three of his fifteen ships.

The fortunes of war are notoriously changeable. Just when things seemed most desperate and discouraging at Ticonderoga, the men at the garrison got the grand news that the British had abandoned their attempt on the fort and on Albany for that year. They had retreated to Canada for the winter. Arnold's gallant battle against their fleet may have delayed their plans just long enough to make it too late to attack. The Lincoln men could return home in December with the satisfaction of having reinforced that vital fort and thankful for having been spared sickness and combat. If Josiah was indeed among them, he now began a long, cold march south to Albany and east into Massachusetts. As the Lincoln men were trudging home, Peter had already left Lincoln for the war.

The fortunes of war brought surprises to Peter, too. His hopes and George Washington's needs coincided in November. Peter was a slave, and the Congress and General Washington had made it clear that slaves were not to be enlisted in the Continental Army. Peter was thirteen; soldiers were to be sixteen. After Dunmore's proclamation inviting the slaves of rebels to join the British, however, Congress and Washington had relented somewhat, and they now allowed free blacks who had served in 1775 to reenlist in the militia. Peter had served. Then again, the Massachusetts militia was not the Continental Army. Anyway regulations, as everyone knew, were often ignored, particularly in times of emergency. The fall of 1776 was one such time.

Peter's life had become increasingly disjointed. He and Josiah made a sad twosome. Nor could Peter really expect any improvement in his prospects. His very presence seemed an indictment of Elizabeth for having left her husband without children or an heir, only this teenaged Negro boy, part slave, part son. In contrast to their gloomy home, the army offered Peter fellowship, excitement, pay, an opportunity to test his courage and prove his worth, to get away and forget. Peggy would, of course, worry about his safety, and Jupiter would doubtless regard the risk as foolish. Josiah might someday free Peter, perhaps when he came of age, but that was uncertain. Josiah was a man of business, and he might regard freeing Peter as a poor business decision. And as Peter grew to manhood he became more valuable on the farm. True, there were numerous examples of slaves who had managed to hire themselves out or even set up in a trade and save enough to buy their freedom as well as the freedom of their children and parents. But Jupiter had not been in that privileged position. His labor was needed on the Brooks farm and in their slaughterhouse and tannery. Nor had Peggy much hope. Looking after her elderly master, even with the aid of her young daughter, kept her occupied.

Peter had no assurance that by enlisting, risking his life for the cause of independence, he would be granted his freedom. Yet there were hopeful signs of a change of heart in Massachusetts about slavery, hastened by the war for white independence. That September, when two blacks captured by an American privateer were advertised for sale in Salem, the Massachusetts legislature forbade the sale. The blacks, the legislature insisted, were to be treated no differently from white prisoners of war, and any sale was null and void for the present and the future.

The enlistment of most of the Continental Army that year, like the last, ended in December. Until a more permanent force was established, Washington was continually worrying about fielding enough men to carry on the war. In September he had complained to Hancock yet again: "It is a melancholy and painfull consideration to those who are concerned in the work and have the command, to be forming Armies constantly and to be left by Troops just when they begin to deserve the Name, or perhaps at the Moment when an Important blow is expected." More regiments must be raised, but in the meantime militia must do.

The Massachusetts General Court responded to the emergency by ordering one-fifth of the state militia not already on active duty, some four thousand men, to be drafted immediately to march to Washington's assistance. By early December, as Washington's situation grew more desperate, they agreed to increase the number of Massachusetts recruits to six thousand.

Whatever their arguments about Peter enlisting, Peggy and Jupiter's lives had been different from his. How could they understand what Peter's childhood with Josiah and Elizabeth had been like or the uncertainty he now felt? With the Nelson family's approval and the agreement of Captain Smith, he enlisted for three months' service. He was duly enrolled as a private and, like the other recruits, was given money for a gun and a blanket. If he already had those things, he could pocket the funds. It was to be a campaign to New York State. In late November he set off with Smith's company.

Peter's enlistment this time was dramatically different from his experience in Cambridge and harsher than the expedition of Lincoln men to Ticonderoga that was just ending. The march to Cambridge in April 1775 had been over familiar ground and could be accomplished in a day. It had been spring, and the weather, if chilly, was pleasant, the excitement high. This time Peter's regiment and the other Massachusetts regiments were to rendezvous with their commander, General Benjamin Lincoln, at Danbury, Connecticut, on that state's western border with New York. They would be marching west across Massachusetts, then veering southwest, cutting across Connecticut. From Danbury they were to proceed south to Peekskill, which guarded the Hudson River just north of New York City. This was new country for Peter. Most of the travels of everyone living in Lincoln were focused on Boston and

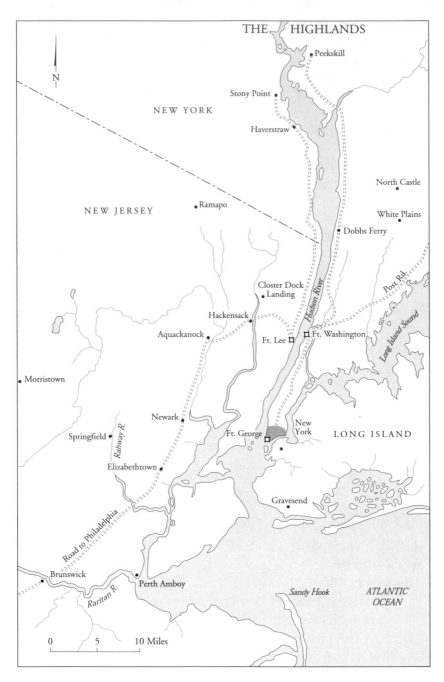

Scene of operations around New York, 1776

the towns surrounding it. Few went overland as far as Connecticut, let alone into New York. It was exciting walking unknown roads into unknown states. That was the good part; the rest was not good.

The first problem was the time of year. Instead of fresh spring weather or a summer march, Peter was marching in the biting cold and occasional snow of a New England December. Their progress was slow at best and often miserable. By January 2, weeks after they set out, not one of the Massachusetts regiments had reached Peekskill. Washington was understandably impatient for these reinforcements and kept sending out dispatches checking on their where-abouts. General Lincoln simply explained that the bad state of the roads had severely slowed their march. Walking and hauling wagons over badly rutted, slippery, and snow-covered roads was exhausting and difficult work.

Making the situation worse, this time the Massachusetts militia regiments were not equipped for a march in good weather, let alone one in bad. The Lincoln men who set out that summer had been fully equipped for service with tents and other basic items. Peter's regiment had nothing. The state was simply unable to furnish the essential gear the new men needed. For a start, there were no tents. Writing to Congress from Harlem Heights in New York for a supply of winter clothes for his regular army, Washington commented that bad as their condition was, it was "much better than the Militia that are coming to Join us from the State of the Massachusetts Bay & Connecticut in consequence of the requisition of Congress—that I am informed, have not a Single Tent or a necessary of any kind, nor can I conceive how It will be possible to support them. . . . These Eastern reinforcements have not a single Necessary not a pan or a Kettle, in which we are now greatly deficient." Had the Nelsons' neighbors been without tents on their march in August they could have coped more comfortably than Peter's regiment, trekking week after week through the bitter December cold, trying each night to find shelter, a nearby barn, perhaps, or at least a bit of straw for cover, then sleeping rough, wrapped in their blankets. Joseph Plumb Martin, a young recruit from Connecticut some three years older than Peter, explained his strategy for keeping warm while sleeping rough without even a blanket:

> To have to lie as I did almost every other night (for our duty required it) on the cold and often wet ground, without a blanket and with nothing but thin summer clothing, was tedious. I have often while upon guard lain on one side until the upper side smarted with cold, then turned that side down to the place warmed by my body and let the other take its turn

at smarting, while the one on the ground warmed; thus alternately turning for four or six hours till called upon to go on sentry, as the soldiers
term it; and when relieved from a tour of two long hours at that business
and returned to the guard again, have had to go through the operation of
freezing and thawing for four or six hours more—in the morning the
ground as white as snow with hoar frost. Or perhaps it would rain all
night like a flood; all that could be done in that case was to lie down (if
one could lie down), take our musket in our arms and place the lock
between our thighs, and "weather it out."

Another problem was food, or rather the lack of it. Peter's supplies from
home wouldn't have lasted long on that weary march, and the regiment had
started out poorly equipped. Martin considered starvation as "a secondary
matter," which it soon became. Sometimes the men went without food for
two days or more and spent time foraging for something to eat. But in
December the orchards were picked clean, the fields bare. Some officers had
little patience with men who grumbled. When one of Martin's comrades
complained to an officer of being hungry, the colonel put his hand into his
pocket and "took out a piece of an ear of Indian corn burnt as black as a coal."
"Here," said he to the complainer, "eat this and learn to be a soldier."

A report that reached Congress in late December of the sufferings of men
at Ticonderoga with tents hint at what Peter and his regiment could expect at
their journey's end: "The poor creatures is now (what's left alive) laying on the
cold ground; in poor thin tents, and some none at all, and many down with
the pleurisy. No barracks, no hospitals to go in. . . . If you was here, your heart
woold melt. At present we have not one pair of shoes or blanket in the store."

Peter and his colleagues were as eager to reach the relative comfort of
their destination as Washington was to have them there. But the changing
situation now made that destination unclear. After November 20 and the
abandonment of Fort Lee, which commanded the New Jersey heights over
the Hudson, Washington's shrinking army had fled south through New Jersey, chased by General Howe's formidable force. In early December they
crossed the Delaware into Pennsylvania, leaving the British on the opposite
side of the river. Washington reckoned that Howe would attempt an assault
on Philadelphia as soon as the Delaware River froze solid enough for his
troops to cross. He called on New Jersey residents to come to his aid, but
shockingly few of the state's men were willing to enlist, at least on the patriot
side. More ominous, few of the state's militia, whose homes were soon to be
in British control, were willing to turn out to help the fleeing ragtag Conti-

nentals. No wonder there was concern from the high command at how long it was taking the Massachusetts militia to reach New York.

As the military situation worsened, Washington couldn't make up his mind where the Massachusetts militia would do best service. So many areas were critical. On December 18 he had wanted them to reinforce the "upper parts of New Jersey and New York below the Highlands." Three days later he ordered that as many of the Massachusetts and Connecticut militia as could be spared be sent to help him defend Philadelphia. The Continental Congress had moved from Philadelphia south to Baltimore, but it would be a great blow were the British to capture Philadelphia. Of the 5,410 Continental troops Washington had when Peter enlisted, the enlistments for 2,060 expired on December 1, and those of 950 more would do so on January 1. "In a word sir," he wrote General William Heath, "my situation is critical & truly alarming, without vigorous exertions & early succours, I do not see what reasonable hope there will be to preserve Philadelphia from falling into the enemys hands." In mid-December Washington wrote in despair, "I think the game is pretty near up."

But Washington was not ready to give up. The day before Christmas, with most of his remaining army about to leave for home, Washington ordered General Lincoln and the other Massachusetts commanders to march their men as speedily as possible "to this place or wherever the Head Quarters may be, with such part of the troops under your command as may be judged expedient."

Then on December 26, before Peter's regiment or the others could possibly come to his aid, and four days before most of his men's enlistments expired, Washington led his troops in a daring raid across the ice-choked Delaware River to Trenton. He had learned that instead of pressing on to Philadelphia, General Howe had sent most of his army to New York City, leaving only small garrisons to hold Trenton and other New Jersey cities. The weather that winter morning was wet and misty, screening the Americans' approach. The Hessian troops at Trenton were taken by surprise. In an hour it was over. Several hundred Germans escaped, but more than nine hundred surrendered. John Glover's Massachusetts seamen had played a major part in the attack. For more than six hours they rowed boatload after boatload of the army across the Delaware. Then they marched eight miles to Trenton, fought, and marched back to the river to row the army and their prisoners back across it. Later, the captured Hessian prisoners were paraded through Philadelphia guarded by Virginia troops on their way home.

This was a marvelous and badly needed victory. "It was a most happy stroke," Benedict Arnold wrote Washington, "and has greatly raised the sinking spirits of the country." A week after the triumph at Trenton, on January 3, Washington followed it with a brilliantly planned and executed battle at Princeton that brought the cause a second victory. The upshot, Washington wrote modestly to Schuyler, was that "by two lucky Strokes at Trenton and Princetown, [the British] have been obliged to abandon Every part of Jersey Except Brunswick & Amboy & the small Tract of country between them."

The victories in New Jersey relieved the pressure on the Massachusetts militia reinforcements still on the march. Nevertheless, the citizen soldiers were wanted and needed everywhere—to shore up Ticonderoga, to reinforce Peekskill, to defend Rhode Island, and to supplement Washington's army in New Jersey. In the event, Washington decided they should reinforce Peekskill. From there they could guard the Hudson River and, if need be, move north to reinforce Fort Ticonderoga or south to threaten the British in New York City and distract them from pursuing Washington or even march into New Jersey to reinforce Washington's evaporating army.

After their harrowing winter march, Peter and his regiment spent the winter at Peekskill. Their life in the fortress was uncomfortable and spartan but seemed a paradise after the misery of their journey to reach it. The fort was a key garrison and supply depot. There was constant tension watching the Hudson for signs of British ships sailing north. Peekskill itself was a target. But with one exception, Peter had little use for his gun. In February, not long after his arrival, the British attacked the fort. With the help of the Massachusetts militia the Americans fought back and repulsed them with little damage. Then on March 1 Peter's enlistment was up and the Massachusetts militia regiments left to begin the more than two-hundred-mile journey home.

After they left, the British attacked Peekskill again. On March 23 British transports suddenly appeared in the river near the fort. Five hundred regulars with four cannon disembarked unopposed. The Peekskill commander, General Alexander McDougall, had only 250 men left to guard the post and saw little alternative but to withdraw. To prevent the precious supplies stored there from falling into British hands, he ordered them burned as he and his men pulled out. A day later a small relief force came to McDougall's aid, and together the Americans forced the British to retreat, but a great deal of damage had been done. The barracks had been burned and the supplies, of course, destroyed. To ensure Peekskill was not captured again, Washington ordered a full eight new regiments sent to reinforce it.

Peter and his colleagues marched north from Peekskill, retracing their steps of three months earlier through the "high country" of New York, then across the rolling hills of Connecticut, heading northeast into Massachusetts. Eventually they turned due east toward Worcester, Concord, Lincoln, and home. The weather was far better than in December and the journey went faster, but the roads in March were still often frozen, especially as they moved north from Peekskill. Occasional fierce snowstorms were common in March, though mercifully snow that time of year melted more quickly. Spring always seemed to come reluctantly to New England. On warmer days the roads became a muddy quagmire, tugging at what was left of their boots. It was a close question whether the icy or muddy roads were worse. Again shelter was a problem every night, and their food supply was inadequate, leaving the men hungry much of the time. They were grateful for any kindness from sympathetic or fearful farmers and townsfolk along the way. At least the men knew their ordeal of cold and hunger would soon be over. Like the militia that left before them to help Ticonderoga, they had survived their enlistment and looked forward to seeing their families and farms again.

Peter came home to Lincoln. It had been a year since Elizabeth's death. A decent interval had passed. He arrived in time to hear the wedding banns announced in church and in time for the wedding itself. On March 31, in the Lexington church where Josiah had married Elizabeth so many years before, and where Jupiter and Peggy were wed, the Reverend Clarke married Josiah and Millicent Bond.

CHAPTER ELEVEN

Getting Back, Getting Even

T HE STATELY VESSELS crowded into New York harbor, the Union Jack flying from the thicket of masts, were a heartening sight to those in Lord Dunmore's bedraggled little fleet as the ships dropped anchor off Sandy Hook. New York City was still in rebel hands, but the best harbor in the rebellious colonies was crammed with the largest force Great Britain had ever sent to the New World. For Titus, one of the few survivors of the Ethiopian Regiment, the size and might of the royal force was in stark contrast to his recent experience as a soldier of the Crown. On August 13 he and his comrades stepped gratefully ashore onto Staten Island.

The past months were a tangle of terrible memories for him, of helplessness in the face of sick and dying friends and of a disheartening and embarrassing retreat. Not that Titus could doubt the choice he had made. For this slave there was no other choice. The British offered a refuge and freedom; the Americans offered neither. He had yet to see a Negro fighting for the Yankee cause, and there were rumors that they were not permitted in the Continental ranks. The army gathering on Staten Island, however, exemplified British military professionalism and confidence. Troops had been converging there all summer. From the north on June 29 came General William Howe, sailing from Halifax, where he had been based since evacuating Boston, bringing his force of more than nine thousand men. Three days later he and his troops captured Staten Island, securing it as a base for the campaign to capture New York.

Next, from the east, came Howe's brother, Admiral Richard Howe, commanding a fleet of 150 ships. They had set sail from Britain in May, reaching Staten Island on July 12. "Black Dick," as he was known from his swarthy complexion, had served in the navy from his youth and had fought with distinction in the French and Indian War. He was the consummate profes-

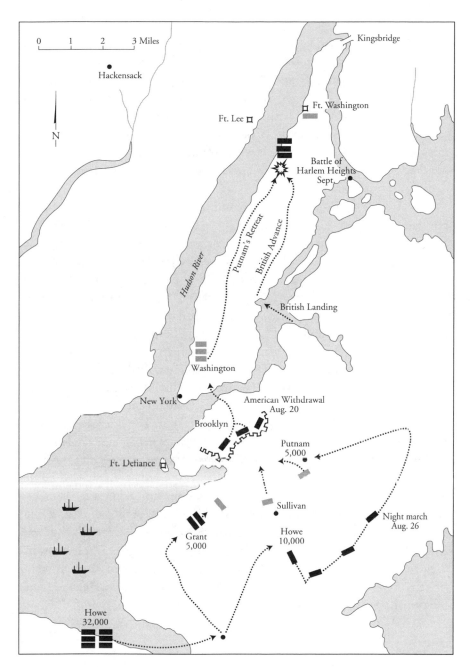

New York, Long Island, and Harlem Heights, August 1776

sional, popular with his officers and, more unusually in the navy, with his men, who were touched by his real concern for them. Richard Howe's hopes for a negotiated settlement to the war were dashed on his arrival when he was handed a copy of the Declaration of Independence, approved while he was at sea. From the south, on August 1, came Major General Henry Clinton and General Charles Cornwallis with Commodore Parker's fleet, fresh from their embarrassing failure to capture Charleston. The total force rose to some forty-five thousand British and Hessian soldiers and sailors and some four hundred vessels. Nearly the last to arrive, Dunmore's little fleet with its 108 men joined this formidable army.

Titus was instantly a part of an international force of English, Irish, Scots, Hessians, American Loyalists, and black refugees—all sporting a dazzling array of uniforms. Most exciting for a black partisan was the presence of the large number of black troops. Even without any proclamation in the North offering freedom to the slaves of rebels, Negro men had fled to the British to gain their liberty and maybe have a chance to fight against their former masters. At first a Loyalist official at New York ordered that "all Negroes Mulattoes and other Improper Persons who have been admitted to the Corps be immediately discharged." But blacks continued to volunteer to serve the British and were now enlisted and trained for combat. By the end of 1776 these "torified Negroes" numbered about eight hundred. Titus and the other survivors of the Ethiopian Regiment were merged into this new Black Brigade.

Among these eight hundred men Titus stood out. The Black Brigade was largely made up of runaways whose training had, at best, begun several months earlier. Titus had nearly a year of military experience, beginning with the first-rate drilling Dunmore's Ethiopian Regiment received. He was also battle tested. His skill and courage were known, and he quickly became a leader of his new group. Just as valuable to the British as his military ability and leadership skills was his intimate knowledge of northern New Jersey, especially the land lying off the western side of Staten Island. This was his old home. He knew its back roads and swamps and could locate the homesteads of its prominent citizens both for and against the British. He knew their slaves. He made sure the British were aware of his background. His moment was arriving.

It was Titus's fate to arrive in a new setting and almost immediately be sent into battle. The British plans to seize Long Island and New York City were well in hand by the time he set foot on Staten Island. Eight days later he and the Black Brigade boarded boats for the grand assault on Long Island. Although they didn't know the troop strength of their enemy, it was obvious they had the advantage. In fact, against the British force of forty-five thousand, Washington was holding New York City and Long Island with only twenty thousand men, many of them raw recruits and untested militia. Congress was insistent Washington defend the city, but the task was a strategic nightmare. Manhattan was an island, bordered by the Hudson, East, and Harlem Rivers, and could be attacked from any direction by an enemy that controlled the sea, which the British now did. To protect the city the Americans had fortified key points in Manhattan, on the highlands overlooking the Hudson, and at Brooklyn Heights, just across the East River on Long Island. Washington considered possession of Brooklyn Heights vital to protect the city. Many of his troops were on Long Island, and during the British attack he would commit half his army to the battle there, dividing an already inferior and scattered force. Despite this commitment, he remained convinced the attack on Long Island was a diversion to permit the main British force to seize Manhattan. As a precaution Washington had the last brigades transported to Long Island take enough boats to get the entire force back to Manhattan quickly if the city were attacked.

Logistics were not his only problem. His intelligence, so reliable in New England, was poor to nonexistent in an area with a majority of Loyalists, leaving him with little knowledge of the size of the British force or their intentions. Personnel were also a problem. The commanders of his Long Island troops had to be changed at the last moment when General Nathanael Greene became ill and General John Sullivan was put in his place. Shortly before the attack old Israel Putnam, wolf-killer, hero of Bunker Hill, was put in charge of Brooklyn Heights. Washington compounded these difficulties by insisting that some commanders whose regiments had been sent to Long Island remain in Manhattan for two days sitting on a court-martial, even though the battle for Long Island had begun.

With Washington's army divided, the British saw an opportunity to destroy the rebel force and grasped it. Long Island was no diversion. They nearly won the war then and there. What that would have meant for Titus and the Black Brigade no one would ever know.

Howe had been waiting for the Hessians to arrive to order the attack. Their convoy appeared on August 15, and he gave them six days to rest. On the night of August 21, the first British regiments moved out. They were transported to Long Island on special barges designed for amphibious tasks, each manned by twenty sailors and capable of carrying fifty soldiers. At six o'clock on the morning of August 22, a bright, hot summer's day, the British warships opened fire on the beaches at the southwest corner of Long Island. After the few Americans in the area fled inland, some fifteen thousand British troops, including Titus and the Black Brigade, landed unnoticed. British strategy involved a three-pronged attack. Two other forces were moving toward the American center and right from the south. That morning British warships battered Brooklyn Heights to the northeast for four hours with a relentless mortar and cannon barrage, "now and then," as one officer quipped, "taking off a head." The idea was to keep the Americans occupied while Clinton and Cornwallis led ten thousand men in an arc north around and behind the American lines on the left. The rebels' one advantage was a steady wind that kept the British warships at a distance for several crucial days, enabling Washington to send reinforcements across the East River. That first day the British units faced little opposition and moved inland quickly. Their first night on Long Island was unexpectedly peaceful. The following day, the slaughter began.

General Sullivan, the new commander of Washington's left wing, was unsure which of four roads the British might use if they were planning a flanking attack. As it turned out, General Clinton, guided by local Loyalists, chose the Jamaica-Bedford Road, the one route Sullivan had left unprotected. Still, Clinton had his own problems. In places the trees and brush were so thick the British troops had to hack and saw their way through. But despite their noisy passage, they arrived undetected on the evening of August 26 and attacked the American left wing from the rear.

It was a rout on all fronts. In the fighting the American tactic of taking aim worked against them: the Hessians waited until the Americans had to reload, then attacked, sometimes simply with the bayonet. General Sullivan and his men were pinned down. Sullivan was captured. His men surrendered or ran. Panic set in. Sixty British infantrymen routed two entire Connecticut brigades. American observers were appalled. Colonel William Smallwood saw Washington and Generals Israel Putnam and Thomas Mifflin caning and whipping troops "from the Brigadier-General down to the private sentinel" to halt their flight. "Even this indignity," he added, "had no weight, they could not be brought to stand one shot." In contrast, Smallwood's Maryland regiment together with a Delaware regiment bravely stood their ground and at the cost of numerous casualties fought off the British, permitting many soldiers to withdraw to Brooklyn Heights. Washington's men faced complete annihilation.

The fighting was brutal. Fleeing Americans were not accorded the courtesies of war. The Scots and Hessian regiments refused to permit them to surrender. They had been intentionally provoked to this dishonorable conduct. An English officer who found the bloodshed "a fine sight" admitted: "We took care to tell the Hessians that the Rebels had resolved to give no quarters to them in particular, which made them fight desperately and put to death all who fell into their hands." "The English did not give much quarter and constantly urged our people to do the like," a Hessian officer wrote. "The riflemen were mostly spitted to the trees with bayonets." But he didn't regard this as a "fine sight," sympathizing, "These people deserve pity rather than fear."

The British officers and troops had deep contempt for their opponents. They dismissed the American soldiers and militia as cowards, and certainly their behavior that day justified the label. The officers, representatives of the upper class, despised the often modest origins of the American officers. One Hessian officer wrote that among those prisoners they did take, "were many called colonels, lieutenant colonels, majors, and other officers, who, however, are nothing but mechanics, tailors, shoemakers, wigmakers, barbers, etc. some of them were soundly beaten by our people, who would by no means let such persons pass for officers." The Americans suffered some 300 killed and 1,970 captured in the attack.

Members of the Black Brigade enjoyed the victory. Raw as most were, they could not have been in more capable hands. Yet Titus and his regiment had been a party to the brutality. And despite the general rout of the enemy, they took casualties they could ill afford. They also witnessed the contempt British officers felt toward American officers and soldiers. If Britons looked down on American aristocrats, what did they really think of slaves? New York State, especially Manhattan and Long Island, had the largest population of enslaved people north of the Chesapeake. There were other doubts. As slaveholders, what would New York Loyalists think of the Black Brigade? And what must their slaves have thought, peering out their windows or glancing furtively up from their work when they spied Titus and his comrades in their British uniforms? Certainly it was prudent for members of the Black Brigade to stay with their unit and avoid any mistakes of identity.

During this battle against northern regiments, Titus saw, for the first time, black troops integrated into American regiments. The British had organized separate black military units, but there were no integrated units. Indeed, most runaway slaves were handed a shovel rather than a gun and did rough labor for the army or acted as servants for the officers. Was it better to be a British officer's supposedly free servant than an American's slave? Was it a distinction without a difference? Once the war was won, would the servant become a slave again? Devoted as Titus was to the British army, it was something to see blacks in the American ranks fighting side by side with whites. How startling a sight for him and even more so for runaways from the South.

Ultimately the weather saved the Americans, as it would do time and again. They suffered greatly from terrible winters during the war, but at that critical moment, bad weather worked to their advantage. A drenching rain the night of August 27 prevented the British warships from coming up the East River, trapping the American force, and closing in to destroy what was left of the American army on Long Island. A British historian described the American army's desperate plight: "Nine thousand disheartened soldiers, the last hope of their country, were penned up, with the sea behind them and a triumphant enemy in front, shelterless and famished on a square mile of open ground swept by a fierce and cold northeasterly gale." They were penned up, but not trapped. After two days in the driving rain, Washington conceded they had no option but to retreat. On the second night they crowded into every boat Washington could assemble. John Glover's tough Marblehead sailors had just reached New York on August 28. Two nights later, shrouded by a deep fog, they rowed the entire army to safety in Manhattan. Among the last to leave, on the last boat, was their general.

The escape of Washington and his army meant the war would go on, but the Howe brothers had taken Long Island. Their next goal was New York City. William Howe was a careful man and took his time planning his strategy. The respite gave Washington two weeks to shore up his defenses, but they were two weeks filled with problems. Scores of Washington's remaining militia were leaving for home. "Our situation is truly distressing," Washington wrote Hancock, pleading for a permanent army. On September 5 the New

York State Convention invited Washington to remove all the bells from the city's churches and public buildings and transport them to Newark, New Jersey, to keep them from falling into British hands. There, if necessary, they were to be recast into cannon. The next day Congress selected John Adams, Benjamin Franklin, and Edward Rutledge to meet with Howe to discuss a settlement. Adams considered it a waste of time and hadn't wanted to participate. The British government, after all, did not recognize Congress. "I presume his Lordship cannot see us," he wrote, "and I hope he will not but if he should, the whole will terminate in nothing." He was right. Howe wanted peace but could not recognize Congress or acknowledge American independence. He even refused to send the committee's proposals to Britain.

On September 15 the British military campaign moved to the next stage, this time striking north of the city, at Kip's Bay. It was a fearsome assault. At dawn the Connecticut militia, peering from their shallow trench, saw British warships clustered just offshore. At 11:00 a.m., eighty-six British cannon opened fire at the beach. When the blasting stopped, flatboats packed with regulars and Hessians, four full divisions, were lowered into the water and rowed toward land. The nervous Hessians, who disliked even this short boat trip, sang hymns to calm their spirits, provoking sneers from British soldiers. The Connecticut militia had no time for hymns or national rivalries. The display of might unnerved them. They panicked and fled, pursued by the British and Hessians, who slaughtered any man they caught. Hearing the noise, Washington rode to the scene and, as on Long Island, did his best to stop the flight and get his men to form a line and face the enemy, but panic is contagious. Two brigades, twenty-five hundred men, morphed from soldiers into a mob right in front of their commander, tossing away any gear that slowed them down. Washington hurled his hat on the ground in fury and began hitting the men as they rushed past. One of his aides seized his horse's bridle, pulling him to safety before the British could capture him.

The army was saved by "Old Put." He dashed to New York City to rescue the men of his detachment and artillery. With the help of young Aaron Burr, who knew the roads in the area, he led his men on an orderly twelve-mile march north to Harlem Heights. His column, stretching some two miles behind him, took the Greenwich Road along the Hudson, the opposite side of the island from the British. That day Putnam marched one-fifth of Washington's army to safety. By five in the evening, under Clinton's direction, another five brigades of British and Hessian infantry had crossed the East River and begun marching north. The two waves of British troops would combine to form a line across Manhattan, blocking the American army in the north. The Americans had lost New York City, lost 17 officers and 350 men dead or missing, sixty-seven cannon, as well as their pride and confidence. The Black Brigade played no prominent role in the victory, but then they didn't need to.

A day later the Battle of Harlem Heights began. The Americans held a strong defensive position on the top of Harlem Heights and busily established three lines, under Generals Greene, Spencer, and Putnam. North of them were Forts Washington and Lee on opposite sides of the Hudson, and beyond that Kings Bridge, which led off Manhattan. Washington sent advance troops to check the whereabouts of the British force. They ended up in an unintended skirmish with the enemy but managed to lure the British into a hollow between the two lines. This time the American units fought valiantly, and the British eventually gave ground. It was only a respite, but it restored American morale. By October 23 Washington was again forced to retreat, this time abandoning the New York area for White Plains. Five days later he was attacked at White Plains. By mid-November the British took Fort Washington, overlooking the Hudson. Washington's flight with his army south across New Jersey had begun.

When American rangers collided with British advance units near Harlem Heights, Titus could not have suspected that his future and lasting fame would come as the most feared ranger of the war. Washington's rangers were a new type of military unit, one devised by Robert Rogers, a skilled New England backwoodsman. During the French and Indian War, Rogers trained his company of locals in Indian-style techniques of scouting, ambush, and hit-and-run missions, the unit often operating independently. His novel force proved so valuable that British officers began studying his tactics. At their urging, he drew up a set of nineteen orders outlining his approach. These included such admonitions as "Don't forget nothing" and "Don't never take a chance you don't have to." He was granted a regular commission but turned out to be a terrible administrator, always in straits over irregularities with his payroll. He traveled to England in 1765 and while there published two books of his exploits and techniques before returning to America. When war broke out, he offered his services to the American side, but after he was turned down because of doubts about his British links, he turned to the British. They commissioned him to raise a Loyalist battalion of rangers. "Rogers Rangers"

or, more officially, the Queen's Rangers, comprised Loyalists from Connecticut and New York and "gentlemen of the southern colonies who had joined Lord Dunmore." In contrast to the scarlet of the regulars, the rangers wore green uniforms to help them blend into the woodland and fields. Rogers was eventually forced out, but the Queen's Rangers went on to become the prototype for a new style of fighting, a style ideally suited to the American war. Both the British and the Americans adopted Rogers's idea. Rangers had to overcome the common opinion of the time, however, that such independent groups of warriors were no more than brigands or thugs.

At some point that winter of 1776 it was decided that Titus and some of the other runaway blacks would be of greater value to the British army in northern New Jersey than attached to the main army. Titus was given the honorific title of colonel and asked to form an independent unit of blacks and runaway whites, usually indentured servants. This was Titus's home ground. He set about organizing his band from a base on Sandy Hook that became known as Refugee Town, ready to try his hand at this different sort of fighting, a kind of hit-and-run guerrilla warfare.

The British had other irregular units of blacks working with their army. Companies of Black Guides and Black Pioneers had been established in North and South Carolina, Pennsylvania, and New York. The top two officers of these companies, though, were white, while other members and the company sergeants and corporals were black. Each company had between sixty and seventy men who took an oath on enlisting that they were joining of their free will and would faithfully serve the British army. Thomas Peters, one of the slaves who belonged to a New York City pioneer company, remembered that they were promised that, when the war was over, they would be "at our own liberty to do & provide for ourselves." The Black Pioneers usually coordinated their activities with the Queen's Rangers. Their knowledge of the local neighborhoods, along with their personal contacts and ability to arouse little suspicion, also made them valuable spies. Pioneers served as guards and occasionally as interpreters with Indians or performed executions.

The British also had units of black fugitives known as "followers of the Army and Flag." Like rangers, they returned to familiar territory to attack militia officers and prominent patriots, practicing guerrilla-style warfare, attacking at night and vanishing as suddenly as they arrived.

Although Titus and his men would often work with local Loyalists and Queen's Rangers, Titus would be in charge. Barely a year after he had fled, John Corlies's slave returned to Monmouth County transformed into Captain Tye, leader of a band of guerrilla fighters.

CHAPTER TWELVE

The Year of Possibilities

JOSIAH AND MILLICENT had seen each other at church in Lexington, Sunday after Sunday, year after year. They knew each other's joys and sorrows memorialized there, the births, baptisms, marriages, deaths, the addition of the black toddler to Josiah's little household. But apart from sharing Sunday services, the vagaries of Lexington life, and now the fright of war, Millicent's home could scarcely have been more different from the Nelsons. Where the entire Nelson clan was child poor, the Bonds were child rich. Josiah, one of only three children, was childless at the age of forty-nine and the uncle of only two. Millicent, by contrast, was fourth of the thirteen children—eight girls and five boys—born to Millicent and Joshua Bond. Pregnancy had followed pregnancy in that home for nearly twenty years. The house was bursting with children.

The Bonds also had more than their share of tragedy. Ruhamah, born the year before Millicent, lived barely long enough to be baptized. The two children born right after Millicent, little Joseph and Mary, died at ages three and four, respectively. In fact, two little Marys died before a third baby Mary survived to adulthood. As one of the older girls Millicent had plenty of experience looking after the younger ones and helping with a busy household. She grew up sharing in the family's repeated sorrow at the untimely termination of young lives. There were teenage deaths as well. In 1773 her sister Phebe died at the age of eighteen. Millicent was keenly aware of the precariousness of life.

This was her first marriage. At thirty Millicent was past the first blush of maidenhood and clearly had been passed up by younger men. Indeed, she had probably given up the idea of marriage, dedicating herself to helping her mother cope. Josiah was a prosperous farmer, still fit, but he was now forty-nine. She was really young enough to be his daughter. However, opportunity didn't knock often at the Bond household. The thought of moving into his large, quiet house, being mistress in her own home, and the pleasure of simply being courted was exciting and ultimately persuasive. She may even have been in love. It seems certain that Josiah loved or soon came to love her.

Josiah could not expect to get any dowry in cash or land with this marriage, but however nice that might have been, it wasn't needed. What he won was the hand of a respectable woman, considerably younger than him though not a girl, a sensible woman who knew how to manage a busy household. And if fertility ran in families, he might even expect, late as it now seemed, to have children of his own. He was lonely and in need of a wife. It seemed an ideal match.

Millicent joined their household at planting time, bringing to the annual task the skills and comfort of a farmwife. Those first weeks, like those for all newly married couples suddenly living and working together, were an anxious time for Josiah and his bride as they slowly and carefully learned each other's ways and the pleasures and awkwardness of shared effort. For Peter these first April days were filled with uncertainty as he tried to sort out his relationship to this new white woman, now living in Elizabeth's house, taking Elizabeth's place. It would have been hard enough for the teenager had he been Josiah's real son, but as a slave his place was far more precarious. Then, before he and Millicent really had a chance to establish a comfortable relationship, she became pregnant. The baby was due in January. What joy for Josiah, what a blessing, and what fussing and preparation in all three Nelson households. Peter's role, already precarious, now seemed doubly uncertain. However kind Millicent might be to her new, teenaged slave-son, once she had her own children he would clearly be the outsider, was now already the outsider. With the birth of this and future babies, real heirs of Josiah's body, Peter's slave status seemed likely to become permanently fixed. He would be nothing more than the "servant for life" as he was originally described, merely a laborer on the family farm. Or that was the fear.

Josiah was not the only one for whom the year was to open new possibilities, dreams about to be fulfilled. Jupiter and other local slaves who had seen little advantage for themselves in the war against Britain suddenly had the opportunity they had been waiting for: an offer to fight for their freedom. After the

military setbacks of 1776 and the difficulty of maintaining an army of short-
term enlistees, Washington finally persuaded Congress to issue quotas to each
state and call on them to conscript men from their militias for the army. The
planned army was to have eighty-eight battalions, each numbering 738 officers and men, some 75,000 in all, with an emphasis on long-term service. It
was a goal that would never be reached, but not for want of trying. Special
bounties, including offers of land and freedom, were used by Congress and by
individual states such as Massachusetts and even small towns such as Lincoln
to encourage men to enlist for three years or, better yet, for the duration. To
fulfill Massachusetts' high quota, fifteen battalions, the officers of the state's
Continental regiments began to recruit black slaves, promising them freedom
for completion of a three-year enlistment. Massachusetts was not alone in
turning to slaves. Before the year was out, Connecticut was actively recruiting
enslaved men and the Rhode Island assembly had passed a resolution inviting
"every able-bodied negro, mulatto or Indian man slave" to enlist in two
segregated battalions the state organized, promising equal pay and freedom.

The Fifteenth Massachusetts Regiment of the Continental Army was
established on the first day of 1777 and placed under the command of Colonel
Timothy Bigelow of Worcester, a former blacksmith. Bigelow was a tall man,
over six feet, with broad shoulders and despite his former trade was now every
inch a commander. Most of Bigelow's men were from the Worcester area or
such townships as Concord, Lincoln, and Lexington to the east. Edmund
Munroe, a Lexington man with a distinguished military background, was
commissioned captain of one of Bigelow's companies. Munroe had been an
ensign in a British ranger corps during the French and Indian War and later
received a commission as a lieutenant in the British army, serving until the
war ended in 1763. Now he filled his company's ranks with local men, including three Munroes. But most men were not keen to sign up for long-term
service, and to complete the numbers, Munroe enlisted a few local slaves.
Those who were willing to serve for three years would earn their freedom.
Among those signing up there was a general opinion that the war was unlikely to last three more years. This was the opportunity Jupiter had been
hoping for. On April 10, 1777, with Joshua Brooks's permission, Jupiter
Brooks enlisted as a private for a three-year term and after a lifetime of
bondage immediately and joyfully changed his name to Jupiter Free.

The young are said to adapt easily to change, but for Peter events were
occurring with disconcerting speed. Less than two weeks after Josiah's wedding, his father, Private Free, was getting ready to march off to war in the

company of friends and neighbors. He could but wish him well. Privates Pomp Blackman, Peter Oliver, Prince Sutton, and Peter Bowes like Jupiter were quick to take advantage of the chance to fight for their freedom, while their community was just relieved to fill its quota of enlistees. The Massachusetts Fifteenth would boast a proud military record. But it would also see hard service, beginning almost at once and including a winter at Valley Forge. For the moment, though, there was keen anticipation as Jupiter, in the plain brown homespun uniform of the Continentals, set off with Munroe's company to master soldiering. If he survived for three years, he would return to Lexington and to Peggy a free man.

That spring was also a season of promise for Captain William Smith, the doughty leader of the Lincoln minute company. Billy Smith had been restless. After the first excitement of war he was disappointed not to have gotten the field officer's commission he had wanted, despite badgering his brother-in-law, John Adams, for help. War was an opportunity for a man of spirit. In April, just as Jupiter was signing up for military duty, Smith's chance for adventure of a new sort appeared. In addition to raising an army, Congress was desperately trying to develop a navy and a corps of marines that could protect the coast and disrupt the flow of supplies the British were shipping to their forces in America. But navies take years to build and train. As a quick way to intercept British supply ships battling their way across the Atlantic, Congress and some individual states licensed privateers. Massachusetts alone issued some one thousand letters of marque licensing them. These private ships, freebooters, were authorized to seize British shipping and were promised a share in the profits from any prizes they brought in. Great fortunes might be won. High adventure was to be had.

On May 6 Abigail Adams sent John the news that her brother William had become a captain of marines and was "going in the Tarter a vessel which mounts 24 Guns is private property but Sails with the Fleet." This was more like it. Off this son of a parson sailed on the aptly named "Tartar," heading, like many other privateers, for the high seas and the waters off Ireland and the Baltic. The winds would soon carry him a long way from Lincoln, from Catherine Louisa and their little ones, from mundane farm life, disapproving parents, and gossipy neighbors. Dr. Samuel Prescott, who had met Paul Revere and William Dawes that fateful night two years before and successfully carried the alarm to Concord, was persuaded to sign on as ship's doctor. Sadly, it was to be a disastrous voyage.

As soon as Jupiter's company was complete, the men marched off to join the rest of the brigade at Peekskill, where Peter had served briefly the year before. Their mission was to block any British attempt to move north up the Hudson River from New York. Their brigade was placed under the capable leadership of John Glover, the heroic Marbleheader, a newly created brigadier general. After Glover's regiment of mariners had ferried Washington's army over the Delaware River in December 1776, the men's enlistments expired and they had disbanded. Seamen at heart, the men preferred signing up for the new privateers rather than the army, especially since privateers offered the chance of riches if they netted an enemy ship. Glover had returned to civilian life. His wife was ill, and his business needed attention. Now he was reluctantly back in service, thanks to Washington's intervention and the prestigious promotion. Glover arrived at Peekskill to take command of the brigade in mid-June. What he saw distressed him. "The troops from our State make the most shocking appearance, without shoes, stockings or breeches," he wrote his brother Jonathan, a member of the Massachusetts legislature. "I have seen soldiers go on duty without . . . nothing to cover their nakedness but a blanket . . . pray let this matter be attended to."

Blankets, knapsacks, and 255 guns with bayonets were already on their way, and Glover's plea would produce more supplies. But Jupiter and his colleagues had more serious concerns than decent clothing. Peekskill was a dangerous posting, yet by late June the brigade was on the march thirty miles south to a far more dangerous outpost, Eastchester, on Long Island. They were just three miles from the British base at Fort Independence and frightfully close to New York City. They were vulnerable and hopelessly outnumbered. Glover wrote in despair that in this perilous and isolated position they had "no dependence under God but on our own strength and [the] situation of the Ground." Fortunately, Jupiter and his other men didn't know their commander had written home with instructions about what should be done were he to be captured.

Washington must have thought better of their deployment, for by early July they had returned to Peekskill. Even there, they were in imminent danger because Howe was expected to attack that fortress at any moment. As it turned out, Howe had other plans.

New York State was the vital link between New England and the Middle Atlantic states, and the British were clearly intent on capturing it. The year before they had seized New York City and General Carleton and his Canadian army had nearly captured Ticonderoga and threatened Albany. In March, shortly after Peter and his regiment left Peekskill, they had captured the Hudson River town and destroyed the supplies and barracks there. Their continued designs on the state were clear. Nevertheless Washington, near Philadelphia with the main force of the Continental Army, remained convinced that British moves on New York were merely an attempt to divert his forces from the real goal of the British to march south. With New York City, New Jersey, and Pennsylvania filled with Loyalists and pacifists, Washington had few sympathizers to inform him and therefore little to no notion of British plans or movements. As it turned out, the British launched two major campaigns that summer, attempting to take both New York State and Philadelphia.

Both expeditions began in June, and their fates were sealed by one man, General William Howe. Howe's very sensible goal was to destroy Washington's main army. According to the grand strategy for the campaign season, however, he was instead designated to play a supporting role in the New York campaign, moving north from New York City to link up with a Canadian army marching south under Major General John Burgoyne. Howe had other ideas. Assuming that Burgoyne would not need his help until mid-September, he decided to move his army south by sea to crush Washington and his elusive army and capture Philadelphia. He pulled his men from New Jersey to New York City. On July 23 he set sail with 16,500 troops, leaving Clinton to hold the city with 7,300 men.

Howe's plan, like every military plan, was excellent until put into practice. Ill winds kept his army adrift for more than a month during the height of the campaign season. The fleet didn't reach the head of the Chesapeake Bay until August 25, and it took another week before they were finally on the march. Both the British and American armies maneuvered for position. Then on September 9 Howe caught up with Washington entrenched and waiting for him on the high ground behind Brandywine Creek. By now, however, Burgoyne's situation in Upstate New York was becoming desperate and Howe's relief force was miles to the south.

"Gentleman Johnny" Burgoyne had lobbied in London to replace Carleton as commander of the Canadian army and lead the campaign to take New York.

He was a good and a bold soldier but had a reputation on both sides of the Atlantic as a vain and pompous man. Horace Walpole, his godfather, dubbed him "Pomposo Hurlothrumbo" because of his odd fondness for issuing proclamations to all and sundry. During the long, warm days of early June, as Peter and Josiah tended their ripening crops in Lincoln and Jupiter was encamped at Peekskill with the Northern Army, bracing for the expected assault, Burgoyne and his men set out from Montreal. The Nelsons back in Lincoln and the troops of the Northern Army might have derived some small comfort from the problems Burgoyne's expedition faced had they known of them. He was short of horses, and his wagons, hastily built of green wood, kept breaking down and were too few to carry tents or the soldiers' baggage. The expedition was only able to carry two weeks' supply of food. Nevertheless, rumor had it that twenty wagons were being used to haul Gentleman Johnny's "necessities," a silver dining service, his wardrobe of fresh uniforms, and numerous cases of champagne. There were personnel problems, too. A small army of no fewer than two thousand women and children were accompanying the troops. The British and Hessian officers disliked one another, and the four hundred Indians who agreed to enlist were fewer than he wanted but hard to control and had brought their women and children with them. Still it was a powerful force by any measure, equipped with 140 cannon being transported by ship. And however poorly supplied the British were, American troops frequently had to manage without food or shelter at all. By June 13 Burgoyne, with eight thousand regulars, Indians, Loyalists, and two companies of Canadian militia, was at St. John's, poised to set sail down Lake Champlain to invade New York.

There was danger in store for New Yorkers from another direction as well. A few days after Burgoyne set out, a second Canadian expedition led by Lieutenant Colonel Barry St. Leger left Montreal with 2,000 men. Only 340 were regulars; Loyalists, Canadians, and Indians made up the bulk of the force. The plan was to create a diversion by advancing up the St. Lawrence River and then south into the Mohawk Valley of central New York before heading east to link up with Burgoyne. Against these forces the Americans had only the small but growing Northern Army, a small garrison at Fort Stanwix in the Mohawk Valley, and any local militia willing to help.

All the news reaching the Northern Army at Albany was bad. Burgoyne's advance was relentless and rapidly bearing down on them. His men quickly

notched up a series of easy triumphs. On June 26 they reached Crown Point.
The small garrison at the fort fled to Ticonderoga with the British only a few
days behind them. In the dead of night on July 6, with British cannon on
nearby Sugar Loaf Mountain poised to fire down on Ticonderoga, that great
fort's garrison also slipped away. Fort Ticonderoga fell without a shot being
fired. Patriots were shocked and dismayed. The fort's commander, Arthur St.
Claire, and his commander, Philip Schuyler, were later to face a court-martial
for its abandonment. But there was more. Just a day after taking Ticonderoga,
Burgoyne's troops defeated patriots in the woods at Hubbardston, Vermont,
and took possession of Fort Ann, which, like the other forts, was abandoned
at their approach. By July 10, the British army was at the north end of Wood
Creek. At this point Burgoyne made what proved to be a fatal error. Rather
than returning to Ticonderoga and putting his men back on ships for passage
to the Hudson, he decided to build a road to that great river through the
wilderness along Wood Creek. There were suspicions that this option was
pushed by local Loyalist Colonel Philip Skene, developer of Skenesborough,
who wanted a road through the twenty-five thousand acres he and some
associates owned there. Whatever the case, Burgoyne chose this option.

The new road Burgoyne's men hacked through the wilderness was a
testament to British engineering. It included some forty bridges and a two-
mile causeway. But roads take time to build. The project slowed the British
advance to a crawl and gave Schuyler and his Northern Army the opening
they needed. Keeping his men out of British reach, Schuyler set them to work
to slow or stop Burgoyne's progress. The soldiers spent day after day felling
trees across paths, destroying bridges, rolling boulders into the creek to
clog fords, and removing food supplies from the reach of the advancing and
increasingly hungry British column. Burgoyne's men, hacking their way
through thick woodland and mosquito-infested swamps, were exhausted by
these simple but aggravating expedients. It took them four weeks to advance
twenty-three miles. They were dogged, though, and on they came. The
British force under St. Leger was also making headway. In early August they
were besieging Fort Stanwix, where a garrison of 720 was holding out against
St. Leger's army of 1,700.

In late July, with Howe sailing south not north and Burgoyne threatening
Albany, Washington ordered Glover's brigade with the Massachusetts Fifteenth Regiment to leave Peekskill and reinforce the Northern Army. John

Nixon's brigade had left Peekskill on the same errand earlier that month. Glover put Jupiter and the rest of his men on boats, and they sailed up the beautiful Hudson, heading from one danger to another. They joined Schuyler's army on August 1 and for the first time faced Indian warriors.

New Englanders and New Yorkers deeply resented the British army's recruitment of Indians, warriors who fought by their own rules. Not that the Americans hadn't tried to recruit Indian help. Still, their outrage seemed justified when they learned in July that a band of Ottawas had murdered, mutilated, and scalped twenty-three-year-old Jane McCrea, a lovely young woman famous for her lustrous, floor-length hair. Jane's brother was a patriot, but she was a Tory and the fiancée of David Jones, a Loyalist with Burgoyne. The Indians claimed they were leading Jane to the British camp when she was accidentally shot by American pickets. If so, why had the Ottawas scalped her and brought that trophy in triumph to Burgoyne's camp? The horror Americans felt turned to fury when they learned that Burgoyne had decided not to punish Jane's murderers lest he offend his Indian allies. Jane's fiancé and his brother returned to Canada in disgust, taking poor Jane's scalp with them. American commanders made sure Burgoyne's behavior was widely broadcast.

Fighting Indian warriors proved more terrifying to Jupiter and his comrades than fighting British soldiers. They were in constant fear of these enemies who slipped unseen through the dense forests of upstate New York and scalped their victims. "This strikes a panic on our men," Glover reported, "which is not to wondered at, when we consider the hazard they run, as scouts, by being fired at from all quarters, (and the woods so thick they can't see three yards before them) and then to hear the cursed warhoop which makes the woods ring for miles." One day two dead men were brought into camp, one still bleeding from the scalp. In a rage Glover sent a four-hundred-man search party into the woods. All they found were three blankets.

After such a promising start to the year, the reports reaching Lincoln by midsummer were uniformly grim. Peggy, Peter, and friends and relatives of those who had marched off with the Lexington company in April were increasingly anxious for their safety. Though they hated to speak it aloud, it looked as if New York State was almost certainly lost. By early August, as the crops of hay, grain, and vegetables were being gathered on the Lincoln family farms and their apples were swelling nicely, St. Leger and his motley Canadian army of regulars, irregulars, and Indians arrived in central New York's Mohawk Valley. Their immediate target was Fort Stanwix, the only substantial strong point between St. Leger's men and Albany. Americans had tried to slow St. Leger's march as they had Burgoyne's, by felling trees and blocking his route as best they could. Fortunately, the fort itself had been strengthened. St. Leger's advance party of Indians and regulars reached the fort just in time to see wagons laden with emergency supplies driven inside. The British commander was confident that a show of force would bring these inexperienced rebels to their senses and paraded his army around the fort's walls. Rather then intimidating the garrison, the sight of the numerous Indians reminded the men of the mutilation of lovely Jane McCrea. That, combined with the British army's obvious shortage of white soldiers, strengthened their determination to hold out. They also knew that some eight hundred militia reinforcements were on the way to rescue them under the command of Brigadier General Nicholas Herkimer, the highly respected son of a German refugee and an experienced soldier.

St. Leger quickly learned of Herkimer's approach and immediately dispatched a party of Loyalists and Indians to intercept him. Herkimer was a sensible man and had been wary of using a direct route to the fort, but his men were eager and time was of the essence. So against his better judgment he and his men took a path that required them to march into a ravine at Oriskany, a spot the Indians called the place of nettles, six miles east of the fort, right into a well-laid ambush. The slaughter was terrible. Herkimer and his men fought fiercely. The battle raged for six hours. The general's horse was shot, and the ball shattered his leg. Propped against his saddle at the base of a tree, calmly smoking his pipe, Herkimer directed his men until the British finally pulled away. But the reinforcement effort had failed. By the evening of August 6 Fort Stanwix's defenders seemed doomed.

In a desperate move to rescue the garrison, Schuyler sent Benedict Arnold west with twelve hundred men to raise the siege. Arnold was afraid the garrison might be forced to surrender before they arrived. He hit on the idea of sending a half-witted Dutchman he had captured on ahead, escorted by two friendly Oneidas. The Dutchman arrived at St. Leger's camp raving that he had come from Arnold, whose force, "as numerous as the leaves on the trees," was about to arrive. St. Leger's Indians held the simple-minded in awe. They promptly deserted, some pausing to break open the rum and loot other supplies. Without their aid, St. Leger had little choice but to return to Montreal. By the time Arnold and his men reached the fort, the British had vanished. News of the success at Fort Stanwix was a badly needed tonic for American spirits.

Washington was busy defending Philadelphia and unable to protect New York State. Although he had sent some of his best officers, including John Glover and John Nixon, Peter's first commander, they would not be enough. Only local militia, the citizen soldiers Washington despised, who had let him down at critical times, were in a position to help. The call went out for men from all nearby states to assist the Northern Army. That army's commander, General Schuyler, had become so resented for his waspish and imperious manner that men were reluctant to enlist. On August 19 Congress replaced Schuyler with Horatio Gates, who had been vigorously lobbying for the post. Gates was able, ambitious, and very popular with the New Englanders. His appointment, coupled with fury over the British use of Indians and the determination to save New York, opened the floodgates. Volunteers from New York, Vermont, and other New England states came streaming in.

Once again Massachusetts called on the men in its militia. Small as Lincoln was, it sent two contingents to New York that autumn, twenty-two men in all.

September came. As Peter and his neighbors braced for their call to join the battle, Gates ordered the Northern Army to advance toward the British. The move instilled the men with new confidence and even heartened glum John Glover. They set up a new camp at Bemis Heights under the guidance of a brilliant Polish engineer. Three days later, on September 11, and miles to the south the confrontation between Washington's Continentals and Howe's regulars took place. The two armies had vied for position for some time before Washington decided to defend Philadelphia by placing his men north of the city at John Chadds's ford on Brandywine Creek and posting men at nearby fords. What he was unprepared for was Howe resorting to the battle plan that had been so successful at Long Island. Part of the British army attacked Washington's center. While the rebel army was occupied, a second group of British soldiers, commanded by Howe and Cornwallis, swung around the American right wing under the command of John Sullivan, hoping to en-

velop it. Just as at Long Island the previous year, Sullivan's men were surprised and smashed. By day's end the Americans suffered some 900 casualties
to Howe's 550. Despite the terrible loss, Washington was keen to charge the
British again. Only a drenching rain that made their gunpowder unusable
stopped him. He was forced to retreat.

Howe was not yet done with Washington. Little more than a week after
the Battle of Brandywine he ordered one of his officers, Charles Grey, to lead
a night raid on General Anthony Wayne's division. Three hundred more
Americans fell in what became known as the Paoli Massacre.

The British continued to advance in Upstate New York. On September 13
and 14, General Burgoyne and his army, now down to some six thousand men,
crossed to the west bank of the Hudson and made camp two miles north of
the village of Saratoga. An expedition Burgoyne had sent to raid Bennington,
Vermont, for supplies a month earlier had been crushed by New Hampshire
militia led by John Stark. It was a costly mistake. Gates's Northern Army now
enjoyed a numerical advantage, although most men were militia and others,
like Jupiter, were untested troops. More militia regiments were rushing to
help him. By September 15 the two armies were just five miles apart. The
British could hear the trumpets and drums of the American camp.

At fourteen Peter was two years too young to be conscripted, but he had been
in the army twice. He counted as an experienced soldier. When the second
call for men came in September, he was permitted to volunteer to help fill
Lincoln's quota. There was every reason for him to stay home and help Josiah
and Millicent, yet by late September the harvest had been gathered, and men
and even boys were urgently needed. Thomas Nelson, who could plead his
age, and Jonathan, who couldn't, were both staying home.

So on September 29 Peter, now calling himself Peter Nelson, was formally enlisted and said his farewells. Farewell to Jonathan, his oldest friend,
Jonathan with all his privileges, white and free. Yet how the teenaged boy
always left behind must have envied Peter the freedom to join the men
marching off to the great adventure of war. Farewell to Mr. and Mrs. Thorning next door and their three daughters, Mary, Abigail, and little Sally. The

Thornings' son, John, had gone off with the first Lincoln group. Now William was preparing to leave. Both had been involved in fighting before, but usually only one at a time. This time their parents and sisters would remain alone at home. Farewell to Millicent, his new mistress, and a moving farewell to his mother, Peggy. She had been praying for Jupiter's safety and would now add Peter to her worries and her prayers. Farewells were hard. There was no knowing whether he would ever return or if he would come home badly wounded or sick. Peter had seen enough of war to know that could happen, but he was young enough to be eager and confident. As September drew to a close Millicent found herself alone with Josiah in her grand new home under the watchful eyes of Nelsons and Bonds as she carried her first child.

Peter was enrolled in Captain Samuel Farrar's company, Colonel Jonathan Reed's regiment. Farrar was a Lincoln man and had served as a lieutenant in William Smith's minuteman company. On September 29 Farrar reported to Lincoln's Colonel Eleazer Brooks that the fourteen men in his company were ready for their assignment. Their company was officially detached from Brooks's command and, like the Lincoln men already in arms, were sent to reinforce General Gates's army "at the Northward." It would mean a march of nearly two hundred miles. Peter was once again with men he had served with before and had known all his life, including Joshua Brooks, Jupiter's owner, now the company's sergeant, and Joseph Mason, Jr., its corporal. After months of comfort in a snug house with regular meals, he was immediately faced with the familiar hardships of life in the American military—exhaustion, hunger, discomfort, and a mixture of fear and excitement. Still, for a boy unhappy at home, it was a relief to be among men who accepted and valued him. And he might get a chance to see his father. As they converged on New York State they joined fifty-two other militia units rushing to reinforce the Continentals in a great confrontation that would, had they but known it, be the turning point in the war.

The Battle of Saratoga was actually a series of deadly clashes between the two armies over about a month. Peter and his regiment nearly missed it. September 19, the day it really began, dawned rainy, foggy, and cold in Upstate New York.

To warm the spirits, the commissary delivered a gill of rum to every man in the camp that morning. Peter was still in Lincoln, but Jupiter's regiment, having finally received needed blankets and firearms with bayonets, were there, and the Lincoln regiment sent earlier had reached the Northern Army. Glover's brigade was posted on the army's right wing and occupied the high ground near the river. To their right were the brigades of Nixon and Paterson. On September 10 Jupiter's brigade had been reinforced by three regiments of New York militia. Reinforcements were welcome, but not the "Yorkers." There was such friction between them and the New Englanders that Glover was reduced to threatening to confine any officer or soldier who swore or struck a soldier from the rival region. The men had little time to nurse their resentments, however. The two days before the battle were spent frantically cutting down trees to construct a breastwork to protect their position.

Burgoyne began the fight, intent on crushing the American forces blocking his road south at Bemis Heights, six miles north of Stillwater. He divided his men into three attack columns and sent them off toward the American army. Gates and the American line watched and waited as the British and Hessians struggled toward them for several exhausting hours through two deep, wooded gorges. General Gates might have left his entrenched position and attacked the British as they were slogging through the ravines and clearly vulnerable. But he didn't. After much signaling, the British columns managed to get into the planned positions.

Like many such battles, the actual fighting started accidentally. Gates had sent Morgan and his famed Virginia sharpshooters to scout out the British positions. By now the sun was high and had burned off the fog. Just after noon Morgan's men spotted the advance British pickets. The famed marksmen couldn't resist opening fire. Their withering attack was deadly, killing or wounding every British officer in the group. In high excitement they threw caution aside and pursued the survivors right back into the hands of a large contingent of British infantry. Now Morgan's men were being bloodied in their turn. Off they ran, leaving Morgan, according to reports, "alone and almost in tears." Pulling himself together, he blew loudly on a turkey call and rallied his men.

At this point the battle became more general. From two until five o'clock in the afternoon it was fierce, especially in the center, where men were fighting in a fifteen-acre clearing belonging to an unfortunate farmer named Isaac Freeman. British artillery and massed ranks of soldiers were firing volley after volley at the Americans, who had the advantage of numbers and trusted to their marksmanship. When some of the British troops fled into the surrounding woods, Morgan's men climbed trees to get clearer shots. In their hunting shirts the sharpshooters blended with the autumn foliage, making it hard for the British to spot them. Six times the men of the Continental Army charged the British lines with, what the earl of Balcarres conceded, was "great obstinacy and courage." Each time the Americans were forced back by a fierce, coordinated bayonet charge. Rifles were deadly, but there was something particularly horrifying about lines of men advancing with the long, bloodthirsty blades, triangular to create a large, unstanchable wound. When it was uncertain who would have the better of the day, the Hessians, with loud cheers and beating drums, rushed to Burgoyne's rescue. Gates's men were exhausted. Their ammunition was running out. Confronted by these fresh troops, they withdrew to their original lines, bringing their wounded and a hundred captives with them and leaving the equally exhausted British in possession of the field.

What role did Jupiter and his comrades play? Through it all, the men of Glover's and Nixon's brigades had been held in reserve and spent the day in camp, doubtless wondering whether to be disappointed or relieved.

"It was a dear-bought victory if I can give it that name," a British lieutenant reflected, "as we lost many brave men. The 62nd had scarce 10 men a company left, and other regiments suffered much, and no very great advantage, honor excepted, was gained by the day." The toll of casualties on both sides was sobering. Some six hundred men on the British side had been killed, wounded, taken prisoner, or were missing, men Burgoyne's expedition could not replace. The Americans were less battered but still had some three hundred casualties of which eighty men were killed, two hundred were wounded, and thirty-six were missing. The Americans lost the field at Freeman's Farm but held their original lines. Upset as they were at losing friends and comrades, more men, hundreds more, were rushing to replace those who had fallen.

In the aftermath of the battle the British were tired and cautious, the Americans disorganized, so for some time both armies dug in. Glover's brigade was moved from the heights down to the river next to the bridge of boats that Gates constructed to span it. Along with the brigades of Nixon and Paterson, they now came under the command of General Benjamin Lincoln. This reorganization resulted from animosity between two proud commanders, Gates and Arnold.

The British built a series of fortified lines and three redoubts and settled down to await help from Clinton, who promised to lead some troops from

New York City to their aid. Meanwhile they were reduced to living on a pound of flour and salt pork a day. Their Canadian and Loyalist allies now began to desert them. The Indians, taking their women and children, vanished, never to return. And thanks to Glover their days and nights were anxious ones. Apparently Glover had suggested to Gates that they embark on a series of raids on the British camp to keep the enemy on edge. Perhaps, having missed out on the battle, he wanted to see some action. At any rate he led the first raid himself. On the evening of September 27 Glover and a hundred of his men set out to attack a British picket of some sixty men posted half a mile away. Another two hundred of his men went to provide cover for the first group. The crisp autumn night was foggy, and they didn't spot the British pickets until sunup. Still, Glover was determined to persist. His men sprang up "like so many Tygers," he reported, and drove the pickets back to their lines, killing three, wounding many more, and capturing a prisoner. None of Glover's men were lost. American raids accomplished their object. One British officer wrote that "not a single night passes but there is firing and continual attacks on the advanced picquets . . . the officers rest in their cloaths, and the field officers are up frequently in the night."

It was at this time that the men of the Northern Army learned the sobering news that Congress had abandoned Philadelphia. The day before Glover's raid on the pickets the British had marched into that city. Washington's shrunken army was intact but disheartened. If the British captured New York State, the war was probably lost.

On October 3 Clinton finally set out from New York City, if not to join Burgoyne, at least to create a diversion by attacking forts in the Hudson Highlands. Burgoyne, still expecting his help at Albany, was now beyond all help. On October 7 he decided to advance again to try to outflank Gates. He left some men to guard his camp and sent others on a foraging expedition for desperately needed supplies. Burgoyne's main force was spread out in a wheat field bordered by woods, just a mile and a half from Gates. His soldiers rested while their camp followers reaped. It was a golden opportunity for the Americans. With the command "Order Morgan to begin the game," Gates sent Morgan's sharpshooters with some infantry regiments to attack the left of Burgoyne's line and a force of Continental regiments and militia, including Nixon's men under General Enoch Poor, to get around the British flank on the right and strike at them through the woods. Ebenezer Learned's brigade was to attack the center. Poor's men arrived first. Despite a British volley and bayonet charge, they overwhelmed the grenadiers, whose position made it difficult to retreat. Both British flanks began collapsing when Learned's brigade hit the Hessians, positioned in the British center. With the outcome still uncertain, Benedict Arnold dashed onto the field. He was furious with Gates for not reporting his role in the previous battle and now, ignoring explicit orders to stay back, galloped to the front lines. With contagious energy and determination, he rallied the Americans and led a charge on the British redoubt. That won the day. During the charge, however, a wounded Hessian lying on the ground shot Arnold's horse at point-blank range. The animal fell, trapping and breaking the same leg Arnold had injured at Quebec.

Jupiter and the other men of Glover's brigade had gotten the alarm about three o'clock in the afternoon and marched to their advanced picket. Around five o'clock there was fighting on their left wing that lasted until sunset. They were finally ordered to attack, but, as one sergeant later reported, "it being pretty dark, and not to our advantage to attack them at that time of night, we returned to our camps again." It was over.

Burgoyne and his men retreated north to Saratoga, sending an advance party farther north. With his dwindling and battered army nearly out of supplies, the general decided to return to Ticonderoga, but discovered, to his dismay, that was no longer possible. Gates had had the foresight to send troops north of the British, effectively surrounding them. On the other hand, Gates nearly snatched defeat from the jaws of victory. Thinking the entire British force was moving with Burgoyne's advance party, he ordered his troops, led by the brigades of Nixon and Glover, to attack what he thought was the lightly staffed British rear guard. Just as Nixon's men were crossing the Fishkill River toward Saratoga, the fog lifted. Thanks to the information from a British deserter, Glover discovered they would be facing the main body of the enemy. Before they could retreat, they were fired on. A cannonball whizzed by Nixon's head, close enough to inflict severe damage to his eye and ear on that side. But despite this small American setback, Burgoyne's situation had become hopeless. In desperation proud Gentleman Johnny sent to Gates for a parley. That is where things stood when Peter and his colleagues arrived.

There was general elation in the American camp. There had been casualties, and many men were simply sick, but the victory was a tremendous relief. Hundreds of militiamen had helped surround and defeat a large, professional

British army. Together with St. Leger's failure to capture Fort Stanwix and his retreat to Canada, the British plan to seize New York was now a shambles. If Peter felt any regret at arriving too late for the fighting, there was also tremendous relief. There would be other fights. The important thing was that a major battle had been won, and Jupiter and so many others were safe.

The negotiations between Gates and Burgoyne dragged on for several days. In the end Gates agreed to a generous settlement. He was worried Clinton might arrive and attack him from the south, so it seemed wise to be cautious. In return for Burgoyne's unconditional surrender, he would escort the British army to Boston and permit its men to sail back to England with the proviso that they would sit out the rest of the war.

There was a formal surrender ceremony. As the American troops watched, the British and Hessian officers and soldiers marched out of their entrenchments and laid down their arms and their regimental banners. "We marched out, according to treaty with drums beating, and the honors of war," a British officer reported, "but the drums seemed to have lost their former inspiring sounds, . . . then it seemed by its last feeble effort, as if almost ashamed to be heard on such an occasion."

On October 17 the Lincoln men with other New England militia regiments and Continental troops joyfully began to escort the vanquished British army back to Massachusetts. They reached Cambridge on November 6. A day later, their enlistments up, Peter and the men from Lincoln walked home. The Continentals, however, turned south for the long trek to join Washington at Valley Forge. The British army, dubbed the Convention Army from the convention Gates had signed, spent more than a year in Cambridge waiting to be evacuated. When a British fleet finally arrived in December 1778, it was refused entry to Boston. It seemed obvious to Bostonians that if the British troops returned to Britain, they would free soldiers there for service in America. The Convention Army would eventually be marched to Virginia. Many men deserted. Few would ever see England or Germany again.

Back in Lincoln, even the inexorable approach of winter's uncomfortable embrace failed to mar the general relief over the amazing victory at Saratoga. Then in mid-November came word that six months out on their voyage,

William Smith and the crew of the good ship *Tartar* had been captured. The man had a knack for misadventure. Poor Catherine Louisa, yet again an object of pity. "My Brother has had the misfortune to be taken upon his return from a cruise up the Baltick," Abigail wrote John. "They had a valuable prize with them loaded with duck and cordage." The mariners and their physician, Dr. Prescott, were taken to Halifax and imprisoned, "since which," Abigail added, "we have not heard from him."

Christmas came and went, then New Year's Day. On January 23, almost thirteen years to the day on which Elizabeth and Josiah had purchased Peter, Millicent gave birth to a healthy baby boy. They named him Josiah.

CHAPTER THIRTEEN

Trials and Tribulations

JUPITER'S HEALTH gave out shortly after the great victory at Saratoga. It was in fact amazing that he had remained fit as long as he had. On October 16, the day before Burgoyne's official surrender, more than a third of the men in Jupiter's brigade were recorded as sick. Jupiter was strong but getting on in years, and the combination of meager and unwholesome food, close quarters that spread disease, exposure to the elements, and exhaustion played havoc with a man's condition. When his regiment turned east to escort the Convention Army to Cambridge, Jupiter hadn't the strength to accompany them and remained at Albany. The division roster tersely notes that he was "sick at Albany" through December and January and sick and absent in February and March, doubtless having braved the long journey to Lincoln in hopes of recuperating. If his personal stake, his bid for freedom, weren't so important, he would have gone home and stayed there. But this was a rare chance. For his new surname, Free, to mean anything, he had to fulfill his three-year commitment. So spring found him back with his regiment at Valley Forge.

Over the winter Washington had ordered the 3,000 to 4,000 men in camp who were susceptible to smallpox to be inoculated. The inoculations began in January. Group after group rotated through the process—inoculation, illness in the hospital, than recuperation. Washington insisted that all new recruits arriving that spring were to be inoculated when they were two to three days' march from the encampment. Having missed the general inoculation in the winter, Jupiter was among those inoculated as he neared camp. The roster lists him as ill throughout April and May, one of some 3,800 soldiers in the camp sick that month, many if not most from their smallpox inoculation. But the scheme worked, and by the end of May, the army was free of smallpox. On June 16, when Washington led his men out of Valley Forge for the new campaign season, Jupiter marched with his regiment.

The men were in good spirits. They had survived the winter and were much better trained. And during the winter their cause seemed more hopeful. With the triumph at Saratoga the French took the American struggle more seriously and in February signed two treaties promoting trade and, more important, officially recognizing American independence. Help would be on the way from one of the world's greatest powers. On May 6 the Continental Army celebrated with a "day of rejoicing" in honor of the alliance with France. Each soldier had been given a gill of rum for the event, and the entire army, gathered on parade, cheered as instructed, "Long Live the King of France. Long Live the Friendly European Powers." Odd that, cheering an alliance with their oldest enemy, an enemy that time after time had swept down from Canada with Indian allies to ravage New England towns until finally defeated in 1763. But real assistance from the French was still in the future. Less than two weeks after leaving Valley Forge a great battle would take place in New Jersey at Monmouth Court House. The French would not be there to help.

The new year began with mixed emotions for Peter's mother, Peggy. In addition to Jupiter's lingering illness, on February 11, William Reed, her old master, died. He was laid beside his wife, Sarah, there to rest for eternity. Reed had reached the grand age of eighty-five. According to the inscription on his headstone, he left ten children and one hundred grandchildren and great-grandchildren "to lament his Death." These and other survivors were exhorted to "Mark the perfect man & Behold the upright."

William's death was less traumatic for Peggy than it might have been. By the time his final will had been drawn up in October 1775, William had already granted his eldest son, William Junior, his share of the estate. Peggy and probably her daughter were his property. Peggy senior could still help look after the old master if needed, of course. He might have been made of sturdy stuff, but he would have required increasing care from familiar and sympathetic hands. The Reeds were a prosperous and respected as well as a numerous family, and there were certainly less pleasant people to work for. Whether Peggy thought her old master "the perfect man" or not, his death ended an era.

After all her years with them, Peggy was a part of that family. But if Jupiter could only manage to fulfill his tour of duty, he would return to her in two years a free man. Then perhaps they might save the money to free her or the Reeds might agree to let her go.

The Reeds had more worries that spring. William Junior's younger brother, Oliver, had sailed as third lieutenant with William Smith on the *Tartar* and had been captured and imprisoned in Halifax with the rest of the crew. When word came in November 1777 of his capture, the family frantically petitioned for his release. Hundreds of men died in such prisons. The result was a letter from Edward Brooks to the Honorable James Bowdoin, Halifax Barracks, asking that Oliver and other prisoners be exchanged. When his father died, Oliver was still languishing at Halifax.

How different the attitude of William Smith's family. Even their brother William's close imprisonment at Halifax failed to exonerate him in the eyes of his sister, Abigail Adams, and the rest of his family. Not even in the privacy of their letters did they dare discuss his woeful failings explicitly. That March Abigail confided to her sister Elizabeth her sympathy for William's daughter, her "Little Neice who I compasinate that She has not a Father Whom She can Honour."

Back home on the Concord Road, Peter's life with Josiah, Millicent, and baby Josiah settled into new routines. The tiny infant made demands on its doting and untested parents, while Peter was left to concentrate on the cycle of farmwork and, when time permitted, relax and visit with friends. The spring months slipped away as he and Josiah readied the land for the new season. It was a sickly season, as spring often is. Perhaps that explains why Josiah's new baby was not taken to church to be baptized. On the other hand, many people believed infant baptism wrong, believed a child should be baptized when old enough to appreciate the significance. Little Josiah would be twelve before he was baptized.

With so many Lincoln men in service, Josiah for the first time began to play a role in town government. Shortly after his marriage a year earlier he had been appointed to a key town committee. Its task was to reckon the "services and expenses of any of the inhabitants of this town in carrying on the present war and to take such measures for equalizing said services and expenses as the town shall think proper." The committee report presented to town meeting in May 1778 made sober reading. The costs of the war had already been high. To meet them the town agreed to grant £3,808 for services for the war, a formidable sum for such a small community. Some seventeen separate campaigns were listed in which Lincoln men had participated. The money was to be paid to men who had served in the various campaigns on behalf of the town and to those who had lent the town funds to meet its assessments for the war effort. The town meeting also agreed to supply the additional shirts, shoes, and stockings now requested by the Massachusetts General Court for its soldiers. In a further vote, townsmen agreed that Lincoln "will be at all future expenses of carrying the present war so far as respects procuring of men when called for by lawful authority." The ever-cautious community was careful to insert the word "lawful," just in case. A group of local military officers was charged to hire men "for the present campaign." If necessary, money was to be borrowed to hire these men. One of those hired would be Peter.

Peter was fifteen now and a strapping five feet, nine inches, a respectable height for that time. He had already served with the militia three times, and although Josiah valued his help on the farm, he was willing to have Peter serve once again. It would enable the town to meet its quota, Peter would earn money for the family—two pounds a month—and Josiah, Millicent, and their baby would be alone in the house. Colonel Thomas Poor of Andover had been appointed to command a regiment for service at Peekskill, New York, that year. The regiment was commissioned May 13, and a month later, on June 14, Peter enlisted in the company commanded by Captain Edward Richardson. Richardson was from the part of Massachusetts that would become the state of Maine. He and his twin brother, Moses, had joined the army in 1775 and served throughout the war. This would turn out to be Peter's longest enlistment yet. The month Peter left home Millicent became pregnant again.

The trek to New York was a long and tiring march of almost two weeks for Peter and his company, with all the familiar hardships of hunger, exposure, and exhaustion. At least the weather was fair in June as they headed west to the vastness of New York State and south to the Hudson Highlands. He was aware that New York had far more Negro slaves than Massachusetts, especially in the area they were heading for, closer to New York City. Did these slaves gazing warily at the patriot army think Peter a fool for risking his life in a war for white freedom? Or did they admire his ability to fight as an equal with the white men of his state? Whatever their views, at least he had the satisfaction of knowing he was not toiling away at some thankless task. He was in the militia because he wanted to be. He was also away from home and worries about his future.

At first the regiment was posted to Fort Clinton rather than Peekskill. Fort Clinton, together with its sister fort, Fort Montgomery, was located at a strategic point on the Hudson near Bear Mountain. In July 1776, before the British had captured New York City, the New York convention had appointed a committee to "devise and carry into execution" measures for "obstructing the channel of Hudson's river, or annoying the navigation of the said River." To carry out that mission Fort Clinton had been fitted with a battery of cannon. A boom and cable had been laid across the river, and fortifications were built on a cliff on the landward side some hundred feet above the water. From Fort Clinton, Peter had a clear view of Fort Montgomery.

The forts had an unfortunate history. During General Clinton's belated effort to help General Burgoyne the previous year, British ships had appeared on the river beneath the forts. While the warships shelled the forts, British troops had attacked from the landward side. In a single day, both forts fell. The enemy was unable to hold the forts and protect New York City but before leaving made sure to destroy them. They burned what was flammable and then tore down the stone buildings. Now the Americans were back guarding the Hudson once again, this time, it was hoped, with better success. Forts Clinton and Montgomery boasted a combined force of about seven hundred men. In the interim the immediate threat had been removed. Burgoyne's army had surrendered, and Clinton, now commander of the British armed forces, was at Philadelphia mulling over his new orders and ominous events.

While Washington's men were celebrating that amazing alliance with France, their doubts quenched by an extra ration of rum, Clinton, Titus's new commander, was trying to adjust to the changed situation. Although the French alliance had been signed in February, he learned of it only in early May when he arrived at Philadelphia to take over command of British land forces from Howe. The French had already dispatched a squadron of twelve warships in the spring, and it gradually became clear they were heading for North America. The alliance had ominous implications. It meant that the British were no longer engaged only in a war to suppress rebellious colonies but in a world war against France. Clinton's men now had to protect their valuable Caribbean possessions as well as defeat Washington's army. The most sensible approach seemed to be to concentrate his forces, abandon Howe's prize of Philadelphia, and return to New York. On June 18, two days after Washington led his men out of their Valley Forge encampment, Clinton led the British army out of Philadelphia for a march across New Jersey to New York City.

The peaceful evening quiet of little New Jersey farming villages that spring was shattered time and again by Titus, now boasting the title Captain Tye, and his band of black and white refugees. They would burst suddenly from the darkness to attack the farms of New Jersey patriots, freeing their slaves, stealing their cattle, burning their houses and barns. Some isolated families slept in the woods at night to avoid his band, returning home at daybreak hoping home was still there. But that June, Clinton would have another use for Titus. He and his band were ordered to join the main British army for its march across New Jersey. Officially known as "followers of the Army and Flag," they were now organized into the Black Brigade. Their detailed knowledge of the terrain and fighting skill would be critical during the trek to New York. As part of the main army, Captain Tye would find himself fighting against black men such as Jupiter who had chosen to win their freedom by serving in the Continental Army. He was used to freeing slaves, not shooting at them. This killing was a painful necessity.

Loyalists were in a panic as the British prepared to leave. Rather than evacuate them with the army, Clinton arranged for three thousand Loyalists, along with sick and wounded soldiers, to be taken to New York by ship. The flotilla would reach the safety of the city just three days before the French squadron appeared in New York harbor.

The rest of the army walked. Progress was slow. It took them nearly seven hours to cross the Delaware River. The baggage train of fifteen hundred wagons stretched for twelve miles. Infantrymen were deployed to guard the baggage train, but the slow-moving procession was fearfully vulnerable. After crossing the Delaware, Clinton divided the men into two divisions—one, under Lieutenant General Wilhelm von Knyphausen, mostly made up of Hessian troops with two brigades of British infantry and some Loyalists, were to accompany the baggage train to New York. The other division, commanded by Cornwallis, comprised the army's elite British and Hessian regiments. Clinton planned to use this division against Washington if the Continentals attacked.

It was exceptionally hot and humid that June, making the march more miserable. Clinton chose a forty-mile-long northeasterly route toward Sandy Hook, where he planned to have his men board ships for New York City. Their journey was plagued by the usual bag of American tricks. British pickets were shot at, trees felled to block the road, and bridges burned. A limited scorched-earth tactic was also used, with livestock being driven out of reach and wells filled in. The desperately hungry and thirsty British soldiers resorted to looting and plundering. As the army approached the coast the road became sandy, slowing progress even more. Men sickened in the heat, others deserted. Five hundred Germans returned to Philadelphia.

Washington kept pace with the British, placing his army to their north, waiting to see which route Clinton chose. Once it was clear he was heading toward the coast, it was time for a decision. At the war council his generals disagreed about what was to be done. Brigadier General Anthony Wayne, Major General Marquis de Lafayette, General Nathanael Greene, and others pressed for an attack while the British army was spread out and vulnerable. General Charles Lee, long a critic of Washington and recently returned from British captivity, argued that the American troops couldn't stand up to the British and should let them retreat to New York. Washington disagreed with Lee and decided to send a vanguard of some twenty-five hundred of his best troops and finest generals to attack the retreating British, then some six miles away. He and the remaining twelve thousand men would be not far behind, ready to come to their support.

Although Lee had opposed the mission, he pleaded for command of the vanguard and Washington acquiesced. It was a serious error. Lee was inexperienced. It was his first independent command. Even though Washington visited him twice the night before the attack to make sure he understood his orders, on the day itself confusion reigned. Lee had no plan of attack, and his commanders were uncertain of their orders. Some regiments began skirmishing with British pickets; some militia attacked the British baggage train. Then at 11:00 a.m. on June 28 Lee ordered an attack by a Pennsylvania regiment and returned to the village where the Monmouth Court House stood. Clinton promptly responded to the attacks, sending Cornwallis to the rescue with four thousand of his men. Just before noon, in intense summer heat, the Battle of Monmouth began. Lee tried a pincer movement, but his orders were confusing, and when his artillery withdrew to get more ammunition, other units thought they were retreating. By one o'clock, when Washington arrived at nearby Tennent Meeting House, he was appalled to see Lee's forces in full retreat. Washington was outraged and set off with his staff to find Lee. As soon as he found the befuddled general, he ordered Lee immediately to organize his men for defense while he deployed the rest of the army on the nearby hills.

The fighting was ferocious. Wayne's men were attacked in the woods by the British but rallied. The New York, Maryland, and Pennsylvania regiments held their line against determined and repeated British attacks, a testimony to the fine training Baron von Steuben had given them over the winter. The British tried again and again to flank the Americans but instead got bogged down in the swamps nearby. An artillery battle that began late in the afternoon lasted for nearly two hours. Around 6:30 p.m. the British turned from the fight and continued their march to the coast. Washington sent men after them, but by nightfall it was all over.

The battle had been costly. Jupiter and the Fifteenth Massachusetts had been in the thick of the fighting. Jupiter's captain, Edmund Munroe, who had offered him, Pomp Blackman, Salem Poor, and other slaves the precious chance to earn their freedom in his Lexington company, died in the battle. The cannonball that killed him also killed George Munroe and left Joseph Cox of their company maimed for life. Captain Ellis, another of the Fifteenth's captains, was also killed at Monmouth. Jupiter survived unharmed and was grateful. If he saw any blacks fighting for the British, he had little time to consider or hesitate. He pulled the trigger and went on fighting for victory and his freedom.

Captain Tye, the most prominent of the former slaves fighting for the British, not only survived but burst on the scene a hero. He and his men fought with distinction. While Jupiter may, by chance, have spotted blacks fighting for the British, Tye surely knew many were fighting in the enemy's New England regiments. But they had made their choice, and he never hesitated in his duty to the British. His most notable accomplishment that day was to capture Elisha Shepard, a captain of the Monmouth militia, and see that he was imprisoned at the Sugar House in New York. Tye's exploits on that battlefield and elsewhere would earn this captain the prestigious rank of colonel.

When the dead were counted, the British had lost between eight hundred and a thousand men, the Americans between five and six hundred. Both sides were convinced they had won. The Americans had stood up to the finest British soldiers and held their ground. The British had wanted merely to cross to the coast and, despite Washington's attack, were able to do so. Really it was a draw. The obvious loser was General Lee. Oddly, he felt he had performed brilliantly and demanded a court-martial to clear his name. There were three specific charges against him: that he did not attack as ordered; that he caused a disorderly and unnecessary retreat in the face of the enemy; and that he had shown disrespect for Washington. After a month of testimony Lee was suspended for a year. He would never serve in command again.

Peter's enlistment proved long, occasionally anxious, ultimately boring. The summer campaign season dragged. The British were busy elsewhere and had little interest in retaking the fortifications guarding the Hudson. Certainly everyone agreed it was better that way, not to have to fight. But if it was peaceful and relatively safe standing watch on the Hudson, it was not so back home in Lincoln. The smallpox epidemic had never really disappeared and now returned to Massachusetts towns with a vengeance. On August 19 tragedy struck. Just a few days shy of his eighteenth birthday, Jonathan Nelson died. It was a blessing that when Peter and Jonathan said their farewells in June, neither boy knew they would never see each other again. Still it was terrible not to have said more, not to have been there to say the final good-bye to his boyhood companion. Not even to be home for his funeral.

If Jonathan's death was terrible for Peter, it was heartrending for Jonathan's parents, Thomas and Lydia. The simple inscription on his headstone stands in mute testimony of their grief:

> In Memory of
> Jonathan Nellson
> The only Son of
> Mr. Thomas Nellson
> And Mrs. Lydia his
> Wife who died
> Augst 19th 1778
> Aged 17 years 11
> months & 22 days.

"Jonathan Nellson, The only Son." They laid him next to his grandfather, who had lived such a long, full life. This loss was almost unbearable. Thomas could not, perhaps no longer even wanted, to manage his small farm and shop alone. A practical solution was found. The month after Jonathan's funeral, his sister, Lydia, now twenty, married her sweetheart, Samuel Hastings, Jr., in the Lexington church.

The Hastings were an old and patriotic Lexington family. Both Samuel and his father were among the little group of minutemen who had faced the British regulars on the Lexington Green. By the time of his marriage Samuel had endured further military adventures. In December 1775 he enlisted for a year in the new Continental Army and was selected to serve as a life guard to the colorful and arrogant General Charles Lee. A year later, when his enlistment was nearly over, news reached Lexington that he was reported "taken." Both Samuel and Lee were captured by the British at Long Island. During that scuffle Samuel was slashed in the neck by an officer's sword. As he told the tale, "His queue saved his life," breaking the force of the blow. A useful pigtail indeed. He was later paroled and returned home, but the following May did a short tour of duty at Ticonderoga to reinforce the Continental Army there.

Now safely home again, Samuel came to live with his bride in her father's modest home. It was a sad beginning to a marriage. Samuel would take over the farm, and their children would inherit it.

But death was not yet done with the Nelsons that year. On October 15 Tabitha Nelson died. Tabitha was fifty-seven and living in the small home she had shared with her elderly parents. How full the Nelson burial plot was becoming. In time Tabitha's little house would be hoisted on sledges and moved next to Thomas's. The two structures would be fastened together to make one somewhat more spacious, if odd-looking dwelling. The kindly spinster owned little else, one cow, a woodlot and small, upland meadow, a house filled with the meager bits and pieces that her parents had not bequeathed to her brothers. Again Peter was away. His enlistment would not be up until February. No chance to say good-bye to Tabitha. No opportunity even to pay his last respects. Just more sadness and loss.

On a happier note, and one was badly needed that fall, the efforts to free Oliver Reed and other captives imprisoned in Halifax finally bore fruit. On October 8 the "silver Eel" set sail for Boston with prisoners to be exchanged for British soldiers. Along with Oliver Reed, Billy Smith was returning home, doubtless to mixed emotions from his family. Perhaps imprisonment would have transformed the prodigal son. They could always hope.

One other event with more significance than Peter could then suspect occurred late that summer. Since the Declaration of Independence had been proclaimed, Massachusetts had been wrestling with the necessity of drafting a constitution by which the state would govern itself, now that its royal charter was defunct. Concord and other towns had been calling since September 1776 for a special elected convention to draft such a document. The state legislature together with the council insisted on taking on the job. At last, in 1778, a constitution was completed and submitted to the people with the promise that once two-thirds of the towns had given their consent it would become the framework of state government. Chief among its flaws as far as the state's slaves were concerned was its specific recognition of slavery. So much for the pleas of the African Americans of Massachusetts to that legislature to eliminate their bondage! But during the summer, by a margin of six to one, the towns of Massachusetts overwhelmingly rejected the proposed constitution. In addition to condoning slavery, many people were upset that the document had no bill of rights and no careful separation of powers. Theophilus Parsons, one of its most active opponents, insisted that a state of nature was preferable to the legislature's proposed constitution. On August 26 eighteen towns met at Pittsfield, in the far northwestern corner of the state, to demand that if a special constitutional convention was not called to draft a new document, they would join another state. It was uncertain what a new constitution might say about slavery, but at least one that clearly condoned slavery had been defeated.

Peter and his regiment were discharged at Watertown, Massachusetts, on February 24 after a service this time of eight months, twenty-one days, including eleven days to travel the 220 miles home. In contrast to the long, hazy June days, when he and his company set out for New York, it was a gloomy and bitterly cold time of year to be trudging home. February was always the worst month in Massachusetts, deep midwinter weather and spring too far in the future to revive the spirits. The winter had been relatively mild, but the journey back, struggling through the wind and snow without adequate food, shelter, or warm clothing, was a trial even for a sturdy adolescent. The camaraderie of fellow sufferers kept the spirits up. But where the other men looked forward to returning to their families, Peter was ambivalent. In addition to the starkly different household that awaited him, there was the loss of Jonathan and Tabitha to come to terms with. These absences would be impossible to forget once he was back.

On February 8, before Peter reached Lincoln, Millicent gave birth again. This time it was a girl. She and Josiah named their little daughter Elizabeth. It was generous of Millicent to honor Josiah's late wife. Later that month Peter, Elizabeth's only child if he could be called that, her stepchild, her "servant for life," returned home to a house fuller than ever before, but one that seemed sadder and oddly emptier and that had little place for him.

CHAPTER FOURTEEN

An Eye for an Eye

But if any harm follow, then thou shalt give life for life, eye for eye, tooth for tooth, hand for hand, foot for foot, burning for burning, wound for wound, stripe for stripe. And if a man smite the eye of his servant, or the eye of his maid, and destroy it; he shall let him go free for his eye's sake. And if he smite out his man-servant's tooth, or his maid-servant's tooth, he shall let him go free for his tooth's sake.

EXODUS 21:23–27

BEFORE THE WAR, little attention was paid to Sandy Hook, a crooked finger of land twelve miles long and barely half a mile wide, pointing from the Jersey shore toward New York City. It was not good farmland, but it was a beautiful place with that lonely windswept beauty of the seaside. In spring the dunes were covered with white plum blossoms and fragrant with sea lavender and bayberry. The sandy soil in its midsection was alive with holly and cedar trees, and by fall the plum blossoms had ripened into juicy purple fruit. The location, on one of the great avian migration routes, kept its skies crowded with raucous seabirds and thousands of other winged travelers. In 1764 an octagonal lighthouse was built at its tip to guide ships safely away from its shallows out into New York harbor. That proximity to New York would give it an unexpected importance.

It remained a desolate spot until June 1776, when fleet after fleet of British warships suddenly loomed off the Hook on their way to Staten Island and New York. Once their presence was known hundreds of New Jersey's Loyalist families rushed to Sandy Hook to place themselves under British protection. Like New York City the Hook would be held by the British for the remainder of the war. Dunes were dug up and fortifications built. A ramshackle community, aptly named Refugee Town, sprang up to house refugees and slaves on

the run. From that convenient spot near Colonel Tye's old home of Shrewsbury, he and his men ventured out to raid his native county of Monmouth.

After the British army extricated itself from the Battle of Monmouth and
finally reached the safety of New York City, Colonel Tye and his black and
white refugee troop returned to their mission of plundering New Jersey villages and farms for food, cattle and enemy prisoners. The thousands of British soldiers bivouacked in and around New York were always in need of
supplies. Night after night that summer Tye led his men along the back roads
he knew so well to revenge himself on patriots and slave-owners. His men's
exploits had already made them infamous and now their fame and Tye's
soared.

By 1779 the war in the so-called neutral grounds of New Jersey had
become increasingly brutal. Although Massachusetts had begun the war, it
now sent Jupiter and Peter and its other men and boys off to fight elsewhere.
New Jersey was often their destination. Indeed, it had more engagements
than any other state during the war. Both armies spent months garrisoned
there, fought major battles on its soil, and went marching back and forth
across its rich farmland and through its tidy villages, buying or plundering as
they went. Residents were understandably angry and afraid. The suffering
endured by the supporters of each side sharpened already pointed differences.
As one army or another took possession of an area, there were confiscations of
land and even murders. Raiding parties such as Tye's repeatedly swooped
down from Sandy Hook or New York to plunder and burn the homes of
patriots who, in their turn, confiscated and sold the property of local Loyalists. In a low moment, desperate New Jersey patriots passed a law authorizing
summary executions of Loyalists. Several were hanged. Washington found
the state often unfriendly. The militiamen were reluctant to turn out at his
request. Many members remained sullenly at home unsure whether it was
wiser to remain neutral or to guess which side might win and join it.

Adding to this turmoil and mayhem that summer of 1779 the countryside
between New Jersey and the New York border was filled with slaves on the
run. On June 30 General Clinton, improving on Lord Dunmore's tactic of
enticing slaves to his army, issued a proclamation offering refuge to "every
NEGRO who shall desert the Rebel Standard" and promising black fugitives
that while they were in territory under the Crown's control, they could "fol-

low . . . any occupation which . . . [they] shall think proper." There was no need to serve in the British army; they could be truly free, at least for the duration of the war. The offer was limited to the slaves of rebels or those fighting in rebel ranks and said nothing of their fate after the end of hostilities. But slaves in New Jersey and neighboring states were willing to take a chance. Anyway, who was to know the political preferences of their masters or where they came from? Hundreds of enslaved men and women, sometimes with children, followed Tye's example and slipped away, bound for New York and the safety of British lines. A military census that year recorded more than twelve hundred blacks living in New York, many of them escapees, and that number would continue to increase.

The flights of slaves were always acts of desperation. In December 1777 a Baltimore newspaper described the escape from one plantation of fifteen men, two women, and four children who broke into their master's barn, stole his boat, and sailed to safety. Others were less fortunate. Boston King, one of the successful escapees, remembered seeing a New Jersey slave who had been caught just twelve miles from his master's home in Brunswick. In the time-honored English manner, the man was led back to Brunswick tied to the tail of a horse. Once there, his hands and feet were locked in the Brunswick village stocks. Much as King deplored this punishment, it was mild compared to those meted out to captured slaves in the South. Four South Carolina slaves who escaped in 1776 and seized a schooner anchored on the Potomac were captured when the crew disobeyed orders and sailed the ship to Maryland. Two of the men, Charles and Kitt, were sentenced to hang; a third, Harry, received thirty lashes on his back. King's own escape from New Jersey to New York had been harrowing. "As I was at prayer one evening," he recalled,

I thought the Lord Heard Me, and would Mercifully deliver me. Therefore putting my confidence in him, about one o'clock in the morning, I went down to the river side and found the guards were either asleep or in the tavern. I instantly entered the water, but when I was a little distance from the opposite shore, I heard the sentinels disputing among themselves. One said, I am sure I saw a man cross the river. Another replied, there is no such thing. When I got a little distance from the shore I got down on my knees and thanked God for this deliverance. I traveled until five o'clock in the morning and then concealed myself until seven o-clock at night, when I proceeded forward thro' brushes and marshes for fear of being discovered. When I came to the river, opposite Staten Island, I found a boat, and although it was near a whale-boat, I ventured into it and cutting the rope, I got safe over. The commanding officer, when informed of my case, gave me a passport and I proceeded to New York.

No wonder Clinton's proclamation and its offer of refuge raised racial tensions to fever pitch in New Jersey and New York. While most slaves were more eager for freedom than revenge, the people of Elizabethtown and other communities were terrified the slaves would rise up and massacre them and their children. Patriots had confiscated the property and slaves of many of their Loyalist neighbors. All were itching for revenge.

Tye and his troop added to the general terror. Their mission now was not only to help supply the British army but to join with local Loyalist Jon Moody and a troop of Queen's Rangers to launch retaliatory raids against Monmouth's patriots, especially their leaders. This was more dangerous and deadly work than raids on farmhouses. In July Tye and Moody led a carefully planned offensive on the town of Shrewsbury. Without warning they swept into the little community, bursting into its homes and barns. They seized nearly eighty head of cattle along with about twenty horses, clothing, and even furniture. The harvest was poor that year and these food stuffs were badly needed to feed the troops based in New York. Shrewsbury was of special interest to Tye. John Corlies lived there and whatever Corlies's personal politics, his home was surely one Tye would take pleasure in targeting. A year earlier when Corlies had still not freed his remaining slaves, the disgusted members of the Friends Congregation ejected him from their midst. Tye and his men had the opportunity to see that those bondsmen made their escape. They also kidnapped two residents, William Brindley and Elisha Cook, before setting off to Staten Island with their booty. Tye and his men were handsomely rewarded for these raids and returned in triumph to Refugee Town although sometimes, when hotly pursued, they first spent an uncomfortable night hiding in the swamps. The successful Shrewsbury raid became the model for other attacks.

The *New Jersey Gazette* and other newspapers kept track of the exploits of the runaway slave and his men. At first Tye was reported to be less brutal than other refugee leaders. This was surprising considering how brutally he himself had been treated. Despite his reputation for relative moderation, though, Colonel Tye was feared and rightly so. By March 1779, as the weather became more hospitable for rapid forays, he and his men seemed to be everywhere. They captured Captain Warner, who managed to purchase his freedom, but two other captured militia officers, Captain James Green and Ensign John Morris, were brought back to Refugee Town. They were eventually imprisoned in New York's Sugar House. When their captives were guilty of crimes against the British, Tye and his men were less lenient. John Russell had been involved in the poorly planned raids on the British at Staten Island. Tye and his men plundered and then burnt Russell's home, killing Russell and wounding his young son. Three weeks later they captured Matthias Halsted, plundering his house situated near Newark.

In June Tye's activities increased and grew harsher and more daring. He carried out three raids against the county militia leaders in a single week. On June 9 Tye and his men attacked the home of Joseph Murray at Colts Neck. Murray had been responsible for several summary executions of Loyalists. Now Tye's troop repaid him in kind. Three days later they attacked the home of the leader of the Monmouth County militia, Barnes Smock. Smock fired off a cannon to summon his men. They came running. This was no plundering raid on hapless families. A pitched battle broke out between Tye's men and Smock's. Amazingly since the fight was on Smock's home ground, it ended in a complete triumph for the refugees. They managed to take Smock and twelve of his men prisoner, carefully destroying the militia cannon before leading their prisoners off to Refugee Town. The *New Jersey Gazette* reported the incident: "Ty, with his party of about twenty blacks and whites, last Friday afternoon took and carried off prisoners Capt. Barns Smock and Gilbert VanMarter, at the same time spiked up the iron four-pounder at Capt. Smock's house, but took no ammunition. Two of the artillery horses, and two of Capt. Smock's horses, were likewise taken off." The newspaper added, "The above mentioned Ty is a negro, who bears the title of Colonel, and commands a motley crew at Sandy Hook." The county's patriots, at their wit's end, called on Governor Livingston for assistance. His response was to proclaim martial law for Monmouth County. It did little good. On June 22 the *New York Journal* reported another raid: "Yesterday morning a party of the enemy, consisting of Ty with 30 blacks, 36 Queen's Rangers, and 30 refugee tories, landed at Conascong. They by some means got in between our scouts undiscovered, and went up to Mr. James Mott, Second Major of the Second Regt of Monmouth Militia, plundered his and several of the neighbors houses of almost everything in them; and carried off the following persons, viz. Mr. James Mott, sen. Jonathan Pearse, Capt. James Johnson and 6 privates—Joseph Dorset, William Blair, James Walling, jun. John Walling, son of Thomas, Philip Walling, James Wall, Matthew Griggs, also several negroes, and a great deal of stock."

But the militia was hot on their trail. The reporter concluded on a more upbeat note, "all the negroes, one excepted, and the horses, horned cattle and sheep, were, I believe, retaken."

Tye's luck was running out. All his brilliant leadership and cunning could not save him on that final raid. That September Tye and his men joined the Queen's Rangers in an attack on Captain Josiah Huddy. The British were especially eager to capture Huddy because of his repeated raids on British positions on Staten Island and Sandy Hook. Furthermore Huddy, like Joseph Murray, had summarily executed captured Loyalists. Until now he had always managed to elude the British.

Tye and his men surprised Huddy at home alone with a female friend, Lucretia Emmons. In a battle worthy of a cowboy film these two kept Tye's troop at bay for two hours. To trick his assailants into believing they were fighting a group of men, Huddy dashed from window to window of his house, firing muskets from one after another while Lucretia Emmons reloaded his guns. In exasperation Tye ordered the house set on fire. Huddy surrendered. But as Tye and his troopers were escaping by boat they were waylaid by the militia. In the confusion Huddy managed to jump overboard and swim to shore, shouting, "I am Huddy," to make sure his rescuers didn't shoot at him.

While Huddy got away, Tye did not. The raid was to be his last. During the fighting at Huddy's house, Tye was shot in the wrist. It was a superficial wound, but several days later, lockjaw set in. Without any effective medical treatment, it proved fatal; his personal war was over. He was just twenty-six.

The slave, Titus, had died a free man, the feared and admired Colonel Tye. He didn't live to enjoy the simple pleasures of freedom, owning his own land and raising a family. But he had managed to free many other men and women and inspired hundreds of others. Did he think much about those blacks, free and slave, who fought against him? Probably not, although later patriots are said to have wished that Tye had fought on their side. He may have considered black patriots foolish or naive, wondering how they could sympathize with men who championed liberty for themselves and kept others enslaved. On the other hand, he may have felt that black men and women should take advantage of any opportunity they had to gain their freedom. In his case and that of most slaves in New Jersey and farther south, there was no alternative to accepting the British offer. Yet Tye knew the British army usually put the runaways to work digging roads and building fortifications, or as servants for British officers. Dunmore had given him the chance he promised, but the Virginia governor would later sell other blacks into slavery in the Bahamas. Tye was fortunate to serve as a soldier, with dignity.

Josiah Huddy's story was not over. Two years after his escape from Tye, the British succeeded in capturing him. They shut him up on one of their notorious prison ships. The situation was miserable but if he managed to remain healthy he could look forward to a prisoner exchange at the end of the war and the war was nearly over. But that exchange never happened. According to the British version of the story some New Jersey Loyalists tricked the British into releasing Huddy into their custody. However they managed to get Huddy, it is clear he was hastily rowed to the shore of Monmouth County and there summarily hanged. Tye would have been pleased to know that a black man was his executioner.

The Americans were incensed that Huddy, a prisoner of war, was ordered to be hanged without even the form of a trial. They pointed out that he was taken to the Jersey shore not by Loyalists but by refugees under the command of a Captain Lippincot. After being hanged a note was fastened to his breast: "We the refugees, having with grief long beheld the cruel murders of our brethren, and finding nothing but such measures daily carrying into execution —we, therefore, determine not to suffer without taking vengeance for the numerous cruelties; and thus begin, and, I say, may those lose their liberty who do not follow on, and have made use of Captain Huddy as the first object to present to your view; and further determine to hang man for man while there is a refugee existing. *Up goes Huddy for Philip White.*"

The refugees apparently believed Huddy had imprisoned their comrade White and viciously broken both his legs then bid him run. But whatever else Huddy may have done, according to Dr. James Thacher, he was in prison when White was captured then struck down and killed while trying to escape.

The ruse to snatch Huddy and the hanging took place while peace negotiations were underway in Paris, where the incident provoked great outrage. Washington demanded the murderer be handed over for trial. When Clinton refused Washington ordered his British prisoners of similar rank to Huddy to choose lots, the loser to be hanged. The lot fell to Captain Charles Asgill of the British guards, only son of a noble English family and just nineteen years old. Back in England young Asgill's father was dying and his distraught mother pleaded with the British king and then the French king to intervene on her son's behalf. A pledge of safety he had been given when he surrendered along with his mother's pleading saved the young man's life.

But all this was in the future. After Tye's death Colonel Stephen Bleuke, one of the Black Pioneers, became leader of the refugee raiders. Their mission continued. Bleuke and others survived to see the British promise of peace and freedom that Tye would never know. But they also learned that even freedom could be disappointing. Despite their contributions to the British cause they were often treated badly. Most black refugees taken to Canada, unlike white Loyalists, received no land. The few who did get land got poorer, smaller, more remote parcels than the land given whites. The blacks were often scorned by the white population in Nova Scotia and those who made the trip across the ocean to Great Britain were shunned in London as well. In the end some returned to their ancestral continent as pioneers and planters to help establish the British colony of Sierra Leone. "The Year of Jubilee is come," Black Loyalists had sung triumphantly, "Return ye Ransomed Sinners Home." Freedom came, but not home.

CHAPTER FIFTEEN

Free at Last

How hard is the soldier's lott who's least danger is in the field of action?
Fighting happens seldom, but fatigue, hunger, cold & heat are constantly
varying his distress.
  SURGEON JABEZ CAMPFIELD, Spencer's Additional Regiment,
  August 4, 1779

P ETER SPENT THE REST of that year at home, trying to blend
back into life in Lincoln. It was difficult to switch from the hardships,
excitement, and camaraderie of military service to the different sort of
hardships in Lincoln. And of course life at home continued to change, and he
was changing with it. Peter was sixteen. The teenage years are always difficult.
Farmers' sons could at least anticipate coming of age, however they might
resent the years before having their own farms and families. But the anxiety
and restlessness is worse when you can't clearly see a happy future for yourself.
Sometimes the world seems open to options, yet at other times it seems to
close in tightly, binding one permanently into a narrow, insignificant role. For
Peter that role was one of a tolerated outsider, a servant for life. Jonathan was
gone, and other childhood friends such as Mary, Abigail, and little Sally
Thorning and their older brothers John and William were no longer playmates. The racial difference and their starkly different destinies intruded. Any
semblance of equality had vanished and with it the comfortable friendships
they had shared. Parents, particularly the parents of girls, were no longer
pleased at the easy familiarity as their children matured. Massachusetts had
strict laws against sexual relations between blacks and whites, and mixed
marriages were prohibited. Both men and women engaging in such relation-
ships were severely punished. A black man, slave or free, would be sold out of
the province, usually to a horrendous fate in the West Indies. Sundays ce-

mented that change in Peter's life, as Josiah and his growing family, with the rest of the Nelsons, settled themselves onto the Lexington church's hard wooden benches on the main floor while Peter clambered up the two flights of stairs to the Negro gallery. He was separated in the community and even before God.

The Nelson family farms, once so bereft of children, began to fill with a new generation. Next door, Thomas and Lydia were distracted from their grief over Jonathan's death by the energy and excitement that young Lydia and Samuel brought to the task of taking over their farm. By midyear a grandchild was expected, the first of ten children who would fill their grand-parents' little house to overflowing with noise, tears, and excitement. And while Thomas's house was filling with grandchildren, Josiah's house was filling with his own children. Late in the year Millicent became pregnant with her third child. Not much room for Peter. From anxiety about the absence of heirs, Josiah now had the problem more familiar to his neighbors of trying to make ends meet and struggling to keep a growing family clothed and fed. It was late in life to learn that lesson, late to adjust to a noisy and hectic home. But he loved his wife and his growing family and seemed to thrive.

Until Josiah's children were older, they added to the burden of work. Like Peter when he entered Josiah's home as a toddler, it would be years before little Josiah and baby Elizabeth were more help than hindrance. On the other hand, now that Peter was a strapping teenager he was a true asset and was desperately needed to work alongside Josiah on the farm. But Peter had been raised with hopes—perhaps vain ones—of a better future than a lifetime of heavy labor as the family slave. Perhaps if Elizabeth had lived, it might have been different. If there had ever been a chance Josiah might have bequeathed him part of his land or treated him in any way as a son, with the arrival of Millicent's first baby that chance was gone. The possibility remained that Josiah might be persuaded to emancipate him. For the present it was as well for the family that he remained home until the very last day of that year, when the harvest had long since been taken in. Slaves like his father had agreed to service in the Continental Army for three years to earn their freedom. Peter couldn't make that commitment and have that opportunity. At first he was too young. Now he was of age, but Josiah needed to agree. When he enlisted for yet another six months that December of 1779, however, it would be under a new surname, a sign he had been emancipated.

The Nelsons were not the only family whose homes had tiny additions arriving or expected. Down the road to the west another baby arrived in the

Smith household. Captain William Smith, the erstwhile privateer back from imprisonment, became a farmer and a new father yet again. On August 22 Charles Salmon Smith was baptized in the Lincoln church. But additional children were no way to keep that restless spirit at home—quite the opposite. A month before his little son was baptized, William was off again, marching west to Springfield for a six-month enlistment in the Continental Army. Apparently he was no longer interested in marine service. Nor this time did he insist on a field officer's rank. It was the last time he would live with his family. Of course, no one knew that yet. They could only speculate. Even before this latest departure, his behavior was disgraceful in the eyes of his father, mother, and sisters, as well as of that God-fearing and family-centered community in which he had lived. In all respects Smith was irresponsible, unable or uninterested in staying out of debt, always on the lookout for the main chance, the higher military commission, a get-rich-quick scheme. He was unsteady, constitutionally incapable of accepting his role as the father of a growing and otherwise respectable family. Once more the long-suffering Catherine Louisa was left to care for her now larger family and substantial farm, an example to all that even the well-to-do had their crosses to bear.

The clock was ticking for Peter's father, Jupiter. Two more years of military service and he would be a free man. The danger of injury, illness, and death was ever present, though. Two years was a long time, and it was best not to look ahead but to take each day as it came. To members of the Continental Congress, the importance to their army and to their cause of men such as Jupiter now seemed clear. In March they recommended that if the legislators of South Carolina and Georgia thought it expedient, they could take immediate measures for raising three thousand "able-bodied Negroes." As an incentive, all "able-bodied Negroes" who would "well and faithfully serve as a soldier to the end of the present war, and shall then return his arms," were promised emancipation and fifty dollars in cash.

There was little time to be lost in recruiting and training these men. The British were eager to capture strongholds in the South and with local Loyalist support build a base from which to attack and subdue the mid-Atlantic and northern states. In November 1778, 3,500 British troops had sailed from New York on that mission. They captured Savannah, Georgia, and with the aid of local supporters returned that state to royal rule. South Carolina was likely to be next. But despite the threat of British attacks, particularly on the port of Charleston, the South Carolina government refused to arm slaves. The ratio of blacks to whites in South Carolina was three to two. That fact ended the argument. The danger of an armed slave insurrection seemed far worse than a British triumph. Some slaves did enlist in the patriot cause as substitutes for their owners, but the official practice in South Carolina was to encourage whites to enlist by promising them a bounty of slaves. Serving as an officer for three years would earn a volunteer three slaves. Three months after southern patriots were asked, and refused, to arm slaves, General Clinton issued the Phillipsburg Proclamation offering refuge and freedom to slaves who deserted the patriot cause or fled from Whig masters.

Happily for Jupiter and the rest of the army, the winter of 1778 to 1779 was mild, at least compared to the record-setting fury of the winter that would follow. It was bitter enough in New England, however, to freeze Rhode Island's Narragansett Bay. Because Washington never knew where the British might attack next, that winter he scattered his troops from New Jersey north to Connecticut and Rhode Island. Jupiter and the Massachusetts Fifteenth passed the winter at Providence with the Rhode Island expedition. Jupiter was physically comfortable, which was important after the illnesses of the past, and relatively close to home. Being based in a city made wealthy by the notorious international slave trade, though, was decidedly uncomfortable.

Rhode Island's port city of Newport on Aquidneck Island had been under British control since December 1776, when a large British fleet entered the harbor followed by an army of seven thousand troops. There had been no real resistance. The site had great strategic value to the British. Newport was the only harbor in the northern states that could be entered by large vessels directly from the sea without having to wait for favorable winds. A garrison there also enabled the British to stop privateers using the bay to prey on British shipping, instead giving the British the opportunity to prey on American ships coming from Boston.

Rhode Island's government and many of its supporters had retreated to Providence, where the state's regiments, the militia of neighboring states, and those regiments of the Continental Army that Washington could spare were housed at the College of Rhode Island, today's Brown University. Militia from neighboring states arrived for three-month enlistments. Friends and acquaintances from Lincoln and Lexington occasionally appeared at the camp. General John Sullivan was in command. Even though the British were unable or maybe uninterested in expanding their territory in the area, their presence was a fearful reminder of that danger. From their base in Newport they raided towns on the mainland, seizing badly needed supplies and sometimes burning houses. In return, the American militia kept up their harassment of the Newport garrison, lobbing cannonballs into it and sending raiding parties to Aquidneck Island. They had a spectacular success in a July raid when they captured the British garrison's commander, General Richard Prescott. He was then exchanged for General Charles Lee.

In 1778, a year before the arrival of Jupiter and the Massachusetts Fifteenth Regiment, Washington had launched a major attempt to drive the British out of Rhode Island with the aid of a large French fleet under the command of Count d'Estaing. D'Estaing was a soldier turned admiral born into one of the most distinguished French noble families. He had a reputation for being arrogant and petty, but he was also brave and ambitious. Whatever his personal qualities, he and his fleet were a godsend. In preparation for their joint assault Washington increased the contingent of soldiers in Rhode Island from about a thousand to ten thousand men and placed them under command of that doughty but luckless officer General John Sullivan. In July, with this army and the French fleet in place, the siege of Newport began. Sadly for Sullivan and his men, his luck ran true to form. D'Estaing disappointed Washington by his unwillingness to engage in a land battle, preferring to fight the British at sea. Sullivan advanced toward British lines, dug in, and began a cannon bombardment. A fierce storm arose as the naval battle took place. Admiral Howe then headed for New York to refit while d'Estaing put in at Newport just long enough to tell Sullivan he was heading for Boston to refit as well. News of the French withdrawal from the battle quickly reached Boston. When, shortly afterward, the French fleet appeared for refitting, it was greeted by angry crowds. Then on November 4, rather than returning to the siege, the French fleet sailed for Martinique to protect their nation's valuable Caribbean colonies.

Sullivan was waiting impatiently in Rhode Island for d'Estaing's ships to return as the men of his militia began to slip off home, when the grim news reached him: the French would not return, but British reinforcements were on the way to relieve the siege of Newport. Sullivan was furious and sent d'Estaing a letter branding his behavior "derogatory to the honor of France." Without French help Sullivan was forced to withdraw. But the British pursued the Americans as they retreated and the Battle of Rhode Island began.

Jupiter would have heard all about it, especially the part played by Rhode Island's all-black regiment, some 130 men. It was the first time an all-black troop had taken the field for the patriot side. Sullivan's men retreated north, pounded by British cannon as they went. They gave as good as they got. American cannon opened fire on the British fleet. The two armies closed, and Sullivan's black troops fought hand to hand with the Hessians. The American line withstood two attacks by the Hessians, held, and then pushed the Hessians back. Sullivan's men triumphed without French aid. They were unable to pursue the British and press their advantage, though, having had no rest for a day and a half. Instead, as so often happened, under cover of darkness the next evening they withdrew to the mainland. It had been a fierce fight. Lafayette dubbed the battle "the best fought action of the war." Congress thanked Sullivan for his efforts, but he had failed to dislodge the British from Newport.

Congress was just as furious as Sullivan about the French withdrawal. It took all Washington's tact to smooth relations between the two peoples. The patriots needed to understand that the French had other interests. This was now a world war. Annoying as it seemed just then, the global battlefield soon proved an immeasurable benefit. The British had colonies and bases around the globe to protect. Parliament would spend much of the next year criticizing the tactics being used in the war in North America and worried sick about the French threat to dispatch a fleet of sixty-six ships of the line into the English Channel to invade Britain. To repel the sixty-six-strong French war fleet the Royal Navy could muster only thirty-five ships. The French alliance, however tricky, was crucial to American success. So in September, tongue in cheek, Congress passed a resolution thanking d'Estaing for his efforts and praising his bravery and zeal. And Jupiter and his regiment spent the winter of 1778 to 1779 with Sullivan and his men keeping watch on the British garrison still ensconced at Newport.

Although the encampment was short of flour and forage for the horses, it was Jupiter's best winter of the war. For once it was the British, not the Americans, who suffered more. The men in the besieged Newport garrison nearly starved when the ships carrying their provisions from New York were several weeks late in arriving. They even had difficulty getting enough fuel to keep warm. In their desperate search for wood, they tore down houses and cut up old ships. The once prosperous town was looking more and more wretched.

Warmer weather eventually returned, and with it the armies were back on the move. In May the Rhode Island commander, John Sullivan, set off for the Pennsylvania frontier to lead an expedition against British rangers and their Iroquois allies. As Sullivan headed south and west General Clinton left New York City, moving north up the Hudson with six thousand men, seventy ships, and 150 boats. His aim was to lure Washington's troops north, then turn south to attack New Jersey and Pennsylvania. It worked. Washington moved his army toward the Hudson. Jupiter and the Massachusetts Fifteenth Regiment were sent to New York to assist. Clinton's first target was Stony Point, and he got there first.

Stony Point was a sheer, rocky peak looming 150 feet above the Hudson River and jutting out into it for half a mile. The river was less than a thousand yards across at that point, so it was the ideal spot to control river traffic. The Point was situated at the southern entrance to the Hudson Highlands and guarded by a small American garrison. The troops stationed there were matched by Captain Thomas Armstrong's seventy North Carolinians on the opposite bank holding Fort Lafayette on Verplanck's Point. By June 1 Clinton's men had captured King's Ferry on the northern side of Stony Point. Faced with the powerful British army and fleet, the American troops abandoned Stony Point. The British then quickly took possession of Fort Lafayette. Although there had been no bloodshed, it was a costly loss for the Americans. With the enemy in control of both banks of the Hudson, supplies had to be diverted to a crossing further north, necessitating an additional thirty miles of hauling over rough country roads.

The British speedily set to work to strengthen the fortifications along both banks, cutting down trees to give them a better view of any ships below, digging earthworks, and placing fifteen cannon at Stony Point. The ship *Vulture* was left to guard the position, and pickets patrolled the shore below. The fort seemed impregnable.

The garrison was a threat. Washington wanted it gone and planned the attack himself. Spies were dispatched. An American officer, dressed as a local, visited the fort and reported that the British defenses were still incomplete.

Washington chose a special group of light infantry led by Anthony Wayne to seize the fort, but first he sent additional scouting parties to examine the terrain. Pompey, a slave serving with the American army, is said to have infiltrated the British lines and obtained the password. Washington got close enough himself to have a look through a spyglass. Satisfied, he ordered the attack.

On July 16 Wayne led his men on a sudden fourteen-mile march. It was a moonless night. To keep their movements a surprise, every dog within three miles of Stony Point was taken and civilians they met were detained. No muskets were to be used, since an accidental firing would alert the garrison. Just after midnight, Wayne and his men attacked. The British troops were taken off guard in the dark. Within thirty minutes it was over. The capture of Stony Point was a triumph and lifted American spirits. For General Clinton it was "a very great affront," truly "mortifying."

Jupiter and his regiment were not part of Wayne's elite troop that captured the fort, but they shared the triumph. Such moments were rare, especially when they occurred with few casualties. Washington ordered the supplies removed and the fort at Stony Point destroyed. Jupiter and the rest of the force set to work to clear the site. It was a happy duty. Regrettably, Washington had no men to spare to garrison Stony Point, and a day after the Americans left, the British reoccupied it and rebuilt the fortifications. But there was joy in Congress nevertheless for a brilliant military exploit. Wayne was awarded a gold medal. The stores captured were appraised at $158,640, and that amount was divided among Wayne's men who had made the initial assault.

Keeping watch in the Hudson Highlands even in summer had its trials. The nights were uncomfortably cold. Joseph Plumb Martin's Connecticut brigade arrived, like Jupiter's, just before the capture of Stony Point. Martin, with his sharp memory for the physical difficulties of military service, vividly recalled their hardships. They were, as ever, hungry and uncomfortable on their arrival, miserable even before being pummeled by a "smart shower of rain with thunder" followed by a brisk wind and cold. He was especially aggrieved that the wild weather had kept him from slipping off to steal a large cheese he had spotted in a farmer's yard. Instead, he had a miserable night. "We were all wet to the skin and had no tents with us, lying on the western side of a cleared hill," Martin recalled. "I never came nearer perishing with the cold in the middle of summer in all my life, before or since." Harsh conditions had already taken a toll on Jupiter's health. He was lucky not to fall prey to one of the deadly diseases that dogged their encampments.

After Stony Point the Continental troops based in New York were preoccupied with sporadic alarms and skirmishes. There was no memorable battle or great breakthrough. True, the British kept New England under threat that campaign season, hoping Washington would feel the need to maintain a large force in the area. British ships swept down on the Connecticut coast, attacking and burning the towns of New Haven, Fairfield, and Norwalk. In Norwalk alone eighty houses, eighty-seven barns, two churches, seventeen shops, and four mills went up in flames. All this was really a feint on Clinton's part. He was intent on carrying out a southern strategy, using his fleet to transport his armies south. To the relief of those New Englanders who were not part of the Continental Army, the war moved south. Happily, Jupiter's regiment stayed in New York.

In late fall Clinton pulled his troops from the Hudson Highlands, abandoning Stony Point and Verplanck's Point for the safety and comforts of New York City. The Continentals set to work again to demolish the deserted fortifications. They spent nearly two weeks at Verplanck "working and starving by day," Martin remembered, "and at night having to lie in the woods without tents. Some of our men got some peas which had been left there by the British, but one might as well have boiled gravel stones soft."

With such constant hardships in addition to the dangers of war, it is no wonder that there were desertions on both sides. During the war some 20 to 25 percent of the Continental Army and state militias left the ranks without permission. With home so close, it was tempting to slip away. Further, the men bitterly resented their shabby treatment, poor supplies, ragged clothing, and miserable conditions. Some sly, enterprising men merely abandoned one regiment to sign on to another and get a second enlistment bounty. Men deserted the British, too. British deserters were often welcomed by the Americans if they were willing to change sides. Those deserters the British caught, however, paid dearly. Recruit Schafer, who had deserted his Hessian regiment while Jupiter was in New York State that summer, was captured and sentenced to run the gauntlet thirty-six times two days in a row. Desertions during the coming winter were frequent but hazardous. Even hiding out was dangerous. A Hessian comrade noted in his diary the fate of Jan Kufner, both of whose feet froze while hiding in New York City. Gangrene had set in, and poor Kufner was slated for a double amputation. His recapture probably saved his life. Another Hessian, a drummer named Meyer, was sentenced to run a gauntlet of three hundred men sixteen times for merely planning to desert. Nevertheless, some Americans deserted to the British in the winter, picking their way across the Hudson when it was solidly frozen, while British troops slid across the same ice to desert to the American side. On the other hand, black soldiers on both sides rarely deserted, no matter how terrible the conditions. Where could they go, after all? Where would they be safer?

Jupiter endured the hardships and survived. On December 31 he had just one more year to go before his enlistment was up. He would be free. The regiment settled into West Point for another winter. Winter came early that year, with snows and cold worse than anyone could remember. But the gaunt and ragged men from Lincoln, Lexington, and neighboring towns did their best to keep warm in their barracks and dreamed of the day they would be trudging along the snow-choked roads on their way home. One more year.

As the tense year at home ended, everything seemed to happen with lightning speed for Peter. More men were desperately needed for the Continental Army. Enlistments were usually up at the end of December. Washington could not be left without troops. Next door Lydia's Samuel was called up in November to serve for a month in New York and then again for another three months, leaving Lydia and her parents deeply worried until he returned. But these were short enlistments, like Peter's earlier enlistments had been. Now Lincoln was assessed to find men for the Continental Army to serve for at least six months, longer if possible. Handsome bounties were promised. Lincoln farmers dug deep to come up with funds to lure recruits. The little town was on the search for men who could be spared and were willing to go. Peter was an obvious choice. He was just sixteen, but sixteen-year-olds were signing up for three-year enlistments. And Peter was already an experienced soldier. It was hard for Josiah to spare him, but harder for someone to be spared who had a wife and children. Peter's help at home would be missed, though probably not the restless, unhappy teenager himself. His bounty and army pay would not come amiss for the Nelsons. Jupiter and other slaves had been promised their freedom if they served for three years. Peter's short enlistments had never carried that promise. Until now he had been too young to be considered for a three-year enlistment. But this time, although he was only to serve six months, Peter's reward would be his freedom, the most precious reward of all. How grand it would be to be free and join Jupiter when his father's enlistment was up. Together they would somehow buy Peggy's freedom, maybe his sister Peggy's, too, and live as a family.

It isn't clear whether he insisted on his liberty—he was not well placed to do that—or whether Josiah or, more likely, Millicent urged that the young man be emancipated. In the emergency the usual emancipation bond would not need to be paid. In fact, on freeing him to serve, the Nelsons were entitled to Peter's bounty. Lincoln needed men, and local pressure on Josiah must have been intense. If Peter went, someone else could stay home. Josiah yielded. On December 31, 1779, Peter was duly enrolled in the Massachusetts Thirteenth Regiment to serve in the Continental Army for an initial term of six months. One more year of service and Jupiter would be a free man. Peter was leaving a free man, but a conscripted one.

The outward sign of Peter's freedom was his new name. In a clear indication of deep anger and dismay, he rejected the name of Nelson and enlisted as Peter Sharon. If Peter's feelings for the Nelsons, especially for Josiah, had been warm ones, he would have kept their name. Many former slaves did. Or he might have chosen Free, his father's new name. But although many former slaves took the name Freeman, "Free" may have seemed somehow tainted, always reminding everyone of a former slave status. Free white men did not use the surname Free.

The choice of the name Sharon was probably Peter's way of confirming his affection for that kindly black couple, Prince and Rose, and their sons, Prince, Silas, and Festus, who lived nearby, slaves of John Headley. All that year, as Peter's home life became increasingly unhappy, he naturally turned elsewhere for comfort and understanding. Jupiter was away, and perhaps Peter did not want to worry Peggy. Prince and Rose's sons, Prince, Silas, and Festus, were quite a bit older than Peter, but they were all part of the close-knit black community of Lincoln. The year 1779 was to be a momentous one for Prince and Rose. Their master, John Headley, and his wife, Mary, were apparently childless. A year after Mary Headley died, John Headley wrote a new will promising that after his death Prince and Rose would have their freedom along with a fund established for their support. The old couple would be able to remain in their home after their emancipation and "to Have ye Bed that they Commonly Lye upon & suitable Covering for ye Same."

In January 1779, when Prince had lived in John Headley's household for fifty years, his master died. Prince and Rose finally got their freedom. Their son Silas, like Jupiter, had enlisted in the Continental Army two years earlier to earn his freedom by fighting. In Silas's case he was recruited for the town of Leominster to the west. On enlisting he took the surname Sharon. Sadly, Silas Sharon never lived to enjoy his liberty. A little more than a year after Silas entered the army, the news reached Lincoln that he had died. Prince and Rose were free, and a Prince Sharon, almost certainly the senior Prince, appeared on the Lincoln rolls for the first time. Silas and Prince may have selected the name Sharon to honor their Rose, as the biblical "rose of Sharon." In choosing the name Sharon for himself, Peter was testifying to his affection for Rose and Prince and perhaps, in some way, making up for the loss of Silas by giving them another son.

Peter Sharon now set off "to the southward" to join Washington's Continental Army for what was to be the worst winter of a frigid century.

CHAPTER SIXTEEN

The Winter Soldier

The winter of 1779 and '80 was very severe; it has been denominated the
"hard winter," and hard it was to the army in particular, in more respects than
one. The period of the Revolution has repeatedly been styled "the times that
tried men's souls."

JOSEPH PLUMB MARTIN, *Ordinary Courage: The Revolutionary War
Adventures of Joseph Plumb Martin* (narrative published 1830)

THIS ENLISTMENT was different. All of Peter's former service had
been with local militia regiments, mostly neighbors, who marched off
for a few weeks of military duty and then returned with relief to
family and farming. It was arduous service, full of danger and discomfort, but
short. Now, he was to be a professional among professionals, a member of
Washington's Continental Army for six months, maybe longer if he reen-
listed. At sixteen, as far as the army was concerned, he was a man, and a free
man to boot. He would be living and fighting alongside battle-tested veterans, with the increased hardships and special camaraderie that meant. Would
he measure up?

Few men were willing to join the ranks in 1779, and it was little wonder.
"These are the times that try men's souls," Thomas Paine had written three
years earlier. If souls were tried in 1776, it was even truer now. The prognosis
for the patriot cause was bleak. Despite the French alliance, the struggle for
independence was at low ebb and often seemed hopeless, quixotic. Just a
ragtag army and fitful militia prevented the British from crushing the American upstarts. And there were other problems. That winter the paper money
the Continental Congress had been issuing with great abandon since 1775
suddenly lost its value. The currency still seemed sound when Peter signed on
and he, or rather Josiah, received his bounty. But within months a captain's
annual pay would buy only a pair of shoes, while an ordinary private's pay, on

the rare occasion when he got it, was virtually worthless. For Peter the fall of the currency was a disappointment, but for married men with wives and children to support, it was disastrous. There were serious repercussions in the decline, however, that did affect Peter and all the men. The fall in value made the soldier's living conditions, already desperate, more precarious still. Local farmers had plenty of food and other necessaries but were understandably unwilling to sell to an army that paid in worthless currency. With the collapse of paper money, the rift between civilians and soldiers widened. Civilians increasingly saw the soldiers as disreputable thieves. James Warren of Massachusetts branded the recruits as "the most undisciplined, profligate Crew that were ever collected" to fight a war. The appearance of the Continental Army's baggage train bound for the middle states was appalling and amusing even to the jaded eyes of Private Joseph Martin: "of all specimens of human beings, this group capped the whole," he remembered. "A caravan of wild beasts could bear no comparison with it." He found their dialect "as confused as their bodily appearance was odd and disgusting. There was Irish and Scotch brogue, murdered English, flat insipid Dutch, and some lingoes which would puzzle a philosopher to tell whether they belonged to this world or some 'undiscovered country.'"

However ragged, though, the soldiers demanded respect and were furious at the attitude of critical civilians. One New Jersey officer spoke for thousands of other soldiers who found it "truly mortifying" to see countrymen "sauntering in idleness and luxury" who "despise our poverty and laugh at our distress." Distress it was. All in all, not a good time to be a Continental soldier. That is why teenaged boys like Peter were needed.

At this desperate juncture, with civilians uncaring or downright hostile to the army, Paine's eloquent challenge boosted the men's morale. "The summer soldier and the sunshine patriot," he wrote, "will, in this crisis, shrink from the service of their country; but he that stands by it now, deserves the love and thanks of man and woman." How fine to be one of those who did not shrink from his country's service, who deserved the love and thanks of man and woman!

Peter's enlistment began at the usual time for Continental enlistments, the end of the year. It was a quiet time for military campaigning, but it was a miserable time to be marching anywhere in the Northeast, or the mid-Atlantic for that matter, especially that winter. Peter and his regiment trudged westward through fierce blizzards along the snow-choked roads of central Massachusetts and across Connecticut to New York's frosty and windswept Hudson Highlands. As usual, Washington was unsure where the British would strike next and divided his army that winter to be ready for any contingency. Of course, it was also easier on the local residents if the entire force was not based in one location. Washington camped with his main force at Morristown, New Jersey, where they were not far from the British army in New York City but were protected from sudden attack by the Jersey swamps and hills. To alert them of any British troop movement they had just completed a new alarm system: a network of poles eighteen to twenty feet high, each topped with a basket for a fire signal that stretched from an observation post near New York City all the way to Morristown. Washington and his chief officers moved into private homes in Morristown. The men were to be housed at nearby Jockey Hollow on Farmer Wick's land. The New England regiments were sent to their familiar posts in the Hudson Highlands to ensure control over the mighty river that linked New York City through Lake Champlain to Canada and New England to the rest of the colonies.

Both the Jockey Hollow and Hudson Highlands encampments shared a miserable winter. Fortunately, no one knew how miserable it would be. Snow began unusually early. There were four snowstorms in November, followed by seven in December, six in January, four more in February, and, just when spring seemed tantalizingly close, another six in March. For good measure, a final blast of snow fell in April. Men arriving at Morristown the first week in December knew that it was already unusually cold and snowy. Eventually some 10,800 soldiers, eight brigades, were camped on the hills at Jockey Hollow. Dr. James Thacher, arriving at Morristown in mid-December, found two feet of snow and the soldiers "actually barefoot and almost naked." "Our lodging last night," he wrote, "was on the frozen ground."

Peter's situation two weeks later was little better. On January 2 while Peter and his regiment were still on their march, a wild blizzard pummeled the New England and mid-Atlantic states. Four feet of snow fell. Gale-force winds sculpted it into fantastic drifts up to six feet deep, smoothing the sharp lines of houses and barns, reaching up doors and windows. The men struggled past maples and oaks with trunks plastered white by the fine, wind-whipped flakes, past white pines with branches drooping and splintering under heavy burdens of snow and birches bent clear to the ground.

"On the 3d instant," Dr. Thacher wrote from Jockey Hollow, "we experienced one of the most tremendous snow-storms ever remembered; no man could endure its violence many minutes without danger of his life." During the night several of the officers' marquees were torn and blown down, trapping their occupants. The officers had to be rescued. The morning after the storm hit, some of the soldiers were found in their tents "buried like sheep under the snow." Snow four to six feet deep covered the camp and prevented supplies from getting through to the men. The soldiers worked frantically, with frozen fingers, to complete the huts that would shelter them for the winter. Plans called for a village of more than a thousand huts in Jockey Hollow laid out in orderly fashion. Each hut was to be fourteen feet wide and fifteen or sixteen feet long with a fireplace in the middle of the back wall, a door in the front, and rows of wooden bunks for twelve men. In the men's hurry to finish the work, some huts were not that large. They also built cabins for their officers, each to house two to four men. When it was finished, the Jockey Hollow encampment was the sixth largest city in North America.

Conditions for Peter and his regiment camped at West Point in the Hudson Highlands were only marginally better. The weather was so bitter the Hudson River—tidal from New York all the way north to Albany—froze solid. Men on horseback could ride across it and even haul cannon over it. With enormous relief, the exhausted men of the Massachusetts Thirteenth Regiment finally reached their winter encampment. At least they didn't have to construct their own shelters; there were already barracks there. Joseph Martin had a short stay in these old barracks at year's end and found "there were rats enough, had they been men, to garrison 20 West Points." Still, it was shelter. Apart from this spartan housing, they found little comfort. Food, clothing, and supplies were scarce and at times completely lacking. They nearly starved to death that winter. Food could be gotten by plundering the local farmers, but plundering was understandably frowned on and often brutally punished. By spring some men in both camps would be reduced to eating bark, shoes, and leather belts.

Amazingly in these terrible conditions Peter, along with nearly all the Continentals, survived. Over the milder winter at Valley Forge in 1777–1778, a thousand men had died of sickness. But at Jockey Hollow only eighty-six of the thousands of soldiers bivouacked there died. And despite the miserable living conditions and hostility of the public, fewer men deserted than in the past. In 1777 there was a desertion rate of 42 percent for the New Jersey Continental line. By 1779 that had fallen to 10 percent. Mutual suffering created a strong bond. Peter was surrounded now by men who had enlisted hoping for a better life. For those who stuck it out, sharing hardships, living and fighting together, created real cohesion. Desertion was a betrayal of comrades. They became, as so many soldiers before and after them, a band of brothers. America would not have another such integrated army until the mid-twentieth century. An odd band it was, though, that Peter became part of. There were slaves earning their freedom and freedmen like himself, white farmers' sons not yet in possession of their inheritance, and men down on their luck. Some soldiers were escaping cranky wives or the law, others getting away from the humdrum predictability of life at home. It was a chance for adventure, to be a part of history. Some men, as in any army, were simply thugs. Maryland forced vagrants eighteen and older to serve for nine months, but Massachusetts never stooped to that level. At one point Washington admitted he believed most of his soldiers had enlisted for the bounty and that those joining out of principles were "no more than a drop in the Ocean."

The soldiers' behavior was as variable as their personalities and motivations. Some men prayed; others whiled away the tedious winter days gambling or drank to excess when drink was available. Some men had brought simple musical instruments with them and formed bands. They even put on the occasional concert. Others skilled at carpentry made furniture. The camp also had camp followers. A few wives, sometimes with children in tow, followed their husbands into the army and helped with washing and cooking. Tedium alternated with tension in winter quarters. One New Jersey captain confessed in exasperation: "I am tired of war and war affairs," of being cooped up in a garrison with "hoggs, Horses, cows . . . & squalling children." Peter was in such a garrison, exasperating but also interesting.

The main fortification in the Hudson Highlands was now at its northern end, at West Point. Peter had served further south, at Peekskill, where Forts Clinton and Montgomery seemed always to be changing hands between the Americans and the British, burned, rebuilt, burned again. Congress finally decided to fortify West Point instead. Years of delay and confusion about the best construction schemes followed until Congress sent a young Polish engineer, Thaddeus Kosciuszko, to take charge. It took him more than two years to complete the task. West Point itself was on a plain that towered over the river at an unusually narrow stretch where the Hudson made two right-angle bends, first west and then north. Sailing ships had to slow down to negotiate the turns and were especially vulnerable to attack. By the spring of 1778 Americans had succeeded in stretching a seventeen-hundred-foot-long iron chain across the river there. The chain itself was impressive. Each of its twelve hundred links weighed between 90 and 120 pounds, the whole weighing some sixty tons. It was attached to a series of logs that kept it at just the right depth to cripple enemy ships attempting passage. Fort Arnold, named for General Benedict Arnold, was built at the end of the West Point plain. The defenses represented the latest in military technology. Three concentric circles with batteries of cannon protected the fort from a land attack. A separate fortification, Fort Putnam, protected Fort Arnold. It had been constructed by the Fifth Massachusetts at the top of a five-hundred-foot hill and named for their colonel, Rufus Putnam. In contrast to the small garrisons at Forts Clinton and Montgomery Peter had been familiar with, Fort Putnam was manned by 420 soldiers. It was protected in its turn by Redoubt Number 4, atop a hill overlooking that fort. To the south West Point was protected by a second set of forts built by three Connecticut regiments. Additional redoubts were built on top of the hills to the southwest of West Point. All these fortifications guarded West Point and the chain strung across the Hudson. On the far side of the river there were more redoubts. This elaborate network was designed to permit cross firing and ensure American control of the river. Never had Peter seen, let alone been part of, such a large and sophisticated military encampment. It was impressive and exciting. Surely if any spot was impregnable, it was West Point.

During the quiet winter months Washington gave orders that the men were to be kept busy. It helped maintain their readiness, reinforced soldierly discipline, prevented boredom, and diverted attention from complaints. They drilled every day, even during snowstorms. They had guard duty and parade. There were occasional excursions to Connecticut to get provisions and sobering interruptions while they all watched men being punished for infractions. Those guilty of insubordination or drunkenness could receive a hundred lashes or more, less than British soldiers got for the offenses but bad enough. Bounty jumpers—men who abused the system by enlisting in a regiment to collect the bounty, then deserting and enlisting in another regiment to collect another bounty—were punished with death. A couple of years earlier a soldier who had collected seven bounties was finally caught, tried, and executed. There was much casual looting by men desperately hungry, but men who continually robbed civilians or who deserted could also be executed. Some offenders were forced to run the gauntlet instead. Groups of soldiers lined up to administer the punishment. In Morristown that winter a board of officers met in the Peter Dickerson Tavern to try Benedict Arnold for accusations of misconduct during his term as military governor of Philadelphia in 1778 after the British left. Arnold was acquitted of two charges but reprimanded by Washington for two others. Washington was careful to recognize Arnold's "distinguished services to his Country" before scolding him for conduct "peculiarly reprehensible, both in a civil and military view." Arnold had nursed resentment over the years for a lack of proper recognition of his stellar military contribution. He was already in secret contact with the British. Later that year as commander of West Point he would commit treason.

News from home was slow in reaching Peter. He was worried about Jupiter's health, which had been poor during his military service. As a free man Jupiter would have to find work to support himself. This meant staying healthy. No letters could be expected unless Jupiter and Peggy found someone to write for them. Peter needed to be constantly on the lookout for any new recruit or traveler from Lexington or someone from Jupiter's regiment, hoping they might be able to tell him how his parents were getting on. But that far from home, how many travelers were likely to have information about a slave woman and her husband? Anyhow this time of year few who didn't have to travel took to the roads. If there was no news, at least there was no bad news.

As for the Nelson families, good news eventually reached West Point. In midwinter, on February 20, Lydia and Samuel had their first child, Thomas's first grandchild, a daughter they named Lydia after her mother and grandmother. At the end of the coming summer Millicent would give birth to her third child. Little Josiah and Elizabeth would have a baby sister, Sarah. In the meantime there was great joy and excitement in the two Nelson households comparing and fretting over babies. Peter wondered where he would sleep if he returned to the house on the Concord Road when his six months' enlistment was up. But he was free now and need never return unless he chose to.

Peter was free, and God willing, Jupiter soon would be, but Peggy remained a slave as did many others in Massachusetts. There was a glimmer of hope, however, that this revolution might yet free them all. That spring, after months of debate, a new draft for a Massachusetts constitution was completed by a special convention sitting at the Old Meeting House in Cambridge. A committee had been chosen to draft the documents, and from this committee a subcommittee of three had been selected, James Bowdoin, Samuel Adams, and John Adams. John would draft the new documents. Peter knew little about its contents other than that, unlike the constitution so emphatically rejected two years earlier, Adams had included a Declaration of Rights. That declaration began with the rousing assertion, "All men are born free and equal." This, in addition to the fact that the new document did not condone slavery, was a hopeful sign. It remained to be seen whether this draft, when submitted to the towns for approval, would meet with a better fate than its predecessor. If ratified and if Adams's words meant what they seemed to mean, there was the possibility that slavery would end in Massachusetts. Of course, should the war be lost, the constitution would be meaningless. Britain would decide how Massachusetts would be governed and who would be free. Winning the war was what he turned his mind to.

The war had taken a new, ominous turn. In late December, while Peter and his regiment were struggling through the snow to West Point, the British general Clinton had set sail from New York City with 7,600 regulars bound for Charleston. There was wild weather at sea as well as on land, and a fierce storm scattered the fleet. The ships eventually reassembled and continued their journey. Charleston was protected by 3,000 Continentals and 2,500 local militia, all under the command of General Benjamin Lincoln. Lincoln understood his danger. Charleston had been a prize the British coveted, and he considered abandoning the city. It wouldn't have been the first time that strategy was used to preserve an American army. But community leaders, the same ones who refused to arm blacks, pleaded with him to defend their city. So Lincoln and his men stayed.

In early May Clinton's troops cut off Lincoln's line of retreat to the north. Then they struck Charleston. The men who insisted Lincoln and his troops remain to protect them now demanded he surrender to prevent damage to themselves and their city. At this juncture there was little alternative. On May 11 Charleston fell. This was the first time in the war that an American army surrendered. With Georgia and now South Carolina's great port firmly under British control, Clinton sailed triumphantly back to New York, leaving Charleston under the command of Charles, Lord Cornwallis.

While Clinton was on this expedition in the South he had left the remaining British and Hessian troops in New York under the command of General Wilhelm von Knyphausen. Knyphausen's junior officers were itching for action and kept pestering him to invade New Jersey. They pointed out, quite correctly, that Washington's army at Morristown was vulnerable, discontented, and poorly equipped. New Jersey also had large numbers of Loyalists eager to help any British force that appeared. There can be little doubt about the extreme exasperation of Washington's Continentals by the spring of 1780. In May the outrage of Joseph Martin and his long-suffering Connecticut regiment boiled over. They had been posted to Elizabethtown and Westfield for some time and returned to Basking Ridge and Jockey Hollow in mid-May hoping to have found better conditions. "We had entertained some hopes," Martin wrote, "that when we had left the lines and joined the main army, we should fare a little better." Instead they found "the old story of starving, as rife as ever." For several days each soldier was given a little musty bread and a little beef every other day but after that "nothing at all." Yet the public continued to expect the army, naked and starving, to do notable things. Martin explained that the men were patriotic and committed to the cause, but felt their choice was either to starve to death or "give all up, and go home. . . . We had borne as long as human nature could endure, and to bear longer we considered folly."

That evening on parade, the frustrated men of Martin's regiment snapped at their officers and refused to obey orders. When parade was over, all but one junior officer left. As that officer turned to leave, he called one of the grumbling men a "mutinous rascal," then stalked off. The "mutinous rascal" pounded the ground with the butt of his musket and called out, "Who will parade with me?" The entire regiment joined him. Another regiment parading nearby came, too. They had no plan of action other than to get other soldiers to join them. They didn't want a leader for fear that he would be singled out and punished. So, shouldering their weapons and with music playing, the mutineers marched off to seek the support of the other two regiments in their brigade. Word quickly spread, however, and the officers of those two regiments ordered their men to parade without their weapons. The officers then alternately cajoled and threatened their angry men and managed to surround them with men of the Pennsylvania line. Once the Pennsylvanians realized what was afoot, Martin writes, they declared, "Let us join them, let us join the Yankees; they are good fellows, and have no notion of lying here like fools and starving." Fearing that the Pennsylvanians might make common cause with the rebels, their officers quickly ordered them back to quarters. Eventually, after many promises of improvement, the would-be mutiny fizzled out. According to Martin, their provisions improved markedly afterward. The following year it would be the turn of the Pennsylvania line to mutiny. Whatever was happening in New Jersey about the miserable condition of the army, the Massachusetts line remained obedient.

The American army seemed ripe for overthrow. Knyphausen finally agreed to invade New Jersey. Clinton was a secretive man, even with his fellow generals, and Knyphausen had no notion what Clinton planned after his triumph at Charleston. He thought it likely Clinton would be marching north from South Carolina to invade Virginia. If so, an attack on the Continentals in New Jersey would be helpful, trapping them between British armies. Knyphausen set out from Staten Island with six thousand men. From Elizabeth's Point they marched toward the Short Hills and the Hobart Gap, just eleven miles from Morristown. Washington summoned the New Jersey militia to his aid. The Jersey militia had never been enthusiastic about the cause, but its men were prepared to protect their homes from invasion. They rushed in and tracked and harried the British vanguard as it marched along the road to Springfield. At the village of Connecticut Farms a fierce battle took place with house-to-house fighting between the two sides. Just as Knyphausen and his main force entered the village, a British soldier, seeing movement in a house window, fired, killing Mrs. Hannah Ogden Caldwell, mother of nine and the wife of the Reverend James Caldwell, the so-called High Priest of the Revolution. The British began systematically looting the houses in the village, then removed Mrs. Caldwell's body from her home before setting the dwelling on fire along with the other houses and the village church.

The sight of the burning village infuriated the Americans. The militia and troops stopped the British advance at the Rahway River Bridge, then crossed it to attack them. Instead of attracting allies, as Knyphausen had expected, he and his troops had enraged the entire countryside. Dismayed, he ordered a retreat.

Washington's response to the British attack and forced retreat was to advance. In late June he led his army out of their winter quarters at Morristown toward the Hudson Highlands, where the New England regiments had been on guard. The French were sending a fleet and troops to Rhode Island to his aid. He was delighted that together they might be able to rout the British from their base at New York City and began assembling his men for the upcoming campaign.

Peter, still at West Point, was nearing the end of his six-month enlistment. The miserably cold winter at the start of his tour had finally given way to spring. The ice on the Hudson slowly melted, and with its disappearance the real campaign season was beginning. So far it had been a relatively quiet tour, just the typical alarms and the customary deprivations—little food, clothing that had started out respectable but grew increasingly ragged, problems staying warm. But these were offset by the camaraderie that came with being one of Washington's veterans learning to be a soldier. "It may seem extraordinary that those who have experienced such accumulated distress and privations, should voluntarily engage again in the same service," Dr. Thacher explained. But "amid all the toils and hardships, there are charms in a military life: it is here that we witness heroic actions and deeds of military glory. The power of habit and the spirit of ambition, pervade the soldiers' ranks, and those who have been accustomed to active scenes, and formed their social attachments, cannot without reluctance quit the tumult and the bustle of a camp, for the calm and quiet of domestic pursuits." Of course, he added, whatever Washington's doubts, the cause itself was a factor: "There is to be found . . . in the bosom of our soldiers the purest principles of patriotism: they glory in the noble cause of their country, and pride themselves in contributing to its successful termination."

With hundreds of other six-month enlistees like Peter about to leave, Washington needed new recruits, and Massachusetts towns had quotas to fill yet again. In June the Lincoln town meeting voted to allocate eighteen thousand pounds to hire eleven men for "the present call to go into the War." The town also agreed to pay another eleven "3 months men" then in the militia. Reenlistment would mean another bounty for Peter, however little that purchased. And really there was little reason to return home. He was no longer Josiah's slave and had little enthusiasm for laboring on the Nelson farm as if he were. In fact, it was no longer certain where home was. If he belonged anywhere, it was in the regiment. So on July 15 he signed on for another six months of military service, one more man to help Lincoln meet its quota.

The Massachusetts Thirteenth was still on guard at West Point in the Hudson Highlands. From time to time the monotony was broken by something pleasant or unpleasant. On July 23 the famous German general Baron von Steuben inspected the regiment. Three days later two men who had arrived with the new "six months' men" were shot for enlisting and deserting several times to collect bounties. Everyone was ordered to watch the execution, an object lesson in honesty. Then at seven o'clock in the evening on July 31 they were suddenly ordered to leave West Point. They crossed the Hudson, always a laborious and risky business for the men, horses, and wagons, and headed south to Peekskill, where Washington had moved his headquarters. Their baggage was sent downstream by boat, by far the quickest route. When they reached Peekskill, the regiment camped in the woods, where their baggage eventually caught up with them.

Washington had hoped that once he had French support he would be able to challenge British control of New York City. The French fleet, however, was slow in coming. In July, after a ten-week journey across the Atlantic, the French ships sailed into Newport harbor with 5,500 officers and men under the command of the Comte de Rochambeau. Rochambeau was supposed to have an additional 2,500 troops but was unable to get them the necessary transport. Sadly, the long voyage had taken its toll on the men he did have. Some had died during the voyage, and another 700 were ill on arrival. To make matters worse, within a few days of their docking, a British fleet arrived to blockade Newport.

Washington was delighted, though, and sent a Frenchman to greet a Frenchman. The Marquis de Lafayette was dispatched to coordinate the effort between the French and American forces. He pressed the French general to help launch an immediate attack on New York, but Rochambeau wanted his men to recover from their journey first. He was also anxious to establish friendly relations with the locals, who found it difficult to shed decades of hostility to the French. Later Washington met Rochambeau in Connecticut to discuss the strategy for the campaign season. Since their combined force was still smaller than Clinton's and they had no additional fleet to support them, they agreed it was unwise to attack New York. Instead they decided to threaten and harass Clinton's northern outposts in hopes of luring him into bringing his army back north, the same strategy Clinton had used repeatedly against Washington. If it worked it would ease pressure on the American commanders struggling against the British in the South. This change meant that the French ships and troops were to remain based in Newport for nearly a year.

Peter and his regiment became aware of the change in plan canceling the attack on New York when the half of their baggage that finally reached them at Peekskill was promptly sent back to West Point. Back they went as well. As the army made the dangerous river crossing once again, doubtless grumbling about the senseless journey, three brigades, including General Glover's and General Starke's and all their baggage, were plunged into the water. One boat sank. Five men and five yoke of oxen were drowned. The other brigades crossed without incident.

No warm welcome awaited them on their return to West Point, only the usual hardships. It was now August and farmers were taking in the harvest, but it was a lean time for the Massachusetts Thirteenth. For many days in a row Peter and the rest of the soldiers had no meat. They became so desperate that some of the men actually crept up to British lines to steal their cattle and other necessaries. They got away with it, but it was a risky way to get food. The major change on their return was the arrival of their new commander, Benedict Arnold.

Washington had offered Benedict Arnold command of the left wing of his army for the attack on New York, but Arnold asked to be granted command of West Point instead. When the plan to assault New York collapsed, Washington agreed to Arnold's request. On August 3 as the Massachusetts Thirteenth and other New England regiments were trudging north back to West Point, General Richard Howe, the fortress commander, was replaced by Benedict Arnold. Arnold's new command stretched from north of the elaborate fortifications at West Point to the southern end of the Hudson Highlands at Stony Point. He now held the key to New York State, the vital link between New England and the mid-Atlantic states and between New York City and Canada.

Arnold was still a hero to the soldiers and to most Americans. His admirers knew little about his problems in Philadelphia. What did that matter compared to his brilliant leadership at Fort Ticonderoga and at Saratoga, his march to Quebec, and other exploits? The man was justly famous. It was easy, at least for enlisted men, to overlook his volatile temperament and sensitivity to slights. Obviously a committed republican, Arnold resented the fact that the army was "permitted to starve in a land of plenty," a common and justified complaint. But his response differed from that of other officers. What his admirers and superiors did not know was that Benedict Arnold was preparing to change sides. He was feverishly negotiating the best deal with the British that he could. His thinking was simple enough. The war was going badly; indeed, it was as good as lost. The British southern strategy was a great success while the French alliance had yet to be helpful. Why go down with a losing cause, one whose leaders never treated him with the respect he deserved; why be a "winter soldier"? He had his future to consider. There was much to gain by throwing in his lot with the British if it was done before the Americans were beaten. To benefit from his treason, he needed to be able to offer the British something of value. The surrender of West Point was just the ticket. Once the fortress was under Arnold's command, the rest would be easy. He might even be able to include the capture of Washington by inviting the commander and some of his generals to visit West Point and dine with him just as the fort was to be betrayed. What a coup that would be. Peter's regiment and the rest of the garrison, with luck even the commander in chief and his staff, would be handed over to the British. Once the British had control of the Hudson Highlands, they would have strategic control of New York State. Together with their domination of the South, the capture of George Washington and his Northern Army would make their victory and the war's end certain.

Arnold laid his plans carefully. He selected the Beverly Robinson House for his headquarters. Its location two miles south of West Point and on the opposite side of the Hudson meant that his activities would not be easily observed. West Point's elaborate fortifications needed repairs, but Arnold made sure they were never made. Throughout August he was preoccupied converting his assets to cash and continuing negotiations with the British. At the end of August he got word from his wife, Peggy, in Philadelphia that the British had agreed to the deal he had requested, twenty thousand pounds sterling and a general's commission in exchange for surrendering West Point. With the bargain struck, he arranged for Peggy and their baby son to be brought to the Robinson House. Details of the handover were to be arranged with Major John Andre, a talented and discreet aide to General Clinton.

On September 21–22 Arnold and Andre met near West Point. Andre had hoped to escape detection by wearing a blue greatcoat over his uniform and calling himself John Anderson. All went as planned, but by the time the meeting ended, it was dawn and too light for Andre to return to the British ship *Vulture*, anchored in the Hudson. In fact, American guns had driven the ship downriver. Andre therefore set off, picking his way south by a round-about route. He was just shy of Tarrytown on the following day, September 23, when he was spotted by three local militiamen and seized. Searching him, they discovered detailed plans of the defenses at West Point and a document from Arnold requesting that Andre be permitted to pass through American lines. Andre tried to bribe his captors, offering a "large sum of money for his release, and as many goods as they would demand." To their credit the militiamen refused and took Andre to Colonel John Jamieson of the Continental dragoons. Jamieson was unsure what was going on. He forwarded a letter to Arnold informing him that Andre had been captured, then sent the documents he had been carrying to George Washington. That was enough for

Arnold. With Washington and his retinue due to arrive at West Point in three days, he had no time to waste. On September 25 Arnold fled to the *Vulture,* waiting for him in the Hudson.

The following day Washington, with Lafayette, Alexander Hamilton, and Henry Knox, reached West Point ignorant of the plot laid to trap them and surprised that Arnold wasn't there to greet them. The discovery of Arnold's flight and, with it, the sudden revelation of his intended treason were deeply disturbing. How close Arnold came to succeeding! Washington and other leaders would have been handed over to the British as prisoners, the key stronghold in New York State would have been taken, and Peter and thousands of his fellow soldiers would be marched off to British prison camps, where thousands of American soldiers had already sickened and died. In his general orders that day Washington put the best face he could on the shocking betrayal by a national hero. "Great honor is due to the American Army," he wrote, "that this is the first instance of Treason of the kind where many were to be expected from the nature of the dispute, and nothing is so bright an ornament in the Character of the American soldiers as their having been proof against all the arts and seductions of an insidious enemy."

The fact that someone of such distinction had defected aroused disbelief and then great anger. Joseph Martin and his corps of sappers and miners saw the *Vulture* sail up the Hudson toward West Point and later down the river "with her precious cargo—Arnold—on board." Martin was astonished when he learned of Arnold's defection. "I should as soon have thought West Point had deserted us as he," he wrote, "but I was soon convinced that it was true."

Arnold made good his escape, but Andre was not so lucky. He was imprisoned and brought to Washington's headquarters to face a court of inquiry. A special board of fourteen general officers convened on September 29. Andre confessed to being a British officer on a mission for his commander but claimed that he was a spy only by accident. This was the truth. Shocked by his admission, the American officers rejected the "spy by accident" defense. Captured soldiers were treated as prisoners of war, but the punishment for spying was hanging. The board was unanimous in its decision that Andre was a spy and condemned him to be executed. Washington wrote Clinton to inform him that Andre would be hanged on October 1. In reply, Clinton offered to exchange anyone in his hands for Andre. Washington wanted just one man, Benedict Arnold. This Clinton refused. Once Andre's fate was clear, he pleaded for a soldier's death by firing squad. This was not granted, and at noon on October 2 he was hanged.

Andre became a hero to the British. In 1821 his remains were dug up and reburied at Westminster Abbey, where a special monument was erected to his memory. The three militiamen who waylaid him were heroes to their countrymen and received silver medals from Congress and pensions of one hundred dollars. There was fury at Arnold selling out his country for money and a commission but a fair amount of sympathy for Andre. Joseph Martin, among others, thought that sympathy misplaced. Martin pointed out how badly the British had treated Captain Nathan Hale, who had been caught spying for Washington in 1776. The British had summarily executed Hale "without the shadow of a trial, denying him the use of a Bible or the assistance [of] a clergyman in his last moments, and destroying the letters he had written to his widowed mother and other relations." It was Hale who, just before his execution, told his captors that he only regretted he had but one life to lose for his country.

After the excitement of September, autumn closed in on the men patrolling the Hudson. Joseph Martin's regiment and others scattered throughout the area marched to West Point for the winter and began building new barracks. As the year ended, Peter's six-month enlistment was also ending. He was paid off and with the rest of his regiment began the long march back to eastern Massachusetts, unsure what he would find or what the future would hold for him. That month Benedict Arnold, now a brigadier general in Clinton's army, led a British raid on Virginia.

CHAPTER SEVENTEEN

Final Battles

Deliver us from evil.
THE LORD'S PRAYER

I T WAS bitterly cold. They had two hundred miles to travel, but the ragged men trudging back to Lincoln and Lexington that January were jubilant. Their enlistments were up. They were alive and heading home. Peter was unclear what awaited him in Lincoln, but the excitement in the haggard, familiar faces surrounding him was contagious. The winter journey from West Point to eastern Massachusetts had become familiar. Their progress was slow this time of year, but they were all delighted to be setting out. They were part of the regular shift at year's end, men leaving the army, others joining. This time, though, many more were leaving camp. All those men who had signed up for three years in 1777, when Congress agreed to the long enlistments, had now fulfilled their commitment. Except for some few who immediately signed on again, the rest were on their way back to civilian life.

Among the cheerful throng was Jupiter Free. He had survived three hard years in the army, withstood major battles and minor skirmishes, sickness, and winters at Valley Forge and other camps, and he was at last a free man. Enlistment had been a gamble, but it had paid off. It had been physically trying. Though his health might never recover, what was that in comparison to being free? He had also made up his mind. He would not return to work for the Brookses in Lincoln. They would be happy to have him back at the family tannery and farm. They were kind people. But he wanted to be near Peggy in Lexington. That meant earning his own way, paying for food and lodging, but surely someone in Lexington could use a willing and steady worker. People knew him there, and Peggy could help him find work. So Peter and his father were returning together, free men.

Their regiments had been disbanded that January. With the drastic loss of

Continental veterans, Washington decided to consolidate his army. Peter's regiment, the Massachusetts Thirteenth, and Jupiter's Massachusetts Fifteenth, were among six Massachusetts regiments affected. Hundreds of men were on the road heading east, tramping along together.

There was joy among those returning to civilian life but gloom at the dismal prospects for the cause they had served, and gloom in the ranks of the men they left behind. Most of Washington's remaining veterans were encamped around New Windsor, New York, above the Hudson Highlands, but the six regiments of the Pennsylvania line had been sent to the old encampment at Jockey Hollow near Morristown, New Jersey. The New Jersey line was camped nearby. The men of both lines were facing another miserable winter. They had not been paid for a year. Without even the customary ration of rum to warm their insides and boost their spirits, they were in no mood to settle for the usual promises of improvements that never materialized. It wasn't just the pay and the intolerable conditions. Many insisted that, like the three-year veterans now returning home, they had signed up for three years, not for the duration. Anyway, who would have guessed in 1777 that the war would go on for more than three years? It was also galling that new recruits were receiving twenty-five dollars in silver while the continuing soldiers had still not been paid. Enough was enough. On January 1, 1781, the men of the Pennsylvania line mutinied. On January 20 the New Jersey line followed suit.

First came the Pennsylvanians. Fifteen hundred men of the state's Continental line marched out of Jockey Hollow, armed with muskets and cannon and heading for Philadelphia. They insisted that they would remain in the ranks only if they received new bounties. It was New Year's Day. The men, a report explained, were "much agitated with liquor." In the confusion, as officers tried to quiet the soldiers, Captain Adam Bettin was shot and killed and two other officers were severely wounded. The line's popular general, "Mad" Anthony Wayne, galloped to the scene. Warning shots were fired over his head. Wayne immediately pulled open his greatcoat, shouting, "If you mean to kill me, shoot me at once—here is my breast!" The mutineers assured Wayne that their quarrel was neither with him and the officers nor with the cause but with Congress.

In preparation for their march on Philadelphia, the soldiers confiscated every horse and ox they could find. According to local tradition, when they tried to seize the fine white horse belonging to Temperance Wick, farmer Wick's daughter, they met their match. Temperance was twenty-one, the youngest of the five Wick children. Like the mutineers, she was not in a conciliatory mood. In December her father had died of pleurisy and her mother was now gravely ill. The two women were the sole adults in the house. Temperance decided to ride to the doctor's for medicine. On her way back, three drunken mutineers blocked her path, grabbing for her horse's bridle. Temperance gave the animal a sharp kick and galloped home. Once back, she brought the horse into the house and led it into a spare bedroom. She put a quilt on the floor to muffle the hoofbeats, and there the horse stayed for several days until the coast was clear.

With the mutineers on the march toward Philadelphia (without Temperance's horse), Congress frantically sent representatives off to negotiate with them. With so much at stake, the representatives had little option but to offer generous terms. Every man who claimed that his enlistment was up was permitted to leave. All the men got their back pay and new uniforms. Most of the men who were discharged, however, promptly signed up again to receive the going bounty.

On January 20 the men of the New Jersey line based at Pompton, near Morristown, decided to try the same tactic. But Washington was angry and afraid of a spreading revolt. He ordered General Robert Howe with five hundred New England soldiers based near West Point to advance immediately to New Jersey and quash the mutiny. Army surgeon James Thacher accompanied them. Howe and his men marched through heavy snow and arrived at Pompton on January 27. He feared that some of his soldiers "would not prove faithful on this trying occasion" but reminded them that the mutineers had to be brought to an unconditional submission, that there would be no temporizing or consideration of terms. The New Jersey men awoke to find their huts surrounded. They were ordered to appear in front of their huts, unarmed, within five minutes. Thacher writes that they submitted quietly. Three of the New Jersey line's ringleaders were selected, tried on the spot, and sentenced to be shot by twelve fellow mutineers. Thacher notes that for these twelve "this was a most painful task; being themselves guilty, they were greatly distressed with the duty imposed on them, and when ordered to load, some of them shed tears." The three men to be executed pleaded for their lives. Two were executed. The third was saved by the intervention of an officer. All the mutineers, Thacher added, were justified to have been dismayed by the hardships they had suffered as soldiers. The wonder was that all the other soldiers remained obedient.

They say bad things happen in threes. Late in December Benedict Arnold, now a British general, had led a raid into Virginia. Now, in January, he and his soldiers captured Richmond, looting its homes and burning its warehouses. Virginia's governor, Thomas Jefferson, and the rest of the government were forced to flee, contenting themselves with offering a reward of five thousand guineas for Arnold's capture. Arnold was never caught.

Peter was now eighteen, capable and strong. He thought of himself as a farmer first, a laborer second; apart from soldiering, he had never been trained in any other craft. Freedom gave him options, but they were limited. Moving back in with Josiah and Millicent and their children after parting in less than ideal circumstances was a last resort. In that house it would be hard to be treated as a free man rather than as Josiah's slave boy, hard to be a marginal worker in the home where he had been an only child, cared for by poor Elizabeth, now five years dead. Jonathan was three years dead. The year he returned home the Thorning girls, his childhood friends, young women now, moved with their family to Lexington. Where to live? Jupiter could not put him up. Rose and Prince would be happy to see him, but they had little room in their small home. He didn't want to be a burden on anyone. It was best just to visit them all from time to time and help out in any way he could.

Lots of families with large farms needed hired help, especially with their men serving in the army or casualties of the war. With two big family farms to manage, the Hartwells could always use additional hands, at least come spring, and Catherine Louisa, abandoned by Captain Billy and with a sizable homestead to run and a house full of children, was another prospect. It was nice being able to choose what he would do but daunting as well. Peter inquired, visited, offered himself for work, and settled down as a hired, live-in farm laborer. There was one other option, the army. A "resolve" had been passed in December 1780 assigning quotas of men to be raised for the army, but they were for the new campaign season, and for the time being Lincoln could postpone that obligation.

In May, as the chance of frost passed in Lincoln and planting season began, a new campaign season was about to begin. Washington met with Rochambeau to plan their strategy. Any major operation against the British required help from a French fleet that could coordinate with their land forces and block

British ships from intervening. Admiral François Joseph Paul, Comte de Grasse, had just such a fleet in the Caribbean. The two commanders wrote asking him to come north for a joint campaign. In the meantime they returned to the old scheme of besieging the British and driving them out of New York City. On July 6 the allied armies met at Dobb's Ferry, New York, to prepare the assault on New York and await news from de Grasse.

At this point the army needed recruits, and Massachusetts towns began frantically seeking men to serve for three years. Lincoln had to raise ten men. It was hard to entice anyone to leave his family and farm for such a long spell under such perilous circumstances. By now everyone had heard of the army mutinies, and veterans were well aware of the miserable conditions that had provoked them. Substantial bounties were needed to lure a man into service. Most towns faced with this dilemma resorted to the same general approach. Small groups of substantial citizens were formed into classes. Each class had to find a recruit and fund his bounty. Money was borrowed, and bargains were made.

Peter was an obvious candidate. He was experienced, well regarded, and single. For him it meant a chance to escape from a marginal, humdrum life in Lincoln and do some good. Life in the army was hard but full of adventure for a young man, and he was treated as an equal. The bonding and feeling of brotherhood among men in war was different from anything he had ever known or would ever know at home. This was also a rare chance to earn a large sum of money. The trick was to drive a hard bargain. Bounties varied with what a man could negotiate. The men who had enlisted for three years in 1777 each got thirty pounds. With Continental currency as good as worthless, you needed to be paid in "hard money" or silver. Amos Adams enlisted for Lincoln for a bounty of sixty-one pounds hard money. Samuel Avery received a bounty of sixty pounds hard money. The average for the three years' service was seventy-three pounds, ten shillings, hard money. Peter did much better.

On June 23 he was officially inscribed as a recruit for Middlesex County. It was the job of Joseph Hosmer, the county superintendent, to record the name and basic description of each recruit. Hosmer described Peter Sharon as "18 years, stature 5 feet 9 inches, complexion, black; hair, black; eyes, black, occupation farmer (also given laborer)." Two days after he was officially listed, John Adams (not William Smith's brother-in-law) and members of his class paid Peter 350 silver dollars to serve three years in the Continental army. This was a huge sum. Only one other Lincoln man, Joel Adams, seems to have received as large a bounty. Three hundred fifty silver dollars could be used to buy property, but Peter bought no property. The bounty was enough to buy his mother's and his sister's freedom. This is almost certainly how Peter used that handsome bounty. When he returned, if he returned, they could live as a family, like other people. For now Peter had two days to get ready to depart. There were hurried visits to friends and loved ones, handshakes and hugs, tears, small gifts, and prayers for a safe return. Then he gathered with Lincoln's other recruits, and they walked off together to the war.

In contrast to Peter's journey home in January, the Middlesex men marching west that July were anything but jubilant. Day after day they trudged along dusty roads, past ripening summer fields, alternately soaked by steamy rains and seared by a blazing sun. At night they slept on the bare ground or, if lucky, in someone's barn. There was good-natured joking, friendships struck up, music from the fifers, a sense of expectation and anxiety, but no real joy. General Washington was concentrating his forces at King's Bridge, only fifteen miles from New York City. That was their destination. Attacking the large British base in New York was a sobering proposition. The British were well entrenched in the great city. They controlled its harbor. The geography made a siege or assault difficult. The British fleet made it even trickier. But who knew what would really happen? There had been plans to attack New York before, and Washington had thought better of it.

The area they were heading for had been devastated by years of warfare. "Casting your eyes over the countryside," mused the Comte de Clermont-Crèvecoeur, a French lieutenant, seeing it for the first time, "you felt very sad, for it revealed all the horrors and cruelty of the English in burned woodlands, destroyed houses, and fallow fields deserted by the owners." The spot chosen for the two armies to camp, however, he found "a very agreeable and advantageous position." On their arrival the new enlistees were welcomed to the ranks, their bounties the envy of the veterans. Clermont-Crèvecoeur was stunned by his first sight of Peter and his comrades, a stark contrast to the French troops in their neat white uniforms. "In beholding this army I was struck, not by its smart appearance, but by its destitution: the men were without Uniforms and covered with rags; most of them were barefoot. They were of all sizes, down to children who could not have been over fourteen. There were many negroes, mulattoes, etc. Only their artillerymen were wearing uniforms." He would come to respect the artillerymen, though. "These are the elite of the country and are actually very good troops, well schooled in their profession. We had nothing but praise for them later." Another French officer found the troops "very war-wise and quite well disciplined." "They are thoroughly inured to hardship," he wrote, "which they endure with little complaint so long as their officers set them an example." He obviously had not met Joseph Martin. He added, "They have supreme confidence in General Washington." The Continentals and their elegant, professional allies settled down to await orders.

They didn't have long to wait. On August 14 Washington and Rochambeau finally got word from de Grasse. He would help, but there were conditions. He was sailing north with a fleet of twenty-nine ships and three thousand soldiers but would travel only as far as the Chesapeake Bay and because of other responsibilities could only remain there until October 15. They had two months. An assault on New York City was out, but there was an opportunity to attack the British army Clinton had based in Virginia under command of General Charles Cornwallis. If the French fleet could blockade the Chesapeake and prevent Cornwallis from getting supplies or reinforcements, there was a chance they might trap him. It meant moving the American and French armies some 450 miles south as quickly as possible. They gave the order to move out. Within four days their canvas tents and supplies had been packed, and they were on the road. To persuade Clinton that New York remained his target, Washington left about three thousand men behind. Campfires were lit every night where the British could see them, boats were collected as if for an attack on Staten Island, and ovens and supply depots were even set up as if poised for an invasion. Clinton was not the only one convinced that New York was the target. As they crossed the Hudson at King's Ferry and marched south along the Jersey shore, Peter and the rest of the army assumed they would be attacking New York. It was not until the end of August, as they drew away from New York, that the men realized they were marching to the Delaware River, then on to Virginia, to confront Cornwallis.

The weather continued oppressively hot. The soldiers marched as quickly as they could, pressing on day after day, battling heat, exhaustion, and ticks. They often slept rough rather than setting up their tents. Occasionally they had a day's break to rest, wash their clothes, and clean their guns. The French and American armies took different routes. This was a wise decision. New Englanders had suffered from French raiding parties over the decades, and the bitter feelings and religious differences between Catholics and Protestants were hard to overcome.

For Peter it was thrilling to be part of Washington's main army, thousands of men marching together all day, camping with their regiments night after night, enjoying the respite from the day's heat, moving steadily south. The marching, though, was exhausting. "I have often been so beat out with long and tedious marching that I have fallen asleep while walking the road," Joseph Martin wrote, "and not been sensible of it till I have jostled against someone in the same situation; and when permitted to stop and have the superlative happiness to roll myself in my blanket and drop down on the ground in the bushes, briars, thorns, or thistles, and get an hour or two's sleep, O how exhilarating."

Thousands of campfires punctuated the dark every evening. Men gathered in their glow, eating, chatting, joking, singing, talking of home, speculating. Sometimes it was nice, though, just to sit alone for a time, studying the stars from a new vantage point, catching the calls of unfamiliar birds and the stirrings of forest creatures. At other times it was a pleasure simply to go to sleep.

Peter had never been further south than northern New Jersey. Traveling south was an alarming prospect for all the blacks in the army. The region was notorious. A northern slave who misbehaved was warned that he or she would be sent south to be sold. Those who were sent away were never heard from again. Slavery was different in the South. Greater distinctions were drawn. Blacks and whites didn't live together or work side by side. One French officer observed that in Virginia, "no white man works in the fields unless driven by poverty to this extremity. An individual's wealth is gauged by the number of negroes he owns." Educating slaves was frowned on and sometimes forbidden. Marriages like Peggy and Jupiter's weren't recognized. The great number of slaves on whom southern whites depended also frightened them and made them cruel. They locked everything up for fear it would be stolen. Peter knew that southerners had objected to slaves, or even free blacks, serving in the American army. The people of Charleston had refused to arm slaves for the fight against the British. They preferred to surrender. The New England regiments, with their mix of races, were unlikely to be well received by either whites or blacks.

Another disturbing thought crept into the mind. Thousands had responded when Virginia's former governor Lord Dunmore and General Clinton had invited the slaves of patriots to abandon their masters and work and fight for the royal army. Large numbers of slaves escaped to New York City and to the British armies in Virginia and the Carolinas. How could Peter judge these fugitives? What other chance did they have for freedom? Maybe the British truly meant to help them. The question was which side in the struggle would keep faith with the blacks who aided them. Jupiter and other

Massachusetts slaves who served three years on the promise of freedom had been freed. But the fate of other slaves, especially those who served as substitutes for their masters in New Jersey, New York, and other states, was uncertain. He was curious about the freed slaves in the South, sorry to be fighting against them. He could only wish them well.

The war had been going badly in the South. The debacle of General Lincoln's surrender at Charleston had led to another disaster. Some four hundred Virginia Continentals who had been on their way to reinforce Charleston had turned back to Virginia when they learned of its surrender. They never reached home. The infamous Lieutenant Colonel Banastre Tarleton and his cavalry galloped after them. Tarleton was a brutal man who genuinely enjoyed killing. He and his soldiers caught up with the Virginians at Waxhaws, near the North Carolina border. The Americans surrendered and pleaded for quarter, but Tarleton ordered his men to butcher them. Three hundred were slaughtered on the spot. The phrase "Tarleton's quarter" was born.

Something had to be done to rebuild an American army in the South. Against Washington's advice, Congress had decided to send the hero of Saratoga, a New England favorite, General Horatio Gates. It was a disastrous choice. Gates used his small, inexperienced force impetuously. Just a few months after Waxhaws, he met with catastrophe. Gates had marched his men right through the night straight at the British outpost in Camden, South Carolina. In the dark they accidentally bumped into British troops. Both sides drew back. But large numbers of Gates's men were ill from bad food and had not fully recovered the next day when Cornwallis came after them in strength. The little army was crushed. There were some 750 casualties. Adding to the disgrace, Gates fled. At the end of 1780, as Washington's three year men were heading home, Congress appointed Nathanael Greene to replace Gates in the South.

In addition to the string of military disasters in the South, fighting between local Loyalists and patriots was especially vicious there. Both sides plundered, raped, and slaughtered. Brutality bred brutality. James Thacher was shocked by the viciousness in Virginia: "Not a day passes but there are more or less who fall a sacrifice to this savage disposition. . . . Some thousands have fallen in this way in this quarter, and the evil rages with more violence than ever." He reckoned, "If a stop cannot be soon put to these massacres, the country will be depopulated in a few months more, as neither whig nor tory can live."

Cornwallis made matters worse. He was not interested in winning the hearts and minds of the local people—quite the opposite. He encouraged his men to terrorize locals, to teach them respect. General Greene, by contrast, was careful to keep his men in check, politely paying for whatever they needed. Winning hearts was essential to success. Greene fought Cornwallis to a draw at Guilford Court House, North Carolina, in March 1781, inflicting a high number of casualties on the British.

In an odd way the Americans were lucky in the British generals now ranged against them. Clinton and Cornwallis disliked and distrusted each other. Clinton had instructed Cornwallis to be cautious and to protect his line of supply. He asked him to ensure that he controlled the land behind his army. But Cornwallis had an aggressive streak and considered Clinton's advice timid. He set out with his army to crush Greene, his men looting as they went. They confiscated six hundred horses and ravaged homes and farms. They also freed, by Jefferson's estimate, some thirty thousand Virginia slaves belonging to patriots. The freed slaves were delighted at first but were left with little protection from their old masters, no way to earn a living, and nowhere to go. Many saw little option but to follow the British army. Hundreds were put to work as laborers or became servants for British officers. Others simply ran off into the woods and swamps, where many of them died of disease, starvation, or exposure.

Cornwallis and his army stormed after Greene, who led them in circles through the countryside. Greene had divided his little force into separate units, each led by one of Washington's finest officers: Daniel Morgan with his crack riflemen, "Light Horse Harry" Lee, and Francis Marion. Each troop set off in a different direction to attack British posts and units. This daring scheme kept Cornwallis off-balance, exhausting his resources and inflicting casualties he could not replace. On top of this Clinton managed to make Cornwallis's life more difficult. In July, while Washington and Rochambeau were still waiting to hear from Admiral de Grasse, Clinton kept changing his mind about where he wanted Cornwallis's army to be. He ordered Cornwallis to take his men to New York, then to Philadelphia, again to New York, and finally to stay in Virginia. No wonder that when Clinton ordered him to fortify Old Point Comfort at the mouth of the James River, Cornwallis ignored the order. Instead, he and his engineers decided to fortify Yorktown on the York River near the Chesapeake Bay. The city was a tobacco port, boasting about three hundred houses, some quite elegant, and a population of 2,500 souls. On August 1, two weeks before de Grasse's message reached Washington and Rochambeau, construction had begun at Yorktown. Freed slaves were put to work constructing fortifications. When the task wasn't going quickly enough, additional slaves were hired from Loyalist masters. Yorktown would be Rochambeau's fifteenth siege. He was a master at it. Everything went as planned. The French fleet appeared at the mouth of the York River on September 1. Cornwallis and his army retreated into Yorktown. A few days later de Grasse's fleet and a smaller British fleet clashed at sea. De Grasse won and with the victory gained control of the Chesapeake. On September 8, as the British ships sailed to New York for reinforcements, the French soldiers on de Grasse's ships disembarked. Three days later, Washington and his men were nearing Philadelphia. They marched through Delaware and Maryland. On September 14 they reached Williamsburg, Virginia, the rendezvous point for the allied armies. What excitement Peter and his comrades felt to have arrived. The entire army paraded, paying Washington the honors due to his rank. He was given a thunderous salute from twenty-one cannon. The weather remained very hot as the men settled down at the encampment, happy to rest after their grueling march. Two regiments from Maryland arrived. The French Legion joined them. General Lincoln and his men appeared. Other scattered units of the patriot army in the south and local militia regiments converged on Williamsburg. Ebenezer Wild of the First Massachusetts reckoned there were about fourteen thousand regular troops and some three to four thousand militia. At sunrise on September 27, the order to move out was given. The soldiers packed up and left Williamsburg. At dawn the next morning they began the short, final march to Yorktown, moving in one long column.

They approached to within a mile of Yorktown, nearly encircling the town. Riflemen began skirmishing at once and kept it up all that day. Peter had never taken part in so vast and powerful an operation. He had arrived at Saratoga in 1777 in time to see the formal surrender, but by then the battle was over. He had fought in skirmishes and defended garrisons, but nothing had prepared him for the scale of the siege, the ferocity of hundreds of cannon pounding earth, rocks, men, and horses to rubble. The noise was horrendous, the sight terrifying. It went on day and night. Cannonballs were "clearly visible in the form of a black ball in the day," James Thacher reported, "but in the night, they appear like fiery meteors with blazing tails, most beautifully brilliant, ascending majestically from the mortar to a certain altitude, and gradually descending to the spot where they are destined to execute their work of destruction." As a ball falls "it whirls round, burrows, and excavates the earth to a considerable extent, and bursting, makes dreadful havoc around." The damage was terrible. Peter was a veteran but in many ways still a boy. In the worst, most frightening, moments there was the comfort of the men around him sharing the danger. You couldn't play the coward in front of them or let them down. Personal honor was important, personal pride was important. The explosions couldn't go on much longer.

The British had constructed elaborate outer works, but on September 30 they abandoned all but two redoubts that were 150 yards ahead of the rest of their fortifications. As they retreated the Americans and French moved closer, taking possession of the abandoned British defenses. Each dash forward placed them nearer to the city with its murderous artillery. The pounding went on all day, day after day, as the British fired on the American and French working parties with, as yet, no answering fire. The trenches were at first some eight hundred yards from the British line. Through the hail of explosions men managed to haul cannon and ammunition to their front lines. The soil was very sandy and easy to dig but for that reason did not pack down well. Hundreds of soldiers not involved in digging trenches and redoubts were sent to the woods to make sandbags. It was hot, heavy work but at least it was farther from the line of fire. The ring around Yorktown tightened. As the British retreated the Americans and French advanced, trench by trench. By October 9 American batteries were able to fire on the British and take their revenge. "I have more than once," Thacher wrote, "witnessed fragments of the mangled bodies and limbs of the British soldiers thrown into the air by the bursting of our shells." Days later they stormed and took two redoubts still in British hands. They dug all night to extend their trenches.

Cornwallis had written to Clinton for help and had been assured it was on its way. But Clinton seemed unaware of the desperate straits his southern army was now in. Food was becoming scarce in Yorktown, and to make matters worse, smallpox had broken out. The blacks in the town were especially susceptible to the disease. To ease both problems, Cornwallis ordered that the blacks who had crowded into the town for protection and to help build the fortifications be thrust out. Into no-man's-land between the British and American forces they were shoved, starving, sick, confused, terrified. Peter saw the freed slaves. He would never forget the sight. "In the woods herds of Negroes which Lord Cornwallis (after he had inveigled them from their proprietors), in love and pity to them, had turned adrift with no other recompense for their confidence in his humanity than the smallpox for their bounty and starvation and death for their wages," Joseph Martin wrote. "They might be seen scattered about in every direction, dead and dying with pieces of ears of burnt Indian corn in the hands and mouths, even of those that were dead." Sarah Osborn, who accompanied her husband's New York regiment, still remembered in old age the sight of "a number of dead Negroes" near their encampment a mile from Yorktown who "the British had driven out of the town and left to starve, or were first starved and then thrown out." The American soldiers, black and white, were appalled and disgusted. If Peter had any doubts about which side slaves should trust, the doubts ended now. The British betrayal of those they had promised to free was horrific. Yet though he could not know it yet, the new nation Peter fought for would betray the blacks, too. It might free those who fought, but in most of the newly independent states there was no intention to abolish slavery.

By dawn on October 15 the American line extended right down to the York River. More batteries were erected and cannon brought forward. The French and American trenches drew a tighter and tighter noose around the town. They were now only two hundred yards from the British works, and both sides were firing at each other all day.

It had become clear to Cornwallis that any reinforcements Clinton might send would never reach him in time. With the French ships blocking the river, a British fleet might not be able to break through anyway. Conditions in the city were intolerable. Seeing it later, Jean-Baptiste Antoine de Verger, a French sublieutenant, found "the din and disorder caused by our bombs in the town defy description. Hardly a house remains that is not destroyed, either wholly or in part, by shells or bombs." Among the devastation were dead freedmen. "One could not go ten steps," de Verger added, "without meeting the wounded or dying, destitute negroes abandoned to their fate, and corpse after corpse on every hand."

Cornwallis tried two more desperate strategies. On October 16 he sent out a party of about six hundred men to spike some of the American cannon to make them useless. Little was accomplished. The cannon were quickly fixed. That night Cornwallis made one final attempt. He and his army slipped out of the town and tried to escape across the river to Gloucester Point. A fierce thunderstorm drove them back. It was over. On October 17, with British cannon nearly silent amid an "almost incessant" American and French bombardment, Cornwallis sent out a lone drummer to parley. It was the anniversary of the great victory at Saratoga.

How sweet victory was after all the humiliating defeats and hardships they had suffered. October 19 dawned a bright, cool autumn day. The American army lined up on one side of the field, their French allies across from them. Crowds gathered to witness the surrender. At two o'clock the British and Hessian troops marched out of Yorktown down the field between the ranks of the allied armies, the smartly dressed French on the right and the shabby Continentals to their left. The British officers led their army and delivered up their swords. Cornwallis feigned illness and left it to his second in command, General Charles O'Hara, to lead the troops. Lincoln officiated for Washington. The British soldiers laid their battle flags on the ground and stacked their guns. More than 7,200 men and 840 sailors were now prisoners. It was humiliating for the British and meant to be, an unconditional surrender without the full honors of war. Washington insisted that all the indignities General Lincoln had endured at the surrender of Charleston be visited on the British at Yorktown. Tears rolled down O'Hara's portly cheeks as he rode along. When his soldiers marched sulkily past, an American band struck up "Yankee Doodle." The British band, their drums covered in black cloth, fifes tied with black ribbons, played the melancholy tune "The World Turned Upside Down," whose lyrics fitted their view of their defeat. They then marched back to Yorktown. On October 27, too late to help, the relief fleet Clinton had sent arrived. Learning of the surrender, the ships turned back to New York. On November 4 there was the parting of ways. Cornwallis sailed for New York. De Grasse left with his fleet for the West Indies. The British and Hessian prisoners were taken inland. And Washington and his men turned north to spend the winter in the Hudson Highlands.

The joy of their triumph was marred for Peter and the other blacks in the army not only by the loss of comrades but by the awful memories of the dead and dying blacks. It was little consolation that after the victory many owners came to look for their slaves, offering a guinea a head for them, little consolation that the returned slaves seemed relieved to resume their former lives. Some of the soldiers, Martin included, helped track the runaways down. To their credit the soldiers refused to help unless they were assured that the poor blacks would not be punished. Colonel Bannister, who had lost eighty-two slaves, assured Martin and others that he had no intention of punishing them, "that he did not blame them at all; the blame lay on Lord Cornwallis." "I saw several of those miserable wretches delivered to their master," Martin wrote. "They came before him under a very powerful fit of the ague. He told them that he gave them the free choice either to go with him or remain where they were, that he would not injure a hair of their heads if they returned with him to their duty. Had the poor souls received a reprieve at the gallows, they could not have been more overjoyed than they appeared to be at what he promised

them; their ague fit soon left them." Martin assisted in finding one of Bannister's slaves, for which he received one silver dollar or its equivalent in paper
money. "It amounted to 1200 (nominal) dollars," he wrote, "all of which I
afterwards paid for one quart of rum."

It was a comfort to be heading north, leaving the painful scenes behind.
But further pain was in store. The news was slow reaching Peter, which was to
be expected. On October 12, while he and the army were fighting the British
at Yorktown, Jupiter had died. His health had never recovered from his years
of army service. He had lived as a free man less than a year. Lexington records
registering his death listed him simply as Jupiter, a Negro. No proud last
name, "Free." But free he now was.

Peter had never really known his father well. They had never lived together as father and son, never had much time to talk as he was growing up.
Seldom even saw each other. Fortunately, they had that journey back to
Massachusetts together when their enlistments ended in January and they
could snatch an hour or two to themselves. Stolen time, seldom out of earshot
of others. He had that. But the dream of living as a family was gone forever.

Sleep was a blessing, not having to remember. The best time of day was
the moment of waking, before the memory of personal loss, the sights of war,
the betrayal and humiliation of southern blacks came flooding back to mind.
Those precious moments of forgetting.

He had two more years in the army. Thanks to his handsome bounty for
the three-year enlistment, his mother and his sister were now free. But with
Jupiter gone they had little reason to stay in Lexington, lots of reason to move
to a city where there were more free blacks and they might hope to find a
better future. All Peter knew was soldiering and farming. His only ties were in
Lincoln. There seemed less and less reason to go home, but where else was
there? Two more years in the army would give him time to think and plan,
two more years to be one of Washington's veterans, part of that band of
brothers.

Afterword

And now we were to be (the greater part of us) parted forever, as uncondi-
tionally separated as though the grave lay between us.
> JOSEPH PLUMB MARTIN, *Ordinary Courage: The Revolutionary War
> Adventures of Joseph Plumb Martin* (narrative published 1830)

First Federal Census, 1790, Lincoln, Massachusetts: *Slaves 0, Others 6*

FTERWARD there was freedom. Freedom for the thirteen colonies
that miraculously won the war and were now independent republics
linked in a confederation. Freedom for soldiers. With the army
disbanded and enlistments ended, they were sent home to resume their former lives as best they could. Most amazing of all, there was freedom for Bay
State slaves. The year the war ended, the Massachusetts Supreme Judicial
Court declared that every slave in the state was free. Emancipation began in
so low-key and legally complex a manner that it would be some time before
everyone was aware of the result. It started with one man's claim that he had
been promised his freedom when he reached maturity but that promise had
not been kept. Massachusetts had seen many such cases in its courts before,
and wronged slaves had been freed. This one had a different ending.

Quock Walker's story began nearly thirty years earlier, in 1754, when
Quock and his parents were purchased by James Caldwell. Caldwell promised the youngster his freedom when he was twenty-four or twenty-five,
Quock wasn't clear which. Unfortunately, Caldwell died intestate in 1763. A
will would have specified Caldwell's plans for Quock. Caldwell's widow
promised Quock freedom when he became twenty-one, but she remarried,
and her new husband, Nathaniel Jennison, had no intention of honoring that
promise. In 1781, when Quock was twenty-eight, he ran away to the home of

John and Seth Caldwell, adult children of his former owner, and began working for them. Jennison tracked him down, seized him, and brought him back. Quock sued on charges of assault and battery. A jury found Jennison guilty and Quock a free man. Jennison then appealed to the state's highest court, the Supreme Judicial Court. At this point the situation became more complicated. Jennison's lawyers did not appear to argue the case before the Supreme Judicial Court, and he asked for a re-hearing. In the meantime Jennison sued the younger Caldwells for luring Walker away. That jury found in favor of Jennison, and it was the Caldwells' turn to appeal to the Supreme Judicial Court. In none of these confusing proceedings was the legality of slavery the central issue, just Quock's personal freedom.

It is curious that although Levi Lincoln, Walker's attorney, did argue passionately against slavery, he didn't base his plea on the Massachusetts Declaration of Rights but on natural law. Lincoln insisted that slavery had never been legal in Massachusetts because it was against the law of God and nature. "We are all born in the same manner, have our bones clothed with the same kind of Flesh—had the same breath of life breathed into us," he pleaded with the jury:

> are all under the same Gospel Dispensation have one common Savior—inhabit the same com[mon] Globe of earth, Die in the same manner . . . we all sleep in a level in the dust—Shall all be raised by the sound of one common trump . . . Shall be arrained at one common bar shall have one common Judge, tried by one common jury—condemned or acquitted by one common law—by the Gospel the perfect law of liberty—This cause will then be tried over again, and your verdict will then be tried Gentlemen of the jury. Therefore gent. of the jury let me conjure you to give such a verdict now as will stand the test, as will be approved of by your own minds in the last moments of your existence—by your Judge at the last day. . . . Is it not a law of nature that all men are equal & free—Is not the law of nature the law of God—Is not the law of God then against Slavery—If there is then the great difficulty is to determine which law you ought to obey—and if you should have the same Ideas as I have of present & future things you will obey the former—For the worst that can happen to you for disobeying the former is the destruction of the body for the last that of your own souls.

The Supreme Judicial Court ultimately determined that Quock was a slave, but in the process of ruling on Walker's rights, the chief justice, William Cushing, found slavery inconsistent with article 1 of the state's new constitution, which declared: "All men are born free and equal."

Cushing's pronouncement that slavery was inconsistent with the Massachusetts constitution caused confusion. The case turned on the narrower issue of whether an individual promised his freedom had been denied it. Moreover, the court opinion with Cushing's comments was not published for some years. But together with several other cases, the Walker case effectively ended slavery in Massachusetts. States like New Hampshire and Pennsylvania instituted gradual emancipation; in Massachusetts it was immediate.

Had Peter not purchased his mother's freedom in 1781, had Jupiter not served three difficult years in the Continental Army, they would both have been free anyway. But who could have known that, and how could one weigh the price of those extra months of freedom both enjoyed? Of course Jupiter was not alone in enlisting in the Continental Army and risking his life for freedom. But at least those who survived to complete their service were freed. Massachusetts slaves who slipped behind British lines on the same errand had a less certain fate. Even more dismal was the fate of slaves in the South enticed by British promises or taken from their patriot masters. The people of Massachusetts were spared close acquaintance with the misery endured by the thousands of southern slaves who escaped to British lines or trailed the British army. Peter and other soldiers had seen them. Frightened, sick, and starving men and women, abandoned by the British before and after Yorktown, left to be hunted down by former owners or to languish in the woods and swamps. Their bodies were left unburied. It was reckoned that between twenty-five thousand and fifty-five thousand southern blacks became fugitives during the war.

Some of these fugitives were fortunate enough to be rescued. A year after Yorktown, the British transported fifteen hundred of them from Savannah and Charleston to New York City. Lord Dunmore, Virginia's former governor and the first British official to offer freedom to slaves who fled to the British army, sold many into slavery in the Bahamas. He also helped transport Loyalists with their slaves to the Caribbean.

The British were more scrupulous in the North, perhaps because the numbers of fugitives there were more manageable or because Sir Guy Carleton, Clinton's successor, was more honorable. Some fifty-six blacks were evacuated in November 1782, many more in April 1783, and when the British finally left New York City, their fleet carried 1,336 men, 914 women, and 750 boys and girls to freedom in Canada. In the months before they set sail, however, a board of inquiry was created under the jurisdiction of General Carleton to settle the conflicting claims of black refugees and their former owners. Both patriots and Loyalists were anxious to retrieve "their property" before the British carried them out of reach. The records are full of their stories—the attempts by former owners to recover escaped slaves and the desperation of the blacks with freedom so close, imperiled up to the hour of sailing.

Rawlins Lowndes was one Loyalist from Charleston who wrote to Carleton in August 1782 on that errand. After reminding the general of his personal service and loyalty to the king, he added: "the continual deprivation of his property is not warranted by any principle of war or policy. What he particularly alludes to is the prevalent practice of carrying off negroes from this province . . . many of his own are now at New York and other places." Lowndes was especially eager to recover "a valuable house servant woman, wife to a man in Captain Durnford's employ." Both husband and wife had been in Georgia with Captain Durnford and were about to be evacuated. Durnford had refused Lowndes's request to return the woman or even permit her to come on shore. Lowndes asked Carleton's help for "the restoration of the woman, to whom his family are much attached, who raised his children and had the care of their infancy." A month later Lowndes received a letter from New York informing him that Captain Durnford's account of matters respecting the black woman differed "materially" from his own but that Durnford was ready "to deliver her to any person authorized to receive her."

The situation was complicated. It wasn't just that former owners wanted their slaves back; British officers who had taken on blacks as servants wanted to keep them. A secret letter to Carleton from a British officer admitted that many officers "look on negroes as their property," adding "the slaves are exceeding unwilling to return to hard labor, and severe punishment from their former masters, and from the numbers that may expect to be brought off, including their wives and children, if to be paid for, will amount to a monstrous expense." He himself had a slave he hoped to keep.

The Hessian general Baron Friedrich Adolf von Riedesel and his wife had three black servants. "At the moment of our departure [to Nova Scotia]," the baroness wrote,

> our good Negroes, a man and his wife, and a young kinswoman of theirs, were reclaimed by their first owner, from whom, as a rebel, they had been taken, on the grounds that he had again become a royalist, and just as the signal for departure was given, he actually arrived with the order that the Negroes be returned to him. Since they were much attached to us, and this man was also an evil master, who had treated them badly, the horror

and lamentation of these poor people were extremely great. The young girl, named Phyllis, fainted, and when she regained her senses would not hear of leaving us. She threw herself at my feet, and, clutching, had to be withdrawn by force. My husband offered their master money, but since he noticed how much we wanted to keep them, he demanded thirty guineas for each, which my husband would not pay him. Had all this not happened at the moment of our departure, I believe that we yet would have kept them. We gave them all their things . . . we had had made for them for the voyage. At this they grew all the more excited, and Phyllis cried, "If I do not die first, I will come back to you, even if it be at the other end of the world!" The good girl had later actually begged two or three persons to take her with them and bring her to me, always adding, "Milady will be very glad to pay my passage." She was quite right, but as no one was assured of this, nobody would burden himself with her. . . . her greedy master would not sell her separately . . . since he was trying to force us to take them all. But this was too stiff for our purse. We regretted our decision later, however, because maidservants in Canada are poor and especially difficult to find.

Until the ships actually sailed, husbands, wives, and their children lived in terror that they or a loved one might be snatched and returned to a former owner. Many were, but in the end thousands of individuals were spirited away to Canada.

The day Washington's triumphal army entered New York, Peter had seen the British fleet in the harbor waiting for a fresh wind. It was not hard to imagine the relief of the emancipated passengers, their exhilaration facing an unknown future as free men and women. How wild a thing is freedom, precious and frightening, not for the timid.

In Lincoln life returned to some semblance of normality. Yet eight long years of warfare had taken their toll. The fighting had moved away from Massachusetts within a year, but its men had followed it in great numbers. Peter and Jupiter had followed. The little family farms and villages of the Bay State had escaped the awful devastation wreaked on the farms and villages of New Jersey and New York, Virginia, and the South, areas through which armies fought, plundered, and burned and neighbor fought neighbor. Local Tories had quickly left Lincoln and neighboring towns for the protection of British Boston and New York. Now they took ship bound for Canada or England.

Thousands of soldiers and militiamen had died in those eight years. Casualties were high. It has been estimated that of the approximately 175,000 men who fought in the American army, navy, and militia, 25,674 died, some 7,174 in battle, another 10,000 from disease in camp and 8,500 more as prisoners in British hands. In fact, though, the fatalities were not evenly spread. Some 30 to 40 percent of those casualties were Continentals. The militia served short stints while the Continentals bore the great weight of the fighting and suffered the most. Many fine officers were killed as well as privates. Peter had seen friends and neighbors die, brave men and boys, some white, some black, all alike hungry and ragged. Some who did return home were ill or maimed or came back to livelihoods ruined by their absence.

Peter didn't know the statistics, nor did Middlesex families. They only knew that many men never returned and others who did were never right again. Jupiter was never right again. He lived only a few months as a free man before his death. There were scores of individual tragedies. Concord's young doctor Samuel Prescott was one. It was Prescott who had given Paul Revere's captors the slip and carried the first alarm to Concord. Later he joined the Continental Army as a surgeon. For some reason, perhaps at Billy Smith's urging, he enlisted with the crew of a New England privateer. His ship was captured by the Royal Navy and its crew taken to prison in Halifax. Life plays no favorites. Unlike his fortunate and profligate shipmate William Smith, who was exchanged, Prescott died in that Halifax prison. He had been courting Lydia Milliken that fateful night of April 18. The house where they had met was burned the next day by the retreating British. Lydia's brother Nathaniel joined the army at Cambridge and died the next year of camp fever. She waited faithfully for Samuel until the war was over and it was clear he would never return. She then married another.

Colonel Timothy Bigelow of Worcester, commander of Jupiter's Massachusetts Fifteenth Regiment, was a fine soldier and a virtuous man. He had famously declared, "While fighting for liberty, I would never be guilty of selling slaves." Bigelow returned from the war to find his blacksmith business in ruins and his finances the same. He was sentenced to prison for debt, where he died.

Others did better. Young Abner Richardson of Lincoln was typical. He was only sixteen when he enlisted with Peter for three years' service in the Continentals. Abner returned home to marry Anna Moore and father thirteen children. The couple moved to Luzerne, New York, where Abner died at the age of ninety-four.

Joseph Plumb Martin, whose salty comments and detailed memories have peppered this history, served in a Connecticut regiment throughout most of the war. Martin survived, still complaining but otherwise unscathed. He bought a farm in a small Maine fishing village, married, was seven times elected selectman, served in the Maine legislature, composed poems, wrote hymns, drew illustrations of wild birds, and died just shy of ninety.

Among the slaves who earned their freedom serving in the Continental Army was Pompey Blackman of Lexington, who served with Jupiter. Once freed he changed his name to Pomp Baldwin. He was baptized in 1782 and died the following year. Brister Hoar, slave of Lincoln's Timothy Wesson, also earned his freedom and fared better. Brister, who changed his name to Sippio Brister, returned to Lincoln and lived there until his death in 1820. He was buried in Lincoln's cemetery, a stone marker placed upon his grave. He was the only former slave in Lincoln to be so honored.

And what of Captain William Smith? After a stint of three months' service in 1780 as a "six month's man," he never returned home. When he failed to pay his taxes the next year, the Reverend Smith, his long-suffering father, refused to permit him to take the farm back into his hands. His sisters were generally "glad" he was gone and thought it best that he did not live "under the same roof with his wife." In 1783 the Reverend Smith died. In his will he provided for his only son "in a small way" but quite handsomely for William's wife, Catherine Louisa, and their six children. "I seldom hear from him," Catherine Louisa wrote a sister-in-law, "and when I do the intelegence is not what I could wish." Some years later, word filtered back that he had stood trial in New York State for counterfeiting but, thankfully, was acquitted. William's sorry tale ended in September 1787, when news reached Lincoln and Quincy that he had died of "black jaundice."

The Hartwell brothers, John, Isaac, and Samuel, survived the war, having served with distinction in the militia. John took over old Ephraim's farm and inn. Samuel and Mary Hartwell remained working their grandfather's farm next door, where Mary enjoyed regaling her grandchildren with tales about the frightening days of the Revolution and especially the part she and Samuel played in its first dramatic battle.

Joseph Mason, Peter's old schoolmaster, died in 1788. His wife, Grace, who served occasionally as schoolmistress, remained on their little farm. When she passed away in 1802, their ten acres, too small to divide among their many children, was left to their oldest son, who immediately sold it to his neighbor John Hartwell.

As for Josiah, he and Millicent had seven children. All were baptized on the very same day in the Lexington church, perhaps to save money. Oddly, the two eldest of their three daughters never married. It was Josiah's fate to outlive Millicent. She died in November 1799. He was clearly distraught by her passing. Millicent was laid to rest in the Lexington churchyard next to Elizabeth. In contrast to the brief inscription on Elizabeth's gravestone, identifying her as the wife of Josiah and recording her age and the date of her death, after those standard facts on Millicent's stone, Josiah added the heartfelt cry, "She lived desired & died lamented." More than a decade later, at the age of eighty-four, he too died. He was laid to rest next to Millicent.

Thomas and Lydia Nelson enjoyed an old age surrounded by grandchildren. Son-in-law Samuel and young Lydia raised five sons and five daughters in that funny little house on the Concord Road. What a lot of Nelsons and Nelson-Hastings there now were. In 1802 at the ages of eighty and eighty-two, both Thomas and Lydia died. Thomas went first and was joined by his Lydia just seven days later.

Peter's mother and sister have vanished from the records, along with thousands of others. One tantalizing hint remains. In the first federal census in 1790, Robert Reed of Lexington had a former slave living with him, and that same year the Lexington records document the death in his household of a mulatto child.

Peter never ventured into the cities like so many other freed African Americans. No, he returned to and remained in his boyhood hometown, if not his boyhood home, where he was known, to do what he knew best, farming.

The first federal census was taken in 1790. The standard form had a column for slaves. In the state of Massachusetts, that column was blank. But unlike white males and heads of households who were listed individually with details about themselves and their families, the free blacks of Massachusetts were simply counted in a column labeled "Others."

There were six "others" in Lincoln. One was Peter. Did the years pass quietly? The records are stubbornly silent. He never married. He could not marry a white woman, and there were so few blacks. And he had no money or prospects. But year after year he tilled that obstinate soil, was part of, but apart from, the community. In the winter of 1791–1792, when various seasonal illnesses and another bout of smallpox were taking their toll of neighbors, Peter died, not yet thirty. They buried him in an unmarked grave in the place reserved for blacks in the old Lincoln cemetery next to the five British soldiers buried there in April 1775.

Essay on Sources

Tracking down the scattered clues to Peter Nelson's life has been an intriguing, arduous, and occasionally frustrating task. I began with research into basic information about Peter's birth and death, the vital statistics for his families, black and white, and their neighbors. Happily, nineteenth-century Massachusetts residents were intent on preserving their state's early records and making them generally available in print. Among the resulting books are collections of early vital records published by the New England Genealogical Society. The most important for my search were Lexington, Massachusetts, *Records of Births, Marriages and Deaths to January 1, 1898* (Boston, 1898); *Vital Records of Lincoln, Massachusetts, to the Year 1850* (Boston, 1908); Concord, *Births, Marriages, and Deaths, 1635–1850* (Boston, n.d.); and Francis H. Brown's *Lexington Epitaphs: A Copy of Epitaphs in the Old Burying-Grounds of Lexington, Massachusetts* (Lexington, Mass., 1905).

The manuscript collections in local, state, and national archives, combined with printed primary materials, enabled me to flesh out this bare picture of births, marriages, and deaths. Archives housed in the Lincoln (Mass.) Public Library include the Nelson Family Papers, ser. 1, 2, 3; Eleazer Brooks Papers; assessors records for the period, ser. 1; Valuation Books, box 1; "The North Book," 1769–1784; and Lincoln Town Meeting Records, reel 1, 1754–1896, which includes a detailed list drawn up in 1780 of the town's costs for the war, including payment to residents who served. At the Lexington Historical Society I was delighted to find the Reverend Jonas Clarke's diary—three volumes of his daily notes written into printed almanacs, covering 1766–1777—as well as Lexington Town Meeting Records for the eighteenth century, George Nelson's "History of the Nelson Family," and the original 1777 recruiter's list of men, separated by race, available for the Third Middlesex

Regiment. The Middlesex County Court House in Cambridge contains the deeds for Lincoln, Lexington, and Concord going back to the beginning of settlement, while the Massachusetts State Archives houses probates and wills, including those of William Reed, Esq., 1778, #18641; Deacon Joshua Brooks, Lincoln, 1768, #2863; and Josiah Nelson, administration, 1826, #15788. Among the large collection of sources at the Massachusetts Historical Society, the most useful manuscripts for my purposes were the Adams Family Papers and documents on slavery listed below. The National Archives Federal Census of 1790 and 1800 for Massachusetts, Rhode Island, and Connecticut, now in print, were also useful. Two reference books very helpful for local information were D. Hamilton Hurd, ed., *History of Middlesex County, Massachusetts,* vols. 1, 2 (Philadelphia, 1890), and Charles Hudson, *History of the Town of Lexington, Middlesex County, Massachusetts, from Its First Settlement to 1868,* 2 vols. (Boston, 1913).

For general information on slavery in Massachusetts and New England, the primary source materials I consulted included the "Petition of many Slaves living in the town of Boston, 6 January 1773 to Thomas Hutchinson, Esq. Governor; to Majestie's Council and House of Representatives in General Court" and "Census of Slaves in Massachusetts, 1754" reprinted in *Collections of the Massachusetts Historical Society,* 2nd ser., vol. 3 (Boston, 1815), housed at the Massachusetts Historical Society. Collections of early Massachusetts statutes were important for laws affecting slaves. See *The Colonial Laws of Massachusetts, Supplements, 1672–1686* (Boston, 1887); *Acts and Resolves of the Province of Massachusetts Bay,* vol. 5: *1769–1780* (Boston, 1886); *Acts and Laws of the Commonwealth of Massachusetts, 1780–1781, 1782–1783* (Boston, 1890); *Judicial Cases concerning American Slavery and the Negro,* ed. Helen Catterall and James J. Hayden, vol. 4 (Washington, D.C., 1936); as well as the landmark English case on slavery, *Somerset v. Stewart, King's Bench, 1772,* 12 Geo III, repr. 98 *English Reports* 499, and the Massachusetts case that emancipated the slaves, *Jennison v. Quork.* For further information on the Somerset case, see William M. Wiecek, "Somerset: Lord Mansfield and the Legitimacy of Slavery in the Anglo-American World," *University of Chicago Law Review* 42 (1974). On the Jennison case, see John D. Cushing, "The Cushing Court and the Abolition of Slavery in Massachusetts: More Notes on the 'Quork Walker Case,'" *American Journal of Legal History* 5 (1961); William S. J. O'Brien, "Did the Jennison Case Outlaw Slavery in Massachusetts?" *William and Mary Quarterly,* 3rd ser., 17 (April 1960); and Rev. Carlton A. Staples, "The Existence and Extinction of Slavery in Massachusetts," *Proceedings of the Lexington Historical Society* 4 (1912).

Long neglected, slavery in colonial and early national America is now the subject of a growing number of fine books and articles, with several focused on New England. These include William D. Piersen, *Black Yankees: The Development of an Afro-American Subculture in Eighteenth-Century New England* (Amherst, Mass., 1988); Edgar J. McManus, *Black Bondage in the North* (Syracuse, N.Y., 1973); Lynda R. Day, *Making a Way to Freedom: A History of African Americans on Long Island* (Interlaken, N.Y., 1997); Robert J. Cottrol, ed., *From African to Yankee: Narratives of Slavery and Freedom in Antebellum New England* (Armonk, N.Y., 1998); Paul Finkelman, *The Law of Freedom and Bondage: A Casebook* (New York, 1986); Philip S. Foner, *Blacks in the American Revolution* (Westport, Conn., 1976); Sylvia R. Frey, *Water from the Rock: Black Resistance in a Revolutionary Age* (Princeton, N.J., 1991); Lorenzo Greene, *The Negro in Colonial New England, 1620–1776* (New York, 1942); Robert Ewell Greene, *Black Courage, 1775–1783: Documentation of Black Participation in the American Revolution* (Washington, D.C., 1984); Herbert G. Gutman, *The Black Family in Slavery and Freedom, 1750–1925* (New York, 1976); Alice Hinkle, *Prince Estabrook: Slave and Soldier* (Lexington, Mass., 2001); Graham Russell Hodges's books *Root and Branch: African Americans in New York and New Jersey, 1613–1863* (Chapel Hill, N.C., 1999), *Slavery and Freedom in the Rural North: African Americans in Monmouth County, New Jersey, 1665–1865* (Madison, N.J., 1997), and *Slavery, Freedom and Culture among Early American Workers* (Armonk, N.Y., 1998); Sidney Kaplan and Emma Kaplan, *The Black Presence in the Era of the American Revolution, 1770–1800*, rev. ed. (Amherst, Mass., 1989); Richard S. Walling, *Men of Color at the Battle of Monmouth, June 28, 1778* (Hightstown, N.J., 1994); Gary Nash's *Race, Class, and Politics: Essays on American Colonial and Revolutionary Society* (Urbana, Ill., 1986), and *The Forgotten Fifth: African Americans in the Age of Revolution* (Cambridge, Mass., 2006); William Cooper Nell, *The Colored Patriots of the American Revolution with Sketches of Several Distinguished Colored Persons* (Boston, 1855); Benjamin Quarles, *The Negro in the American Revolution* (Chapel Hill, N.C., 1961); George Quintal, Jr., *Patriots of Color: "A Peculiar Beauty and Merit"; African Americans and Native Americans at Battle Road and Bunker Hill* (Washington, D.C., 2002); David O. White, *Connecticut's Black Soldiers, 1775–1783* (Chester, Conn., 1973); and Arthur Zilversmit, *The First Emancipation: The Abolition of Slavery in the North* (Chicago, 1967). For research on blacks in Manhattan, see Thelma Wills Foote, "Black Life in Colonial Manhattan, 1664–1786" (Ph.D. diss., Harvard University, 1991). Two fine recent books on slaves during the Revolution, concentrating on blacks who sided with the British, are Simon Schama, *Rough Crossings: Brit-*

ain, the Slaves, and the American Revolution (London, 2005), and Cassandra Pybus, *Epic Journeys of Freedom: Runaway Slaves of the American Revolution and Their Global Quest for Liberty* (Boston, 2006).

There are excellent manuscript and print materials on the military history of the war and local participation in it. *Massachusetts Soldiers and Sailors of the Revolutionary War* (Boston, 1907), a huge collection compiled from local, state, and federal sources, is indispensable. Here I found details of Peter's enlistments as well as those of his family and neighbors and not only reference to Peter's bounty of 350 silver dollars but even his receipt of the funds. The "General Index Military Service Records of Revolutionary War Soldiers" at the National Archives was very helpful, as was Fred A. Berg, *Encyclopedia of Continental Army Units* (Harrison, Pa., 1972). For information about the war with detailed accounts of battles, Richard L. Blanco's *American Revolution, 1775–1783: An Encyclopedia*, 2 vols. (New York, 1993), unfortunately out of print, is an outstanding source. James Kirby Martin and Mark Edward Lender, *A Respectable Army: The Military Origins of the Republic, 1763–1789* (Arlington Heights, Ill., 1982), provides a shrewd analysis of Washington's army. For specifics on casualties, see Howard H. Peckham, ed., *The Toll of Independence: Engagements and Battle Casualties of the American Revolution* (Chicago, 1974). David Hackett Fisher's prize-winning book *Washington's Crossing* (Oxford, 2004) provides much information and insight in addition to a detailed narrative of that major event.

The Library of Congress manuscript collections are a splendid source for the military history of the Revolutionary War. Collections I found particularly valuable were "The Board of Commissioners Superintending Embarkation of British Army from New York Minutes," vol. 1783, PRO 30/55; "Silas Burbank: Massachusetts Regiment, January 1777, Military and Public Accounts"; "Continental Army Payroll Records: For absentees of various regiments from payrolls July 1779-July 1780"; "4th Massachusetts Regiment, 1779–1783," 4 vols.; and two volumes of quartermaster receipts: Schuyler, Major General, Continental Army Commander, Northern Department, 1775–1777, accounts and warrants for units under his command; and United Kingdom, Colonial Office, Plantations General, vols. 7, 8.

Lacking a journal from Peter, I consulted those of other soldiers to fill in many details of military service. One of the best for my purposes was Joseph Plumb Martin, *Ordinary Courage: The Revolutionary War Adventures of Joseph Plumb Martin*, ed. James Kirby Martin (1830; reprint, St. James, N.Y., 1993). Although written in his old age, Martin's memory was remarkable, and his memoirs are full of interesting detail. Equally valuable was the journal of the Continental army surgeon James Thacher, *A Military Journal during the American Revolutionary War* (1862; reprint, New York, 1969). Other useful journals and diaries for understanding the war on the patriot side were Elijah Fisher, *Elijah Fisher's Journal while in the War for Independence and Continued Two Years after He Came to Maine, 1775–1784* (New York, 1909); John Nixon, "The Military Records of Brigadier General John Nixon," ed. John M. Merriam, American Antiquarian Society (Worcester, Mass., 1926); James Robert, "Narrative of James Roberts," Heartsman's Historical Series, 71 (n.d.; reprint, Chicago, 1858); *A Journal of the Operations of the Queen's Rangers* (New York, 1844), John Graves Simcoe's book on ranger techniques that guided Captain Tye's troop, among others; and Sir John Johnson, *Orderly Book of Sir John Johnson during the Oriskany Campaign, 1776–1777*, ed. William L. Stone (Albany, N.Y., 1882). To these I gratefully add two collections of papers: the magnificent series *The Papers of George Washington: Revolutionary War Series*, ed. W. W. Abbot, Dorothy Twohig, Philander D. Chase, et al., vols. 1, 2 (Charlottesville, Va., 1985, 1987), and the fine collection *The Letters and Papers of Edmund Pendleton, 1734–1803*, ed. David John Hayes, 2 vols. (Charlottesville, Va., 1967).

On the British side are other valuable collections and journals, among them Marion Balderston and David Syrett, eds., *The Lost War: Letters from British Officers during the American Revolution* (New York, 1975); Sir Henry Clinton, *The American Rebellion: Sir Henry Clinton's Narrative of His Campaigns, 1775–1782, with an Appendix of Original Documents*, ed. William B. Willcox (New Haven, 1954); Thomas Gage, *The Correspondence of General Thomas Gage with the Secretaries of State, and with the War Office and the Treasury*, ed. Clarence E. Carter, vol. 2 (Hamden, Conn., 1969); Johann Conrad Dohla, *A Hessian Diary of the American Revolution*, ed. and trans. Bruce E. Burgoyne (Norman, Okla., 1990); Sir James Murray, *Letters from America, 1773–1780*, ed. Eric Robson (Manchester, U.K., 1950); *Peter Oliver's Origin and Progress of the American Revolution: A Tory View*, ed. Douglass Adair and John A. Schutz (Stanford, Calif., 1961); and *Baroness von Riedesel and the American Revolution: Journal and Correspondence of a Tour of Duty, 1776–1783*, rev. and trans. Marvin L. Brown, Jr. (Chapel Hill, N.C., 1965), the fascinating journal of Baroness von Riedesel, who accompanied her officer husband to America. Bernhard A. Uhlendoff edited and translated a series of letters and diaries of Hessian officers, *The Siege of Charleston* (Ann Arbor, Mich., 1938). Also see John Gray Bell, ed., *American Revolutionary War:*

Catalogue of an Extraordinary Collection of Original Documents Connected with the British Army (Manchester, 1857), and *The Gentleman's Magazine and Historical Chronicle*, vol. 47: *1777–1781* (London). For official materials, see Historical Manuscripts Commission, *A Report on American Manuscripts in the Royal Institution of Great Britain*, 4 vols. (London, 1904–1909). Two useful dissertations on the British effort to entice slaves to join the royal cause are David Brian Crawford, "Counter-Revolution in Virginia: Patriot Response to Dunmore's Emancipation Proclamation of November 7, 1775" (M.A. thesis, Ball State University, 1993), and John Anthony Zurlo, "The Influence of the Slave Evacuation by the British on Anglo-American Relations: 1775–1795" (M.A. thesis, University of Texas, Arlington, 1975).

For French memoirs, see the fascinating accounts in *The American Campaigns of Rochambeau's Army, 1780, 1781, 1782, 1783*, ed. and trans. Howard C. Rice, Jr., and Anne S. K. Brown, vol. 1: *The Journals of Clermont-Crèvecoeur, Verger, and Berthier* (Princeton, N.J., 1972).

An impressive amount of work has been done on the first battle of the American Revolution. Douglas P. Sabin's extraordinary manuscript, "April 19, 1775: A Historiographical Study" (September 1987), produced for Minute Man National Historical Park, may soon be available online. David Hackett Fischer's *Paul Revere's Ride* (New York, 1994) is a tour de force. Also see Frank Warren Coburn, *The Battle of April 19, 1775*, 2nd ed. (Lexington, Mass., 1922); Robert A. Gross, *The Minutemen and Their World* (New York, 1976); Frank Hersey, *Heroes of the Battle Road: A Narrative of Events in Lincoln on the 18th and 19th of April, 1775* (Boston, 1930); George A. Billias, *General John Glover and His Marblehead Mariners* (New York, 1960); Edward Harris, *Andover in the American Revolution* (Marceline, Mo., 1976); and Frank A. Gardner, "Colonel John Nixon's Regiment," *Massachusetts Magazine* 2 (1914). For more general local history, see John C. MacLean's splendid book, *A Rich Harvest: The History, Buildings, and People of Lincoln, Massachusetts* (Lincoln, Mass., 1987), and Richard Buel, Jr., *Dear Liberty: Connecticut's Mobilization for the Revolutionary War* (Middletown, Conn., 1980).

Among the excellent books on various aspects of the war that I found particularly valuable are J. H. Benton, *Warning Out in New England* (Boston, 1911); Elizabeth Fenn's groundbreaking work *Pox Americana: The Great Small Pox Epidemic of 1775–82* (New York, 2001); Rupert Furneaux, *The Battle of Saratoga* (New York, 1971); Peter Charles Hoffer, *Law and People in Colonial America* (Baltimore, 1994); Stephen Innes, ed., *Work and Labor in Early America* (Chapel Hill, N.C., 1988); Richard M. Ketchum, *The Winter Soldiers*

(Norwalk, Conn., 1973); Mark E. Lender, *The New Jersey Soldier* (Trenton, N.J., 1975); George Emery Littlefield, *Early Schools and School-Books of New England* (New York, 1965); Charles Patrick Neimeyer, *America Goes to War: A Social History of the Continental Army* (New York, 1996); John W. Shay, *A People Numerous and Armed: Reflections on the Military Struggle for American Independence* (New York, 1976); Charles Royster, *A Revolutionary People at War* (Chapel Hill, N.C., 1979); Henry Wiencek, *An Imperfect God: George Washington, His Slaves, and the Creation of America* (New York, 2003); and William B. Willcox, *Protrait of a General: Sir Henry Clinton in the War of Independence* (New York, 1962).

Useful articles on the war are Don Higginbotham's "The American Militia: A Traditional Institution with Revolutionary Responsibilities" in his edited volume *Reconsiderations on the Revolutionary War* (Westport, Conn., 1978), and, in another Higginbotham volume, Maurer Maurer, "Military Justice under General Washington," in *Military Analysis of the Revolutionary War* (Millwood, N.Y., 1977). See also Michael Riccards, "Patriots and Plunderers: Confiscation of Loyalist Lands in New Jersey, 1776–1786," *New Jersey History* (Spring 1968), and more generally John R. Sellers, "The Common Soldier in the American Revolution," in *Military History of the American Revolution*, Proceedings of the Sixth Military History Symposium (Washington, D.C., 1976).

Scholars and readers of the Revolutionary War era in all its aspects are exceedingly fortunate to have such valuable works at their disposal. This essay does not contain a complete list of those I have consulted but is sufficient, I hope, to give the reader an understanding of the research that has gone into uncovering Peter's world and his role in it. Clearly, I am indebted to hundreds of talented individuals without whom this book would have been stillborn.

Index